BETWEEN PAST AND FUTURE

EVANGELICAL MISSION ENTERING THE TWENTY-FIRST CENTURY

OTHER TITLES IN THE EMS SERIES:

BETWEEN PAST AND FUTURE

EVANGELICAL MISSION ENTERING THE TWENTY-FIRST CENTURY

Edited by
Jonathan J. Bonk

Evangelical Missiological Society Series
Number 10

William Carey Library
PASADENA · CALIFORNIA

EMS Series No. 10

Published by
William Carey Library
P.O. Box 40129
Pasadena, CA 91114
(626) 720-8210

ISBN: 0-87808-384-7

PRINTED IN THE UNITED STATES OF AMERICA

Dedicated

to

Kenneth B. Mulholland

in whose life we see

His life

Contents

Author Profiles

Dwight P. Baker is Program Director at the Overseas Ministries Study Center, New Haven, Connecticut. Previously he served for seven years at the U.S. Center for World Mission, Pasadena, California, much of that time as director of the World Christian Foundations study program. He received the M.A. in English from Bemidji State University, the M.Div. from North Park Theological Seminary, and the M.S. and Ph.D. in cultural anthropology from Purdue University.

Jonathan J. Bonk is Executive Director of the Overseas Ministries Study Center, New Haven, Connecticut. He is also Editor of the *International Bulletin of Missionary Research* and Project Director for the *Dictionary of African Christian Biography*. He grew up in Ethiopia, where he and his wife later served as missionaries. He served for twenty-two years as chairman and professor of global Christian studies at Providence College and Seminary in Manitoba, Canada.

Argentina-born **Luis Bush** and his wife Doris have four children, three of them married. After working for a business consulting firm Luis Bush entered the Christian ministry, serving first as a pastor in El Salvador, then as a mission mobilizer with an emerging Latin American organization called COMIBAM, then as international president of Partners International, prior to becoming the international director of the AD2000 Movement. Sponsored by the School of World Mission and Fuller Theological Seminary and in collaboration with the Lausanne Committee for World Evangelization, Bush now leads a three-year-long World Inquiry among Christian leaders in hundreds of world-class cities to help construct a missiology capable of empowering the global church for participation in God's mission for the twenty-first century.

Bruce K. Camp spent six years as missions pastor under Charles Swindoll and then thirteen years as a church missions consultant for the Evangelical Free Church Mission, where he supervised the entire staff of church missions consultants and launched and edited two EFCM publications. Currently he is Global Outreach Pastor for Ocean Hills Community Church in San Juan Capistrano, California, as well as the founder and President/CEO of DualReach. Bruce has served on the board of ACMC and trained dozens of mission agency personnel as part of the Training Church Mission Consultants program. He holds a Doctor of Missiology degree from Biola University and has written numerous articles and church missions resources.

Charles L. Chaney is retired vice president of church extension for the North American Mission Board of the Southern Baptist Convention. He previously served as president of Southwest Baptist University, as director of the Missions Division of the Illinois Baptist State Association, and, for twenty years, as a pastor and church planter in Illinois, Kentucky, and Texas. The last five years he has been research professor of missions at Southwestern Baptist Theological Seminary, Fort Worth, Texas, in the seminary's Minister in Residence program. He has written five books, including *The Birth of Missions in America* (William Carey Library) and *Church Planting at the End of the Twentieth Century* (Tyndale). He is a graduate of Howard Payne University (B.A.), Southern Baptist Theological Seminary (B.D., Th.M.), and the University of Chicago (M.A., Ph.D.). He is currently working on a history of home missions in the United States and Canada—Catholic, Protestant, and evangelical—over five centuries.

Michael Jaffarian is a missionary researcher with CBInternational and an associate research editor of the *World Christian Encyclopedia* (2d ed., Oxford University Press, 2001). He and his wife, Dawna, have served in India and Singapore and now live in Richmond, Virginia.

Todd M. Johnson has been a missionary with Youth With A Mission (YWAM) since 1978. Since 1989 he has been a full-time missionary researcher and is presently director of the newly-formed Center for the Study of Global Christianity at Gordon-Conwell Theological Seminary. He is co-author of the two-volume *World Christian Encyclopedia* (2d ed., Oxford University Press, 2001) and *World Christian Trends, AD 30–AD 2200* (William Carey Library, 2001).

Gary B. McGee is Professor of Church History and Pentecostal Studies at Assemblies of God Theological Seminary, Springfield, Missouri. He wrote *This Gospel Shall Be Preached* (1986), a two-volume history of Assemblies of God international missions, and edited *Initial Evidence: Historical and Biblical Perspectives on the Pentecostal Doctrine of Spirit Baptism* (1991). He also serves as visiting professor at seminaries in Belgium and Singapore.

John Moldovan is Associate Professor of Missions and Evangelism at the Criswell College, where he has served since 1989. He endured harsh persecution in Romania and was forced into exile for his ministry by the Romanian dictator Nicolae Ceausescu. His understanding of suffering offers a constructive perspective on missions.

Paul E. Pierson is Senior Professor of History of Mission and Latin American Studies at Fuller Theological Seminary School of World Mission. He served as dean of the School of World Mission from 1980 to 1992 and before that as a missionary to Brazil (1955–70) and Portugal (1970–73), working in church planting and theological education.

John Mark Terry serves as the A. P. and Faye Stone Professor of Missions and Associate Dean for Doctoral Studies in the Billy Graham School of Missions and Evangelism at the Southern Baptist Theological Seminary in Louisville, Kentucky. He earned a Doctor of Philosophy in Missions degree at Southwestern Baptist Theological Seminary in Fort Worth, Texas. He and his wife, Barbara, served as missionaries in the Philippines for fourteen years under appointment by the International Mission Board of the Southern Baptist Convention.

Foreword

The study and practice of mission stands on three foundations. First is the Bible, which is the basis of all we do—providing vision, giving us our marching orders, and maintaining the standards against which we measure our efforts in mission. The second foundation is the social sciences, the use of which enables us to better understand people, cultures, and societies, providing the tools that enable us to communicate clearly the message of Christ found in the Scriptures. The third foundation is comprised of the great story of God's work through the church over the course of history. It is a story of tragedy and triumph, success and failure. Learning to draw from the lessons of the past is crucial for the work of the future.

Earlier volumes in the EMS series have focused attention on the foundations of Scripture (EMS 1: *Scripture and Strategy: The Use of the Bible in Postmodern Church and Mission*; EMS 5: *The Holy Spirit and Mission Dynamics*), the social sciences (EMS 4: *Missiology and the Social Sciences: Contributions, Cautions, and Conclusions*), or both (EMS 2: *Christianity and the Religions: A Biblical Theology of World Religions*). It is the third foundation, history, that is the focus for this collection of papers from evangelical missiologists. Through them we remember the past in ways that are helpful for evangelical mission in the present and the future. From ecumenism to Pentecostalism, from activism to education, from the local church to William Carey, this volume provides important missiological "bricks" with which the future of mission will be built.

While I was a student in college and seminary I confess that history was not my favorite subject. Memorizing names and dates, identifying the myriad of controversies that seemed to revolve around the change of a letter here or a word there left me feeling inadequate and uninspired. Since my days of study, however, again and again I have been forced to return to the pages of history to draw lessons so that I could gain focus on things we all face in the present.

Harvard philosopher George Santayana's oft quoted "Those who forget the past are condemned to repeat it" applies to missiology as well as it does to any other discipline. The past provides the foundation on which the present stands and the future will build. May God give us grace to draw from the lessons presented in this book in ways that will enrich us as people, as a church, and as a community calling others to come worship Jesus Christ.

A. Scott Moreau
Chair, Missions and Intercultural Studies
Wheaton College
Editor, *Evangelical Missions Quarterly*

Introduction

This volume traces its origins to the 2001 annual meeting of the Evangelical Missiological Society, held in conjunction with the Godsmisson.commUNITY 2001 conference that convened September 20–23, 2001. The theme of the EMS meeting was Lessons in Mission from the Twentieth Century, and three papers in this book—the offerings by Todd Johnson, Luis Bush, and Jonathan Bonk—were prepared for that occasion. It being the custom of EMS to make of its annual meetings the kernel for the volumes in their ongoing series, it became necessary to supplement this modest trilogy with contributions from other EMS members. Accordingly, a selection was made from papers prepared for EMS 2001 regional conferences. These essays, in turn, were supplemented by still others whose authors were especially invited to contribute. In all but a few instances, the names will be familiar to evangelical readers of this volume. The contributors to this volume provide a helpfully reflective, wide-ranging survey of evangelical missionary endeavor past. One glaring deficiency should be noted: not a single female contributor could be found. This is instructive, indicating that evangelical missiology is still severely hampered by its gender myopia.

The volume's collective title is evocative of a collection of Hannah Arendt's essays. Quoting Faulkner's wry observation, "The past is never dead, it is not even past,"[1] Arendt draws attention to something that is routinely forgotten, overlooked, or denied by those of us whose social conditioning has caused us to be—at the functional level—highly critical of the past. For several centuries at least, proofs mustered to demonstrate that the present is superior to the past have noted that "we" (European tribes and their offspring) live more comfortably, move more swiftly, consume more greedily, waste more conspicuously, devastate more terribly, destroy more indiscriminately, and live more insularly than ever before. Such has constituted the proof positive of the superiority of our way of life and the genius of our Gospel. Western missionary activity—whether political, economic, scientific, social, or religious—held out the prospect of a world that soon would be, or at least should be, like us. Only "development"— a concept that stands as the natural mutant of another word found frequently in the discourse of our forebears, "civilization"—is needed. Persons and societies no longer need civilizing, but they do require developing. Both concepts are rooted in our Western doctrine of progress. For a culture fixated on the future (nostalgia aside), the *good old days* are the *bad old days*. While we often romanticize the past, our children, youth, and trendsetters are taught to feel a strong distaste for and even aversion to anything deemed out of date—including material goods and comforts, social and ethical values, cultures, societies, and even the elderly; for nothing could deal a more lethal blow to consumer culture than an outbreak of widespread contentment in North America.

But in embracing this vision of progress—and in devising and employing the various instruments of "development" for those whose "progress" is so inconspicuous as to be regarded as regress—we can forget that ours is a fundamentally moral universe and that the measure of progress according to God is *not* how fast we travel, how comfortably we live, how many varieties of food we consume, or how quickly and thoroughly we exhaust this planet's nonrenewable resources. The real test of progress is how we love God and our neighbor. Everything else is fluff, and potentially dangerous fluff, at that. It gets in the eyes, so that we no longer see clearly as God sees.

While history proves that the past is no sure guide to the future, it is all we have. We are reassured in the knowledge that we serve the eternal living God of past, present, and future. It is the prayerful hope of the publisher, the authors, the Evangelical Missiological Society, and the editor of this volume that it may somehow yield fresh insights to our understanding as God's missionary people as we live faithfully into the century ahead.

A word of grateful acknowledgment must be rendered to my colleagues Pamela Sola, Angela Scipio, Kim Healy, Lois Baker, Dwight Baker, and Dan Nicholas, whose editorial attentiveness and skill contributed incalculably to the satisfaction that readers of this book will experience. Thank you.

Jonathan J. Bonk
Editor
January 2003

Note

1. Hannah Arendt, *Between Past and Future: Six Exercises in Political Thought* (New York: Viking, 1961), p. 9.

Chapter One

The AD2000 Movement as a Great Commission Catalyst

Luis Bush

The following essay provides a summary of a late-twentieth-century catalytic movement, birthed in the late 1980's and completed by predetermined intent at the end of that century. This movement, the AD2000 Movement, was predominantly a vision-casting endeavor, riding on the "winds of change" coming from the Christian and secular ethos of that period. Primary efforts of the movement based on the biblical mandates of the Great Commission as found in the foundational texts of Matthew 28:18–20 and Mark 16:15 were focused on the unreached peoples, building networks for prayer and for resources. The genesis of the 10/40 Window as a geographical frame of reference occurred in the early 1990's, later precipitating four "Praying Through the Window" month-long concentrations of prayer by millions around the world. Key communication materials were used to catalyze greater understanding and motivation, along with major consultations, both national and global. GCOWE '95 in Korea and GCOWE '97 in South Africa were the major consultations, attended by some four thousand persons from 186 and 132 nations, respectively.

By January of 1989 more than two thousand individual plans for global evangelism had been identified, each focusing on the year 2000! One-third of these originated in Africa, Asia, and Latin America, which until recently had been viewed as the major foci of missionary concern. The church planted in those areas was now on the move, reaching out with the same Gospel to reproduce itself throughout the whole world. Authors of the plans met in Singapore early in 1989 to exchange notes. Despite great diversity in the group, there were four significant outcomes. First, people realized that the 2000 vision was something God had placed on the hearts of many Christian leaders throughout the world. Second, there was duplication in many of the plans. Third, an overarching committee or group was needed to facilitate cohesion of initiative and reduce duplication. Fourth, there was a united commitment to what was called *The Great Commission Manifesto*. This manifesto was an expression of commitment to cooperate among existing and emerging evangelization AD2000-focused initiatives in dependence on the empowerment of the Holy Spirit, and in compassionate servanthood to seize the moment toward fulfillment of a saturation church planting movement among every people and the proclamation of the Gospel to every person.

A few months later, Christian leaders from around the world embraced the spirit and words of the final paragraph under the eleventh affirmation of the Lausanne II Manila Manifesto. "The year 2000 has become a challenging milestone. We commit ourselves to evangelize the world during the last decade of this millennium."[1]

AD2000 was born—a servant catalyst—to encourage, network, inspire, research, and disseminate information about what the Holy Spirit was doing through the church globally. The intention was to encourage cooperation among existing churches, movements, and structures to work together towards this same vision.[2] This essay will examine the catalytic contributions of the AD2000 movement to the spread of the Gospel during the movement's decade of existence.

In what way did AD2000 serve as a Great Commission catalyst? The term *catalyst* is defined in the online *American Heritage Dictionary of the English Language* first within the semantic field of chemistry as a "substance, usually used in small amounts relative to the reactants, that modifies and increases the rate of a reaction without being consumed in the process." In the more generic sense it is defined as "one that precipitates a process or event."

To what extent did AD2000 serve catalytically to *precipitate* and *increase the rate of reaction* of the Great Commission process to advance the Christian movement? A number of Christian leaders were hopeful at the beginning of the decade, such as Patrick Johnstone, author of *Operation World*, who observed in 1992, "I believe that God has given us the best opportunity in all history to gain a wide level of support among Christians committed to world evangelization in the AD2000 vision."[3] At the end of the decade Johnstone's assessment was as follows: "In retrospect we believe that we have had the privilege of being involved in the greatest focused global Great Commission movement in history."[4]

The stated purpose of AD2000 was to motivate and network male and female church leaders by inspiring them with the vision of reaching the unreached by the year 2000 through consultations, prayer efforts, and communication materials.[5]

It is the contention of the author that the continuous efforts by AD2000 leaders to implement the various parts of this purpose precipitated involvement in the Great Commission. The catalytic effect of AD2000 on response to the Great Commission can be seen by considering the primary elements in the AD2000 purpose statement:

1. Motivating for the Great Commission
2. Networking for the Great Commission
3. Focusing on the unreached and the Great Commission
4. The year 2000 and the Great Commission
5. Consultations and the Great Commission
6. Prayer efforts and the Great Commission
7. Communication materials and the Great Commission

We will look at each of these points below, in a slightly different order.

Motivating for the Great Commission

The two key catalytic words contained in the AD2000 purpose statement were *motivate* and *network*.[6] Men and women were motivated by inspiring them with a compelling vision. Out of the many plans by denominations, mission agencies, global conferences, national movements, and other Christian organizations, the vision watchword became *A Church for Every People and the Gospel for Every Person by the Year 2000*.

AD2000 was a vision-driven movement. Thomas Wang, while serving as the international director of the Lausanne Committee for World Evangelization (LCWE), observed the number of major denominations and mission groups with plans for evangelization with the a.d. 2000 time target and wrote an article, "The Year 2000: Is God Trying to Tell Us Something?"[7] Christian leaders with plans were motivated to share their own visions and listen to others. They came together in Singapore in early 1989.

The vision did not change or become diluted during the course of the decade. Those involved remained focused on the original vision. As a servant-catalyst, AD2000 involved Christian leaders by serving existing structures that shared the same vision. This common purpose multiplied and broadened implementation efforts. The resulting total was greater than the sum of the individual parts. One example of this effect occurred with the call of Bill Bright. He called for a meeting with the Campus Crusade for Christ (CCC) directors of affairs to present the vision of AD2000, with the prospect of finding common ground that could mutually enhance the broader initiative of God in both ministries. The resulting cooperative relationship between the two entities enhanced AD2000 while boosting the New Life 2000 project being undertaken by CCC.

Christian leaders responded worldwide from large, medium, and small organizations, ministries, churches, denominations, and movements. Laymen and -women became involved. Formal and informal relationships were established. Involvement included spiritual and operational aspects.

AD2000 was fueled by the distinct giftedness of the leaders and their organizations. As each mission leader considered aligning with the movement, he or she faced the same question, both internally and from others: Is there enough added value from involving myself and the ministry/organization I represent in the AD2000 process to merit the cost in terms of time, money, and risk of criticism? As leaders plunged or waded into the movement, we learned from and grew to respect one another.

Networking for the Great Commission

The primary building block for the first half of the decade, enabling AD2000 to operate as a grassroots, bottom-up movement, was the functional network. Networks were formed on local, state, national, regional, and global levels. Communication took place during network and national consultations, through e-mail, on the Internet, at annual status meetings, through track/network newsletters, and at GCOWE '95 and '97.

Through functional networks, and within the general purpose of AD2000, there was a global multiplier effect. Each of the tracks, by design, stood as a semiautonomous unit, with respective chairpersons and coordinators responsible for the organization, personnel, style, funding, and activities of their track. The specific track objectives were in support of the overall objectives of the movement. The result reinforced the vision of presenting the Gospel to every person in every nation and people group and establishing an indigenous church planting movement in every country and people group by the year 2000. Annual meetings with track and task force leaders kept the loose structure from dissolving. Track leaders worked out among themselves the ways and means of helping each other, engaging in joint projects, eliminating unnecessary redundancy, and synchronizing their activities. Each track sought ways to support and encourage other tracks.

Focusing on the Unreached and the Great Commission

At the first meeting of the international board of AD2000 in July 1990, it became clear to all that if we were serious about providing a valid opportunity for every people to experience the love, truth, and saving power of Jesus Christ, we must concentrate on the most spiritually resistant region of the world. Board members were referring to what has become widely known as the 10/40 Window.

The 10/40 Window

The primary but not exclusive focus of AD2000 became the 10/40 Window, a term coined for the area of the world between ten degrees and forty degrees north latitude, stretching from northern Africa and southern Spain to Japan and the northern Philippines.[8]

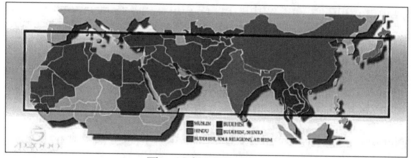

The 10/40 Window

Critics argued that to focus on the 10/40 Window was to skew the biblical call to the whole world. "Too many expressions of reductionist thinking (oversimplifications of the complex task) have influenced the Evangelical missionary movement for the last fifty years. They include . . . a limited geographic focus," wrote William Taylor.[9]

There were compelling reasons, however, for focusing on the 10/40 Window.[10] This area represented the least-evangelized peoples and countries of the world. Ninety-seven percent of the people living in the fifty-five least evangelized countries in 1989 resided in the 10/40 Window. This was also the area where 85 percent of the poorest of the poor lived.

Joshua Project 2000

It was the conviction of participants at GCOWE '95 that a global effort was needed to focus attention and provide tools for implementing the vision of a church for every people by the year 2000 by developing a selected list of unreached peoples. Christian leaders came together several months later for what was called The Launch. The Launch represented the initiation of the implementation phase of AD2000 for the second half of the decade, following the vision-casting phase of the first half. In order to work together toward the vision, participants adopted two approaches: (1) national initiatives until the year 2000 that would emphasize pioneer church planting among the unreached, and (2) Joshua Project 2000.

Joshua Project 2000 was a global cooperative strategy, focused on the least evangelized peoples of the world, that sought to engage every church, agency, denomination, and Christian from every country in the world in an effort to implement the goal of *a church for every people and the Gospel for every person by the year 2000*. The goal of Joshua Project 2000 was to establish a pioneer church planting movement within every ethnolinguistic people of over 10,000 individuals within every country of the world by December 31, 2000. [11] "The Joshua Project . . . is the largest strategic mobilization of Christians in history to disciple the people of the world. Support and enthusiasm has come from across a wide spectrum of denominations, agencies and countries. In the latter, the involvement has been predominantly non-Western."[12]

National Initiatives and the Unreached: A Case Study from Kenya

The GCOWE '97 African National Initiatives (ANI) Consultation produced a vision to build on the momentum by holding five or six key regional and national consultations throughout Africa by the end of 1998. Speaking on behalf of the Kenyan delegation, made up of more than eighty leaders, Stephen Kabachia said, "When the Kenya delegation was confronted by lists of unreached peoples in Kenya, they determined that never again would a Kenyan delegation attend a global consultation to be embarrassed by such lists." They called their plan Finish the Task 2000. As a result of this plan a nationwide consultation with five hundred leaders was held, all the unreached peoples identified were adopted by denominations, churches, and seminaries, and prayer efforts and pioneer church planting efforts were initiated.

The Year 2000 and the Great Commission

The fall of the Berlin Wall in 1989 symbolized a dramatic turning point in human history. The breakup of the former Soviet Union, the movement of some nations toward democracy, the migration of hundreds of thousands of refugees across national borders, and the intensification of tribalism and nationalism have altered the geopolitical landscape. The dismantling of the old Soviet Union's centralized authoritarian regime resulted in a proliferation of nations open to new ideas. One of the consequences is that since 1990, the United Nations has grown 28 percent in number of nations. It was as though God were shaking the nations, giving access to Christian messengers that had not existed in a hundred years. The contextual conditions surrounding the end of the second millennium served to provide a suitable platform to launch a global Christian movement.

Secularist Sees a Decline of the Age of Unbelief in the 1990's

Early in the decade *Time* magazine published a four-page essay entitled "The Year 2000: Is It the End or Just the Beginning?" The author, Henry Grunwald, is a former U.S. ambassador to Austria and is *Time*'s former editor-in-chief. Writing from a secular perspective, Grunwald summarized his thesis in the introduction by saying, "People feel as if the hand of God were turning a page in human fate. We have a sense of things ending and others beginning." He made three observations: "First, of course, we are witnessing the end of communism. Second, we are witnessing the end of nationalism, as we have known it, and beginning to look for new international arrangements; and third, we are witnessing the end, or at least the decline, of an age of unbelief and beginning what may be a new age of faith." This last point was the major point of his article. "Many people seem to want a faith that is more rigorous and demanding, or else more personal. . . . Throughout the Third World, Christian churches, especially the Evangelicals, are gaining more converts than ever before."[13]

Futurists Predict Spiritual Awakening for the 1990's

Not only secularists but also futurists predicted a spiritual awakening in the 1990s. In his best-selling book titled *Megatrends 2000* John Naisbitt described the "unmistakable signs of a worldwide multi-denominational religious revival."[14] Upon observing the significance of this trend, he wrote a follow-up book titled *Religious Revival of the Third Millennium*. "The bond we share today with the people of past millennial eras is the sense of living in a time of enormous change. . . . When people are buffeted about by change, the need for spiritual belief intensifies. The 'God is dead' philosophy of the past is being quickly replaced. With the millennium in sight, the powerful countertrend of the religious revival is repudiating blind faith in science and technology. Huge increases have been experienced in church membership, especially among Evangelical and Charismatic denominations."[15]

Significance of the Year 2000 to Believers

Beginning in the late 1980s thousands of Christian leaders and laymen anticipated a time of divine visitation. Many prayed for God's direction. Some planned. The editors of the Manila Manifesto, the expression of three thousand Christian leaders representing 170 countries gathered at Lausanne II in mid-1989, posed the question: "Now the year 2000 has become for many a challenging milestone. Can we commit ourselves to evangelize the world during the last decade of this millennium? There is nothing magical about the date, yet should we not do our best to reach this goal? Christ commands us to take the gospel to all people. The task is urgent. We are determined to obey Him with joy and hope."[16]

The year 2000 instilled a sense of urgency. It spurred many on to decisive action. Many were impelled to ask: What can we do to seek to fulfill the mandate of Jesus, given to his followers two millennia ago, to make disciples of all the nations and to preach the Gospel to every creature so that there is a church for every people and the Gospel is made available to every person?

Prayer Efforts and the Great Commission

Prayer was the major strategy of AD2000. It undergirded every planning meeting, every event, the launch of every initiative. The approach to the meetings followed a pattern: divide the time equally among the challenges and reports of various AD2000 Christian leaders; allow time for response from other leaders to those challenges and reports; initiate a time of seeking God about the things that were shared and discussed.

Prayer Triplets and the AD2000 Women's Network

By the time of GCOWE '95, women leaders in more than 150 countries had become involved in the AD2000 and Beyond Movement. Evelyn Christenson, author of the bestseller *What Happens When Women Pray*, wrote a prayer study guide for use by the AD2000 women's track. By 1995 it had been translated into twenty-three languages. Among the women's track goals for the year 2000 was to have prayer triplets functioning in 180 countries.[17]

Praying Through the 10/40 Window

Praying Through the Window I, a global prayer initiative for the month of October 1993, focused on the countries located within the 10/40 Window. Praying Through the Window II, in October 1995, focused prayer on the one hundred "gateway cities" of the 10/40 Window. Praying Through the Window III, in October 1997, focused prayer on the 10/40 Window's 132 unreached people clusters, most of whom had never heard the Gospel in their own language in a culturally sensitive way. Praying Through the Window IV, in October 1999, focused once again on the countries of the 10/40 Window, with prayer teams assigned to one thousand major cities.

Upon adding the total number of intercessors in the first three efforts along with about forty million, as recorded in the minutes of the last meeting of the 1999 Praying Through the Window Steering Committee (chaired by Michael Little, president of CBN), the number exceeded 120 million.[18] Bev Pegues recorded and tabulated thousands of prayer journeys and millions of home-based intercessors involved in the Praying Through the Window emphases.

New Approaches to Prayer Encouraged and Disputed

As was pointed out in a 1994 article in *Christianity Today*, the mass prayer movement has not taken place without controversy. Andreas Tapia described spiritual warfare as a "highly controversial subject among Christians."[19] Prayer-related expressions that began to be used in the prayer track included strategic-level spiritual warfare, spiritual mapping, and identificational repentance.[20]

United Prayer Track leader Peter Wagner explained the reason for the emphasis on spiritual warfare: "I believe that the major reason why more people haven't become believers through the centuries is that the 'god of this age' has successfully blinded their minds (see 2 Cor. 4:3–4). Nevertheless, steady progress has been made and today Satan is backed up in what could possibly be seen as his last geographical fortress, the 10/40 Window (not denying, of course, that Satan is also much too malignantly active in virtually every other part of the world as well)."[21]

Wagner wrote a series of books over the course of the decade called the Prayer Warrior series in which he reported to the body of Christ some observations on the prayer movement worldwide and on the spiritual tools being used.

Prayer at GCOWE '95

One example of the significant role of prayer in relation to mobilizing Christian leaders was noted at GCOWE '95. It was highlighted by the schedule of the plenary sessions. Sprinkled throughout the minute-by-minute outline was "praying for the unreached peoples in twos and threes," "Korean-style prayer for every country to have a national initiative focused on the unfinished task," "prayer and weeping for the cities," "prayer for mobilization," and so on. Prayer was not only planned but also spontaneous, as time was taken to pray whenever the Spirit led during the meetings. Two or more delegates with hands joined praying in the hallways was a common sight.

Intercessory prayer "covering" was also seen as key to progress. Over a hundred prayer intercessors paid their own way to Seoul to pray around the clock for GCOWE '95. The Sunday evening worship service was a highlight for many as the delegates were led in a "concert of prayer." Fifty children interceded throughout GCOWE '95. Vonette Bright, former chairperson of the Lausanne Prayer Committee, said: "I have never experienced so much prayer in an international gathering of Christians before."[22]

Communication Materials and the Great Commission

Great Commission efforts were catalyzed not only through consultations and prayer efforts but also through communications. Communications were generated both formally and informally as a vital part of the process of involving Christian leaders. For significant events, a few timely, quality press releases were produced and distributed. Reports were generated of what God was doing through national and network initiatives. These communications allowed far-flung Christians to feel a part of the movement's progress.

Newsworthy reports of AD2000-related events, progress, and perspectives were distributed through electronic conferences, via e-mail, and, upon approval by the national coordinator, later on the Internet. Due to the public nature of the Internet, however, on several occasions these Internet-published reports stirred up opposition by groups opposing Christian witness in their nations. This led to a discussion on appropriate and inappropriate terminology, which in turn led to a consultation on the appropriate language of mission.

The provision of low-cost or no-cost electronic communication tools was seen as a specific provision by the Lord for the advancement of the Gospel. This technology allowed speed and facility of communication across the world unimagined just a decade ago.

Listing of Unreached Peoples

One primary piece of information that developed over the years was an integrated listing of the peoples of the world. A first draft was created for GCOWE '95. It was a rough list, compiling every known "least evangelized" ethnolinguistic people within every country of the world. It was only a beginning. It contained all the known peoples (about 4,800) that were deemed to have the most need of a church planting movement in their midst, had insufficient access to the Gospel, were less than 2 percent Christian, or were identified as unreached peoples for purposes of prayer and mission. The value of the list was dependent upon readers' active participation in updating, correcting, and joining in the effort to make it an effective tool. With this participation, it became of value for country and regional strategy and planning in addition to its value for mobilizing the worldwide church for prayer and for mission involvement.

After two years of global dissemination and subsequent improvement, a new list was prepared for GCOWE '97. The process involved networking, which continually revealed the list's deficiencies as well as the need to refine classifications and terminology.

Patrick Johnstone wrote:

> This volume is unique for the following reasons:
> *   It gives the most widely discussed and agreed-upon list of signifi-
>   cant unreached peoples ever published.

- It shows the list of 1739 peoples of over 10,000 population among whom there is an inadequate or non-existent church planting movement, and where the Great Commission to make disciples of all peoples has yet to be fulfilled.
- It lists the Joshua Project peoples by country of residence, name, People Cluster and Affinity Bloc. This enables more effective national and global planning for cooperative efforts to plant mature, witnessing churches among them.
- It provides, for the first time, fairly full information on the extent of adoption of peoples and present or planned Christian ministries among them.
- It provides a mechanism for assessing progress towards the goal of a church for every people by the year 2000 so that we may be accountable to the millions of Christians who are contributing in some way to these goals.[23]

By November 1999 almost four thousand editorial changes had been made to the list, which now included information from more than fifty thousand "work-among" records from agencies and churches in over 110 countries of the world, recording the church planting efforts among the Joshua Project 2000 peoples. The information on this list made it possible to monitor progress toward the goal of a church for every people. (See graphs and tables at the end of this chapter.)

Prayer Profiles Used by Churches and Cell Groups Worldwide

In 1995 Bethany World Prayer Center, a church in Baton Rouge, Louisiana, accepted the challenge of producing prayer profiles from the Joshua Project list of unreached groups. These small booklets, containing basic information and prayer requests about specific unreached peoples, have been used in local churches to pray for these peoples widely throughout the world. Each profile contained a photo, a map, and information about the lifestyles, customs, and beliefs of the people. It listed spiritual strongholds and addressed specific prayer needs. The prayer profiles were distributed globally through a worldwide network of cell-group churches.

Consultations and the Great Commission

Great Commission efforts were also catalyzed through consultations and conferences. These were gatherings to consult with other Christian leaders who embraced the AD2000 vision. There were augmented city consultations, such as were held in Miami and Calcutta. There were regional consultations and state consultations within a country, as occurred in North India and Nigeria. Regional consultations also took place by continent, as in the Latino America 2000 meeting in 1996. There were also consultations by language, as in Francophone Africa. In addition, there were three Global Consultations on World Evangelization by the Year 2000 and Beyond (GCOWEs) that exponentially multiplied the mobilization impact on Christian leaders.

National Consultations

In most countries where AD2000-type consultations were held, the result was the launching or reinforcement of national initiatives to the year 2000. There were several basic assumptions related to national consultations based on previous enquiries and evidence. The first assumption was that every country of the world contained Christian leaders, committed to the fulfillment of the Great Commission, who desired fellowship and needed to network with those outside of their country who shared that same vision.[24] The second assumption was a commitment to strengthen existing national movements based on faith goals for the year 2000, along with recognition of a need to design viable strategies for all interest groups to work together toward that end. A third basic assumption was the existence in each country of the desire to foster and nurture a viable national initiative where there was none, in whatever way possible—but particularly through the process of national consultation. In the national consultations key questions frequently included the following:

- What is the Great Commission (Matt. 28:19–20) saying to us?
- What does the Great Commandment (Mark 12:30) say to us?
- How did the Gospel get to this country and how did it spread?
- What is the country's profile (political, economic, social, and religious)?
- What are the key issues facing the church?
- Who and where are the unreached people and cities?
- What and where are the unreached peoples outside this country to which the church in this country could send missionaries?

- Who and where are the harvesters?
- How do we train those harvesters?[25]

National Christian leaders were encouraged to listen to other national leaders within their countries and not to set goals for world evangelization arbitrarily on their behalf. This process usually involved bringing together for working consultations or short retreats a variety of leaders from various theological persuasions, geographical settings, and social strata, some of whom had never met due to their differences.[26]

Global Consultations

Prayer, reconciliation, partnerships, strategic planning, empowerment, and mobilization were the hallmark outcomes of the 1995 Global Consultation for World Evangelization. Some of these were planned outcomes, but others, such as empowerment and reconciliation, were planned only on the Holy Spirit's agenda. These spiritual initiatives had far-reaching effects in mobilizing AD2000 leadership. George Verwer stated, "I believe that GCOWE is a catalytic atomic bomb."[27]

To a number of participants, reconciliation between Christian leaders was life- and ministry-changing, unleashing a wave of reconciliation among Christian leaders around the world. An editor wrote: "One of the most powerful forces unleashed at the recent Global Consultation on World Evangelization (GCOWE '95) was the power of reconciliation which broke out like a wildfire, spreading from one meeting to another as various groups forgave each other for the past sins of the people or group they represented. ... The totally diverse members of the Israeli delegation representing Palestinian and Israeli Arab Christians and Messianic Jews were seen holding hands and hugging each other as they pledged to work together."[28]

These public expressions of repentance and reconciliation ignited dozens more, as delegates were convicted of generational animosities and individual bitterness that had to be repented of and cleansed before real partnership could occur. The significance of this reconciliation was that it was neither predicted nor orchestrated but was a natural outcome of the prayer and bonding which occurred among individuals, ethnic groups, mission agencies, denominations, and countries. "Many of the leaders recognized that they could not hope to evangelize the world without first being reconciled with each other," observed *Australian Presbyterian Life Today*.[29]

Avery Willis, Southern Baptist Foreign Mission Board vice-president of overseas operations, said in a speech to the GCOWE '95 delegates: "We want to ask forgiveness from you for thinking we could do that kind of job [reaching the world by the year 2000] without you. We recognize that it's going to take the whole body of Christ to reach the people of this world. Business as usual will not get the job done."[30]

The U.S.A. delegation prepared their own statement, which read in part: "We acknowledge and confess our sins of omission and commission, the arrogance expressed in undue national pride, the unjust treatment of minority groups within our own nation, the insensitivity to other nations and cultures, the undue dependence on our own plans and technology, our unteachability, the extravagant appropriation of God's resources for our own use, the conspicuous consumption of global resources, the fragmentation of the Body of Christ, and the imposition upon others of our cultural forms as though they comprised the gospel itself. In sincere humility and in the spirit of reconciliation expressed in 2 Corinthians 5, we ask forgiveness for the negative impact upon others of our sinful attitudes and actions and we express our commitment to the unity of the Body of Christ. Will you forgive us?"[31]

The spirit of repentance and reconciliation between Christian leaders flowed into GCOWE '97, the next global conference, held in South Africa in June 1997. By this time it had become clear that reconciliation was a *prerequisite* for world evangelization. One of the most powerful moments was the reconciliation that followed the official written request for forgiveness presented publicly by a contingent from the host country. A representative from the thirty-five-member Salvation Army delegation reported on the scene:

> I am thrilled to share with you the powerful outpouring of God's Holy Spirit during my recent visit to South Africa while representing the Salvation Army at the Global Consultation on World Evangelization (GCOWE '97). Over 4000 delegates from 130 countries gathered for six days in Pretoria.
>
> There were times of anguish and calls of repentance. There was recognition of our own sinfulness, pride and prejudices. On the last day as all the consultations gathered for the finale a leading representative from the South African Dutch Reformed Church calmly and somberly read a statement of denominational repentance for the decades of racism tolerated by that church. At the conclusion of the statement—as he received forgiveness from a black pastor—the overwhelming sense of the presence of God was almost unbearable.

One sensed that this was so deep, that centuries of injustice and sin were beginning to be healed, that it was too awe inspiring to watch. The white pastors around me from South Africa were heaving enormous tears of sorrow and pain.[32]

The reconciliation between Christian leaders that took place at GCOWE '95 and '97 impacted participants deeply, paving the way for working together in the national initiatives and resource networks and the Great Commission.

Conclusion

AD2000 served as a Great Commission catalyst by focusing tightly on its purpose, which was to *motivate* and *network* men and women church leaders by *inspiring them with the vision of reaching the unreached* by *the year 2000* through *consultations, prayer efforts,* and *communication materials.* The catalytic impact of AD2000 on Great Commission efforts was a result of the implementation of the primary elements of this purpose.

Following GCOWE '97 in South Africa a Christian leader listed the unique contributions of the AD2000 Movement to world evangelization, which included the following items:

- Has empowered an unprecedented global awareness of and commitment to completion of the Great Commission.
- Has produced an unprecedented, global Third World, non-Western awareness of, commitment to, and involvement in leadership for fulfillment of the Great Commission.
- Has provided an unprecedented global platform on which mission/church leadership from East/West and North/South have been able to meet for action plans related to fulfillment of the Great Commission.
- Has provided an unprecedented global awareness of the need for national and people-group specific strategies for evangelism in contrast to the traditional ad hoc approaches.[33]

Another Christian leader wrote: "The AD2000 and Beyond Movement has been raised up by God as the chief force for catalyzing the multiple churches, agencies, ministries, and denominations around the world for a concerted effort to complete the task for world evangelization."[34]

From the very first formative AD2000 meeting, it was agreed that this would be a catalytic movement seeking to encourage the global Christian community toward the goal of "a church for every people and the Gospel for every person" in the decade of the 1990s, and to disband beyond. A disband clause, to be effective by the year 2001, was incorporated into the AD2000 handbook and the corporate by-laws. Although implications of the commitment to disband have been questioned in light of the ongoing vision and mission momentum the AD2000 movement generated, in keeping with the agreement, AD2000 disbanded.

Notes

1. "The Manila Manifesto," in *Proclaim Christ Until He Comes*, ed. J. D. Douglas (Minneapolis: World Wide Publications, 1990), p. 37.

2. Luis K. Bush, ed., *AD2000 and Beyond Handbook*, 3d ed. (Colorado Springs, Colo.: AD2000 and Beyond Movement, 1993), p. 1.

3. Patrick Johnstone, letter to the author, 1992.

4. Patrick Johnstone, "Summary Report: Unreached Peoples Network," *AD2000 Announce*, September 7, 2000.

5. Bush, *AD2000 and Beyond Handbook*, pp. 1, 44.

6. Ibid., p. 44.

7. Thomas Wang, "The Year 2000: Is God Trying to Tell Us Something?" in *Countdown to AD2000*, ed. Thomas Wang (Pasadena, Calif.: AD2000 Movement, 1989), xiv-xx.

8. Luis Bush, *The 10/40 Window: Getting to the Core of the Core* (Colorado Springs, Colo.: AD2000 Movement, 1992), p. 3.

9. William D. Taylor, "Global Consultation on Evangelical Missiology" (paper presented to the World Evangelical Fellowship Missions Commission, October 10–16, 1999, Iguassu, Parana, Brazil).

10. Bush, *The 10/40 Window*, p. 1.

11. Criteria for inclusion on the Joshua Project 2000 list of selected peoples required that a group be ethnolinguistically or nationally distinct, have a population of over 10,000 in a given country, and have less than 2 percent evangelicals and less than 5 percent Christian adherents. Hundreds of churches, mission agencies, denominations, and theological institutions from around the world have become involved in the Joshua Project.

12. Patrick Johnstone, *The Church Is Bigger than You Think* (Ross-shire, U.K.: Christian Focus Publications and WEC, 1998), p. 107.

13. Henry Grunwald, "The Year 2000: Is It the End or Just the Beginning?" *Time* 139, no. 13 (March 30, 1992): 73–76.

14. John Naisbitt and Patricia Aburdene, *Megatrends 2000: Ten New Directions for the 1990s* (New York: Morrow, 1990), p. 270.

15. Quoted in Jay Rogers, "*Megatrends* Authors Predict Spiritual Awakening for the 1990s," Media House International Online, Internet, http://forerunner.com/forerunner/X0290_Megatrends_authors.html.

16. Douglas, ed., *Proclaim Christ Until He Comes*, p. 37.

17. Luis K. Bush, ed., *GCOWE '95 Handbook* (Colorado Springs, Colo.: AD2000 and Beyond Movement, 1995), p. 125.

18. Luis K. Bush and Beverly Pegues, *The Move of the Holy Spirit in the 10/40 Window*, ed. Jane Rumph (Seattle, Wash.: YWAM Publishing, 1999), p. 228.

19. Andreas Tapia, "Is a Global Great Awakening Just Around the Corner?" *Christianity Today* 38, no. 13 (November 1994): 80, 85–86.

20. C. Peter Wagner, "Contemporary Dynamics of the Holy Spirit in Missions: A Personal Pilgrimage" (paper presented at the triennial meeting of the Evangelical Foreign Missions Association/Evangelical Missiological Society, September 20–23, 1996, Orlando, Fla.), p. 8.

21. Ibid., pp. 7–8.

22. Quoted in David and Mary Hardgrove, "GCOWE '95—A Ripple Effect," unpublished manuscript.

23. Patrick Johnstone, "The Importance of This Global Guide," in *Global Guide to Unreached Peoples*, ed. Dan Scribner (Colorado Springs, Colo.: AD2000 and Beyond Movement, 1997), p. iv.

24. Bush, *AD2000 and Beyond Handbook*, p. 15.

25. Ibid., pp. 13–14.

26. Ibid., p. 15.

27. George Verwer, "GCOWE '95," *Mission Frontiers* 17, nos. 7–8 (July–August 1995): 9.

28. Rick Wood, "GCOWE '95," *Mission Frontiers* 17, nos. 7–8 (July–August 1995): 18.

29. David Hardgrove, *Australian Presbyterian Life Today* (July 1995).

30. Douglas, ed., *Proclaim Christ Until He Comes*, p. 37.

31. Bush, ed., *GCOWE '95 Handbook*, p. 125.

32. R. J. Munn, "South Africa Victory Report," e-mail to Salvation Army global leaders, July 19, 1997.

33. Phill Butler, "Unique Contributions of the AD2000 Movement to World Evangelization," e-mail to author, August 17, 1997.

34. C. Peter Wagner, *Breaking Strongholds in Your City* (Ventura, Calif.: Regal Books, 1993), p. 12.

People Group Criteria	Groups	Population	Percent
Above 10,000 population > 2% Evangelical > 5% Adherents	4000	3,690 million	61.50%
Above 10,000 population < 2% Evangelical < 5% Adherents	1600	2,280 million	38.00%
Below 10,000	7400	30 million	.50%
World Totals	13000	6,000 million	100.00%

Church Planting Status	Population	Percent
Targeted for Church Planting by December 31, 2000	5,925 million	98.75%
Church Planting Team currently on-site	5,889 million	98.15%
Reported Fellowship of at least 100 indigenous believers	5,620 million	93.67%
World Totals	6,000 million	100.00%

Joshua Project – Least Reached Peoples		
Church Planting Progress: % of People Groups	October 1997	October 2000
Targeted for Church Planting by December 31, 2000	77%	85%
Church Planting Team currently on-site	43%	68%
Reported Fellowship of at least 100 Indigenous believers	4%	31%

Key Observations:

1. There are approximately 13,000 people groups, more than half of which are smaller than 10,000 in population.

2. The Joshua Project list represents about 2.2 billion individuals living in about 1,600 people groups that are less than 2% Evangelical and less than 5% Adherents.

3. As of December 31, 2000, nearly 99% of the world's population lived in a people group that had an actual or planned on-site church planting team.

4. Conversely, approximately 1% of the world's population lived in a people group without a church planting effort.

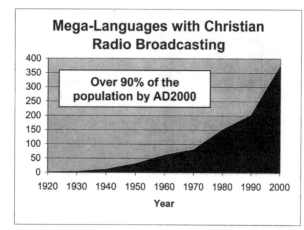

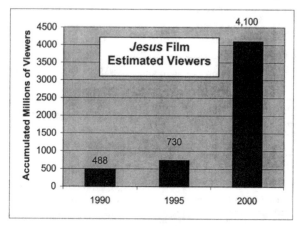

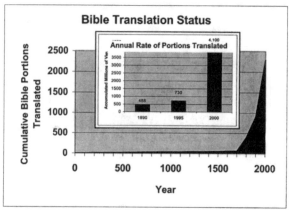

Key Observations:

1. As of December 31, 2000, 8 out of every 10 people had access to the entire Bible in their own language. Nine out of 10 had access to the New Testament.

2. As of December 31, 2000, Christian radio broadcasts covered an estimated 90% of the world's population.

3. As of December 31, 2000, there had been over 4.1 billion viewers of the *Jesus Film* and it was available in languages known by 99% of the world's population.

4. As of December 31, 2000, 4.8 billion or about 80% of the population of the world had heard the Gospel.

Chapter Two

"It Can Be Done": The Impact of Modernity and Postmodernity on the Global Mission Plans of Churches and Agencies

Todd M. Johnson

The movement to evangelize the world by A.D. 2000 adopted the same slogan proposed by evangelist D. L. Moody one hundred years earlier: "It can be done. It ought to be done. It must be done." This slogan, as well as the supreme confidence expressed throughout the twentieth century in global plans, makes one suspicious that these plans are thoroughly "modern" in their orientation—a product of their times. Yet now that it is clear that modern assumptions are giving way to postmodern ones, it is worth investigating how this change will impact missionary strategy.

In 1988 I completed an analysis of evangelization in the late nineteenth century, documenting a movement to evangelize the world by 1900.[1] I had hoped that lessons learned in this period could be particularly instructive to a meeting of Christian leaders in Singapore in 1989 who contemplated evangelizing the world by A.D. 2000. A great swell of confidence was expressed by these leaders in their ability to reach the A.D. 2000 goal. The movement that coalesced at the Singapore meeting eventually adopted the same slogan proposed by evangelist Dwight L. Moody one hundred years earlier: "It can be done. It ought to be done. It must be done."[2] This slogan, as well as the supreme confidence expressed throughout the twentieth century in global plans, makes one suspicious of the plans' cultural and philosophical foundations. Upon closer examination, these plans appear to be thoroughly "modern" in their orientation—a product of their times. Yet now that it is clear that modern assumptions are giving way to postmodern ones, it is worth investigating how this change will impact missionary strategy.

What Is a Global Plan?

A global plan can be defined as "a documented, christocentric plan, proposal, or program that starts with the Great Commission and articulates concern for evangelizing the world's entire population."[3] Beginning with Jesus one finds that throughout the history of the church its leaders have continuously proposed global plans. Specific, written, proposed, announced global plans easily number in excess of fifteen hundred, and the vast majority of these (83 percent) were proposed in the twentieth century. After glancing at nineteenth-century proposals, we will concern ourselves primarily with these twentieth-century global plans.

Evangelizing the World by 1900

My research revealed that a large number of Christians had formulated global plans set on evangelizing the world by the year 1900. Their rationale was most clearly articulated in "An Appeal to Disciples Everywhere," a document penned in 1885 by a committee that included Dwight L. Moody and Arthur T. Pierson. That same year the editors of *The Gospel in All Lands* commented, "The great need of urging forward at once the army of Christ in its contest with heathendom, ought to overshadow all minor considerations, and we welcome any plan which will the more speedily bring about the desired result."[4] During the years 1885 to 1895 missionary journals, especially the *Missionary Review of the World*, published articles on both sides of a debate about whether or not world evangelization should be attempted, what it would mean to accomplish it, and how many years it might require (estimates ranged from ten years to a million years!). A missionary conference in London in 1888, called partly in response to Moody and Pierson's "Appeal," proposed to solve once and for all the problem of world evangelization. Pierson believed that the conference could portion out all the remaining unevangelized territories among the different agencies. He was bitterly disappointed when the bulk of the presentations there focused on reporting progress among the already evangelized masses in contact with the Christian West. By 1895 he, and most others, had given up hope on the year 1900 as a viable goal.

Actual Progress by 1900

By 1900 over half of the world's population had still never heard of Jesus Christ. Optimistic projections about reaching all with the Gospel had not been attained. German missiologist Gustav Warnack, in a letter to the Ecumenical Missionary Conference meeting in New York City, warned of rushing evangelization and not paying enough attention to indigenization. That same year John R. Mott published *The Evangelization of the World in This Generation.* He tried to address Warnack's concerns, but the tone of his book was one of supreme confidence and faith that the whole world could and would be evangelized in a relatively short period of time.

Global Plans Proliferate in the Twentieth Century

Mott's book envisaged a massive movement that would span all Christian traditions and include the entire world's population. Shortly after the turn of the century every major Christian tradition began to articulate its vision for world evangelization in the form of proposals, programs, and plans. Consider the following:

- The Pentecostal movement was launched, initially with a plan to evangelize the whole world by means of workers speaking in tongues without the need for learning languages.
- The Consolata Missionary Fathers, a new Roman Catholic order founded in Turin, was one of numerous orders charged specifically to evangelize the unevangelized. By 1980 it had over a thousand missionaries.
- James Dennis completed a global statistical analysis of Christian missions, extended over the century by dozens of major statistical updates from all Christian traditions.
- National councils of churches and mission agencies were set up all over the world focused on Christian unity and evangelistic coordination.
- Emphasis on the second coming of Christ intensified through the writings of William E. Blackstone, Popes Pius X and Benedict XV, and later Hal Lindsey, Tim LaHaye, and Jerry Jenkins.
- The faith missions movement received a boost through C. T. Studd's new missions society, Christ's Etceteras (later Worldwide Evangelization Crusade, then WEC).

In 1910 the World Missionary Conference in Edinburgh, Scotland, opened with the words: "It is a startling and solemnising fact that even as late as the twentieth century the Great Command of Jesus Christ to carry the Gospel to all mankind is still so largely unfulfilled. It is a ground for great hopefulness that, notwithstanding the serious situation occasioned by such neglect, the Church is confronted today, as in no preceding generation, with a literally worldwide opportunity to make Christ known."[5] This same motif of unparalleled opportunity was revisited time and time again in twentieth-century plans, culminating in 1989 with the appropriation by the Global Consultation on World Evangelization (GCOWE) of its "kairos moment" in mission history.

Graphing Twentieth-Century Global Plans

Graph 1 on the facing page illustrates the status of some two hundred of the largest plans to evangelize the world. The vertical axis at left shows the status of each plan, and that on the right shows the percentage of the world's population that is Christian or unevangelized. The first thing to strike the eye is that most of these larger plans proposed since 1900 are still active, and many are doing quite well. With the plans juxtaposed against the slow decline in the percentage of the unevangelized, however, it is clear that these plans, even though healthy, were unable to attain their stated goal of evangelizing the world. Second, one sees the proliferation of plans in the last decade of the century. It is perhaps too early to measure their impact.

Assessing the Impact of Twentieth-Century Global Plans

At the end of the twentieth century just over 33 percent of the world's population professed to be Christians. Contrary to the optimistic expectation one hundred years ago of a "Christian century," this percentage is actually slightly lower than it was in 1900. One might conclude that global plans have made virtually no progress in enlisting followers in the past one hundred years.

Positive Achievements of Global Plans

Such a conclusion would, however, miss the radical changes that have impacted the world Christian movement in the twentieth century. First of all, in 1900 more than 80 percent of all Christians were white. Most were from Europe and North America. Today

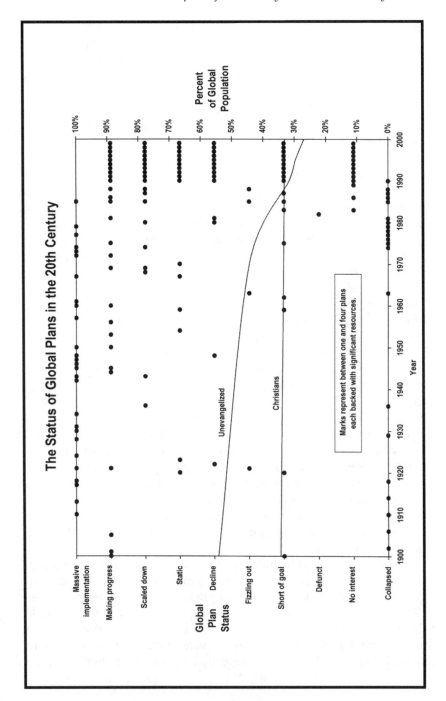

that figure has dropped to 45 percent. The demographic mass of Christianity is now found in Latin America, Africa, and Asia.[6] Over the next twenty-five years the "white" portion of global Christianity is expected to continue to decline dramatically. Global plans are also following this shift with an ever-increasing number originating in the non-Western world.

Second, in 1900 only a handful of Christians were involved in renewal movements. By A.D. 2000 over 500 million, or 25 percent of all Christians, were participants in the Pentecostal/charismatic renewal. Over the century the first wave of renewal, the Pentecostal movement, has grown into 750 denominations in 225 countries with 65 million members. Later, a second wave, the charismatic renewal, hit the mainline churches encompassing 6,500 denominations in 235 countries with over 175 million members. Finally, a third wave, termed here the rise of the neocharismatics, emphasizing a break with Western denominationalism, has spread into over 18,800 networks in 225 countries, claiming over 295 million members. The majority of these are in Africa and Asia. Altogether these three waves of renewal mark a radical transformation of Christianity in the twentieth century.[7] Global plans are emerging from all three waves.

Third, Christians of all major traditions have grown increasingly committed to the Great Commission of Jesus Christ. One out of three Christians in the world today is active in obedience to this Commission. The number has grown from 78 million Great Commission Christians in 1900 to over 650 million in A.D. 2000.[8] As a result, hundreds of new mission agencies have been formed and thousands of new missionaries sent out. The independent churches, barely a factor in mission in 1900, are now providing a new infusion of workers as many of the more traditional sending bodies continue to decline. An entirely unexpected surge of workers has emerged from the non-Western world—thousands of new churches and agencies formulating global plans and sending out foreign and home missionaries.

Fourth, Christians have stepped up their evangelistic efforts particularly in line with advances in communications technology, beginning with radio broadcasting from 1921 and progressing to satellite networks and the Internet today. We estimate that in 1900 Christians generated enough evangelism on earth for every person to hear the Gospel six times every year. By 2000 that figure had skyrocketed to 155 times—a gospel presentation for every person on earth every other day all year long.[9] Global plans increasingly take advantage of technological advances.

Goals of Global Plans Not Met

Remarkably, these dramatic changes have not achieved a fundamental goal of Christian missions—proclaiming the Good News to every people in the world. In 1910 a major study by Samuel Zwemer was commissioned by the World Missionary Conference in Edinburgh and then published the following year as *The Unoccupied Mission Fields of Africa and Asia.* Zwemer clearly outlined the unfinished task and the opportunities the churches had for contacting the unevangelized. He even emblazoned an early version of the 10/40 Window on the cover. This call was largely ignored. Similar clarion calls, many as global plans, were issued throughout the twentieth century, culminating in a concerted global effort in the 1990s focused on a now-popularized 10/40 Window. Nonetheless, at the end of the twentieth century 1.6 billion people in several thousand ethnolinguistic peoples were without access to a culturally relevant church community.

This shortfall is largely the result of the choice of locations where missionaries went to work during the twentieth century. Nine out of ten missionaries were sent out to work among peoples already contacted with the Christian message and, in many cases, already heavily Christian. This pattern is being repeated today by the new independent missionaries and, to a large extent, by non-Western missionaries.[10]

Another unanticipated trend has been the tremendous resistance non-Christians have shown to Christians and Christian missions in the twentieth century. The rise of Communism early in the century provided most of this dynamic. For over sesventy years not only were Christians in Communist lands under intense persecution, but millions lost their lives prematurely as a result of their witness—the standard definition of Christian martyrs. With the collapse of Communism in the latter part of the century, one would think that martyrdom and persecution would now be rare. Unfortunately, this is not the case. Outside of the Communist world, governments that now persecute Christians are run by secularists, Muslims, Hindus, and, surprisingly, other Christians. In fact, the twentieth century has been the bloodiest on record, not only for all of humanity, but for Christians as well. In these hundred years more Christians lost their lives as martyrs than in all the previous centuries combined.[11]

Modernity's Impact

Global plans of the twentieth century were for the most part modern. They shared the characteristics of the age in which they were conceived. Most were overconfident in the statements of what they hoped to achieve. Some were racist; others marginalized women. Nearly all expressed modern overconfidence coupled with a belief in inevitable progress—the cornerstone of Enlightenment thought. Even the popular missionary hymns from the turn of the century reflect this: "For the darkness shall turn to dawning, and the dawning to noonday bright, and Christ's great kingdom shall come on earth, the kingdom of love and light."[12] A rehearsal of the names of global plans shows this tendency clearly. Consider the following chronological procession:

1900   The evangelization of the world in this generation
1908   The modern crusade
1910   The whole church taking the whole gospel to the whole world
1912   Reaching every home
1914   Inauguration of the Kingdom of God on earth
1929   Each one teach one
1930   Bringing Christ to the nations
1934   Evangelize to a finish to bring back the king
1943   Into all the world
1946   Complete Christ's commission
1950   Help open paths to evangelize
1956   The gospel to every creature
1957   Global conquest
1959   Two thousand tongues to go
1963   The master plan of evangelism
1967   Crusade for world revival
1974   Let the earth hear his voice
1976   Bold mission thrust
1980   A church for every people by the year 2000
1984   Strategy to every people

1986   One million native missionaries
1990   Decade of evangelization

Each of these global plans proposed in the twentieth century emphasizes an aspect of the Great Commission, but each also contains hints of a modern worldview. D. L. Moody's slogan, mentioned earlier, also typifies the modern impulse in global plans. Although the slogan applies to Christian initiative, it can be interpreted to contain strong modern undertones. "It can be done" expresses the modern emphasis that all problems have a solution. "It ought to be done" expresses the modern sentiment that man has a moral or humanitarian responsibility to others. "It must be done" expresses the modern belief in inevitable progress. Moody and his successors stopped short of "It will be done," which would be the epitome of modern hubris.

Postmodernity's Impact

It is not too early to make a preliminary evaluation of postmodernity. Its impact on global plans is clearly beginning to be felt. First of all, critiques of modernity are emerging. The most vocal have focused on the alleged "managerial missiology" of the Western world. This theme was taken up at the World Evangelical Fellowship–sponsored Iguassu Missiological Consultation held in Brazil in October 1999. The compendium that emerged from the meeting is clearly focused on critiquing forms of missions strategy that have modern roots.[13] This critique is helpful insofar as it highlights areas where self-critical reflection is long overdue and much needed. Unfortunately, the compendium also illustrates how difficult it is both to distance oneself from the past and at the same time to integrate essential elements of a comprehensive missiology into the "new" way of doing things. For example, while decrying the quantitative approach throughout, the authors also present a jumble of statistics in and out of context. More prevalent is the trend (warned against in social science literature[14]) of replacing overconfident quantitative statements of fact with overconfident qualitative statements of fact. In this sense, authors throughout the compendium tend to critique one modern weakness but then to replace it with another.

Second, decentralization of church and mission authority has begun to stifle overly enthusiastic plans from top leadership. Middle managers are beginning to emerge as key players in strategy.[15] An important development in this area is the worldwide rise of the independent churches. As these have begun to participate in missions, they have done so without many of the trappings of centralized planning. The process has included more collaboration with local churches.

Third, decentralization has led to an increase in church-based initiatives. Individual churches are beginning to have an impact on mission strategy by becoming more directly involved in reaching peoples. Unreached peoples are adopted, teams are sent to visit and pray, and, in many cases, long-term personnel are deployed, often without reference to mission agencies.

Fourth, decentralization also encourages individual initiative. Whereas in the modern pattern, Christians with resources tended to support existing institutions and programs, today one sees more direct involvement by individuals, ranging from their being given a voice in projects to the development of completely independent projects.

Fifth, perhaps the most significant development is the rise of specifically nonglobal plans. Without centralized planning, agencies and churches are focusing more on specific peoples, countries, and regions. Except for the largest agencies, most work in thirty or fewer countries. As churches begin to work directly on the field, their emphasis is not global but local. The advantage of this type of strategy is the availability of far more resources for reaching unreached peoples. The disadvantage, which has already been observed in places like the former Soviet Union, is massive duplication of resources. What happens when thousands of individuals, churches, and agencies all have their eye on the same new opportunity?

Twenty-first-Century Plans

The challenges that the new missions force of the twenty-first century faces are legion. The world of A.D. 2001 is radically different from that of 1901. The overconfidence exhibited early in the twentieth century by secular leaders of the Enlightenment project has been completely deflated by the collapse of Communism and a general loss of faith in science and the idea of inevitable progress.[16] Theologians and mission leaders who borrowed heavily from the modern paradigm find themselves at a crossroads. Although some advocate an even stronger "modern" approach, many see the changing times as a corrective to the overconfidence of twentieth-century strategies.

With that in mind, some see the ethos of twentieth-century mission creeping into twenty-first-century initiatives. First, they point out a tendency to convene big conferences with impressive slogans in which the implications of the slogans are not seriously addressed. Second, the hoped-for century of church union has become instead one of schism and lack of cooperation. Instead of existing denominations uniting, hundreds of new organizations have emerged, each with its own independently stated plans. Third, the number of missionaries available for frontier missions may be impacted by an increasing uneasiness over the efficacy of Christianity in already-discipled peoples—with Rwanda as a premier example. As a result, more mission effort is advocated among the 141 countries that are already 60 percent or more Christian—already the locus of 97 percent of current missionary deployment.[17] Fourth, short-term missions is now a driving force in missions. Although this means that more Christians are exposed to mission fields, it seems to be having the effect of injecting a short-term emphasis into long-term church planting strategies. Fifth, although much has been learned in contextualization of the Gospel, emerging short-term mentalities foreshadow a de-emphasis on language and culture learning—the backbone of the foreign missionary enterprise.

Positive Achievements of Twentieth-Century Plans

Nonetheless, positive developments in twentieth-century global plans are also being appropriated in the new century. First and foremost has been the formation of two kinds of partnerships. One, we see increasing cooperation between Western and non-Western missions. Whereas there have been many false starts along the way, valuable lessons have been learned relating to the use of money and the sharing of control of personnel and funds. Two, strategic partnerships between mission agencies have been formed specifically around unreached peoples. For example, a Bible translation agency might work closely with church planting efforts and radio broadcasters. Although these partnerships are few in number, they represent a major step forward in frontier missions strategy. Closely related to this is the rise of strategy coordinators. This new breed of missionary steps back far enough from a specific people to enumerate all the possible ways they might be reached. He or she then chooses ten or so of the best strategies and advocates among specialized agencies (such as media ministries) for their accomplishment.

Perhaps the most astonishing development in frontier missions in the twentieth century has been the unanticipated rise of nonbaptized believers in Christ.[18] Akin to the fabulous growth of the Chinese house churches or African independent churches in the latter half of the twentieth century, several million Hindus, Muslims, and Buddhists have given their primary allegiance to Jesus Christ but have chosen not to leave their cultural traditions to join Christian churches. Their growth and development as individual believers and movements is not to be taken for granted. It may depend largely on the ability of key leaders within the churches to study and understand the implications of this kind of radical contextualization. Their challenge in their role as ambassadors will be to try to anticipate how the new believers can interact with the churches. They may also be able to unlock contextualized strategies in reaching peoples currently beyond the Gospel.

All of these developments underscore the fact that the missionary strategist or planner of the twenty-first century will likely have a much greater load to bear than his or her twentieth-century predecessor. Faced with information overload in a networked environment, multiple agencies from multiple countries taking multiple approaches, the impact of globalization and postmodernism on seemingly remote peoples, an increased need for cultural, ethnic, and religious sensitivity, the emergence of almost-unrecognizable new forms of Christianity, and a host of other new factors, global plans will need to be more carefully constructed in the twenty-first century. Only then will the churches of the world be able to fulfill the initial requirement of the Great Commission and the true goal of the global planning process—the effective penetration of all peoples with the Gospel.

Notes

General note: All statistics in the text are documented in David B. Barrett, George T. Kurian, and Todd M. Johnson, *World Christian Encyclopedia: A Comparative Survey of Churches and Religions in the Modern World*, 2d ed., 2 vols. (Oxford and New York: Oxford Univ. Press, 2001), cited in the notes as *WCE*; and David B. Barrett and Todd M. Johnson, *World Christian Trends, AD 30–AD 2200* (Pasadena, Calif.:

William Carey Library, 2001), cited in the notes as *WCT*. For an annual summary table of global statistics see www.globalchristianity.org.

1. See Todd M. Johnson, *Countdown to 1900: Evangelization at the End of the Nineteenth Century* (Birmingham, Ala.: New Hope Press, 1988).
2. This quotation appears, among other places, in Luis Bush, ed., *AD2000 and Beyond Handbook: A Church for Every People and the Gospel for Every Person by AD 2000*, 3d ed. (Colorado Springs, Colo.: AD2000 and Beyond Movement, 1993), title page. The story of the Singapore meeting is related on pp. 1–2.
3. Global plans are examined in great detail in *WCT*, part 26, "GeoStrategies."
4. "Dividing the World for Evangelization," *The Gospel in All Lands*, November 1885, p. 517.
5. See *World Missionary Conference, 1910:* Report of Commission I: *Carrying the Gospel to All the Non-Christian World* (Edinburgh: Oliphant, Anderson, & Ferrier; and New York: Fleming H. Revell, 1910).
6. See *WCE*, part 8, "EthnoSphere."
7. See *WCT*, part 5, "GeoRenewal."
8. See *WCT*, part 21, "GeoPersonnel."
9. See *WCT*, part 24, "Microevangelistics."
10. See Global Diagram 62, "Where should missionaries work?" in *WCT*, part 1, "GeoStatus."
11. *WCT*, part 4, "Martyrology."
12. H. Ernest Nichol, "We've a Story to Tell to the Nations," 1896.
13. William D. Taylor, ed., *Global Missiology for the Twenty-first Century: The Iguassu Dialogue* (Grand Rapids: Baker Academic, 2000).
14. See Isadore Newman and Carolyn R. Benz, *Qualitative-Quantitative Research Methodology: Exploring the Interactive Continuum* (Carbondale: Southern Illinois Univ. Press, 1998).
15. See S. J. Wall and S. R. Wall, *The New Strategists: Creating Leaders at All Levels* (New York: Free Press, 1995).
16. For characteristics of modernity see Lawrence Cahoone, ed., *From Modernism to Postmodernism: An Anthology* (Cambridge: Blackwell, 1996).
17. See James F. Engel and William A. Dyrness, *Changing the Mind of Missions: Where Have We Gone Wrong?* (Downers Grove, Ill.: InterVarsity, 2000). The 97 percent figure appears in various sources, for example, the pamphlet "The Invisible Majority in the 10/40 Window" (Brampton, Ontario: CNEC–Partners International, n.d.), and a similar brochure, "The 10/40 Window: Getting to the Core of the Core" (Colorado Springs, Colo.: AD2000 and Beyond Movement, n.d.).
18. See *WCT*, part 6, "Independency," for a description of these movements.

Chapter Three

Surprises of the Holy Spirit: How Pentecostalism Has Changed the Landscape of Modern Mission

Gary B. McGee

Pentecostalism has pressed virtually every branch of Christianity to review its understanding of the ministry of the Holy Spirit in the life and mission of the church. Pentecostal missions have thrived on an unbridled confidence in the restoration of the spiritual dynamics of early Christian evangelism, coupled with a robust pragmatism in methodology. Emerging out of the experiential piety of the nineteenth-century Wesleyan/Holiness and Higher Life movements, the Pentecostal movement has emphasized the affective dimension of Christian living in part by teaching that baptism in the Holy Spirit (characterized by glossolalia) is a postconversion experience intended for every believer. Other "surprises" of the Spirit have included the charismatic renewals in the mainline Protestant churches and the Roman Catholic Church, the empowerment of women, the ease with which Pentecostal spirituality has been contextualized in Third World countries, and the vast numbers of Christians who have embraced it.

"We have depended too much on man, too little on God," confessed John L. Nevius to the Shanghai Missionary Conference in 1890. "We have rested too much on human agencies and methods and too little on the direct power of the Holy Spirit."[1] At the time, fewer than two hundred thousand Protestants could be found in China out of a population of well over a quarter of a billion people.[2] One cynic quipped, "More die here every minute than are converted in a century."[3] Nevius and his colleagues had every right to be concerned. Though Christianity had gained its greatest advance around the world, the results still seemed disappointing given the huge investment in missionary personnel and funds.[4]

Dramatic changes on the international scene, the potential that could be achieved through united action, and the belief that a new era in history had begun drew mission leaders twenty years later to the World Missionary Conference at Edinburgh, Scotland, to plan for the future. Now that the Protestant missionary enterprise had entered its second century, what would the future hold? Some hoped the meeting would rise above the mechanics of cooperation, recruitment and training of missionaries, and fund-raising to center attention on the work of the Holy Spirit in mission. Jonathan Goforth, the redoubtable Canadian Presbyterian missionary to China, prayed that the conference would spark a "new Pentecost." In his estimation, the possibilities seemed endless: "The home churches, empowered by a mighty Holy Ghost Revival, would send out men fitted as were Paul and Barnabas. With their enormous resources in men and means the world would be evangelized in a generation." However, much to his dissatisfaction, "of the many who spoke to that great missionary gathering," he recalled, "not more than three emphasized God the Holy Spirit as the one essential factor in world evangelization. Listening to the addresses . . . one could not but conclude that the giving of the Gospel to lost mankind was largely a matter of better organization, better equipment, more men and women."[5] For "radical evangelicals" like Goforth, increasingly perturbed over the slow pace of conversions and the number of peoples not yet reached with the Gospel, the only hope for accomplishing the Great Commission lay in a special infusion of spiritual power in the church.[6]

For whatever reasons, the leaders of the mission establishment who planned the conclave failed to see—or possibly underestimated—the interest in the Holy Spirit that had been steadily growing for decades. Calls to prayer for the outpouring of the Holy Spirit as predicted by the Old Testament prophet Joel (2:28–29) had echoed back and forth across the continents in the second half of the century, encouraged in part by revival movements and the mounting global influence of the Wesleyan Holiness and Reformed "Higher Life" movements. The urgency reflected a sense of spiritual powerlessness in sectors of the missionary community. A long-standing debate over how far the "apostolic methods" of first-century evangelism could be adapted to the modern era added to the dilemma. An uneasiness arose when the effectiveness of contemporary mission methods were compared with those of the early church. Thus, in his keynote address to the first international convention of the Student Volunteer Movement for Foreign Missions at Cleveland, Ohio, in 1891, A. J. Gordon lamented the "deplorable weakness" of the church: "Have we forgotten that there is a Holy Ghost, that we must insist upon walking upon crutches when we might fly?"[7]

Little did the Edinburgh conferees in June 1910 realize the significance of the Pentecostal revival that had begun earlier in the decade. No one at the time could have foreseen how the surprises of the Holy Spirit that came with Pentecostalism in its various forms would impact the Christian world mission. Catholic charismatic theologian Peter Hocken finds the term "surprises" to be particularly appropriate: "The focus on surprise is not a concentration on extraordinary phenomena, but a reflection on the unexpectedness of these interventions of God. Surprises result from the disparity between the greatness of the divine work and the limitations of human understanding. God's works surprise us because they do not conform to our expectations and do not fit into our received categories." Therefore, "attention to the surprises is important because they show where we need to revise our thinking and expand our categories to the scope of God's acts."[8]

Following a short historical introduction, this essay will briefly analyze selected aspects of ways in which Pentecostalism has influenced spirituality, fostered an egalitarian concept of ministry, affected relationships between Christians, and contributed to the growth of indigenous churches.

Pentecostalism in the Twentieth Century

Pentecostalism emerged from the experiential piety of revivalism and the confluence of the nineteenth-century Wesleyan/Holiness and Higher Life movements, the evangelical healing movement, and the premillennial eschatology of the Plymouth Brethren.[9] Holiness advocates, endeavoring to restore the spiritual dynamics of the New Testament church, turned to the Book of Acts and defined baptism in the Holy Spirit as a postconversion experience intended for every believer. To the Wesleyans it furnished sanctifying grace, while Higher Life teachers held a closely related understanding of "full consecration" that empowered the faithful to witness. Put together, they constituted the "Four-fold Gospel" or "Full Gospel," a crystallized statement of basic Holiness beliefs pointing to Christ as Savior, sanctifier (baptizer in the Holy Spirit), healer, and coming king. To these radical evangelicals, successful evangelization required "Spirit-filled" missionaries in whose ministries displays of divine power would be the norm rather than the exception.

Looking back after a century, we find the course of history becoming clearer, and little-known happenings taking on greater magnitude. Two such events occurred on the first day of the century, on different continents, on opposing battlements of theology, and with vastly different outlooks on church and mission. On January 1, 1901, Agnes Ozman, a student at Charles F. Parham's Bethel Bible School in Topeka, Kansas, testified to speaking in tongues— and not just the "tongues of angels," but the Chinese language to prepare her as a missionary to China.[10] Unbeknown to the Topeka enthusiasts, on the same day in Saint Peter's Basilica in Rome, Pope Leo XIII solemnly intoned the hymn "Come, Holy Ghost" in the name of the whole church. This invocation was not done by happenstance; he did it at the urging of Elena Guerra, a woman as obscure as Ozman but later dubbed the Apostle of the Holy Spirit by Pope John XXIII.[11] If either party had known about the other event, they would have instantly dismissed its importance. However, six decades later when John XXIII opened the Second Vatican Council and prayed for a "new Pentecost," the Pentecostal movement had become the fastest growing Christian movement worldwide. Within just twenty more years Catholic charismatics would number in the tens of millions, and the two movements of the Spirit would at last intersect where each had begun.

Parham, a Midwestern Holiness preacher, had opened Bethel Bible School to prepare Spirit-filled missionaries. To him and his students, as well as the participants at later Pentecostal revivals around the world, including William J. Seymour and the "saints" at the Azusa Street revival (1906–09) in Los Angeles, California, the end-time outpouring of the Spirit had started. Living just days, weeks, or months before the return of Christ for his church, they experienced the "Apostolic faith" of the early Christians restored in its fullness. God had bestowed spiritual power and the languages of the nations to expedite evangelization; long years of preparation in language school could now be bypassed to begin preaching immediately when one arrived on the mission field.[12] Topeka looked at power to witness, while Azusa Street, with its interracial and intercultural makeup, expanded the revival to encompass reconciliation.[13] Seymour's perspective denoted the Spirit's conferral of dignity and empowerment on black Pentecostals and Hispanics in America and oppressed peoples overseas. Azusa's "prophetic witness" against the prejudices and racism of the prevailing culture would later challenge white Pentecostals who, though deeply committed to mission—even holistic mission—hesitated about the role of social justice in mission.[14]

By the time Edinburgh convened, over two hundred Pentecostals labored abroad, mostly in the traditional sites of Protestant mission activity.[15] Topeka/Azusa and Edinburgh represent contrasting visions of mission: one populist and the other establishment, one explosive and the other orderly, one focused on proclamation and the other on holistic mission, one with a wide streak of independence and the other seeking cooperation, one with a stopwatch and the other with Big Ben.

Without doubt, the flourishing of Pentecostalism proved to be one of the most astonishing developments in modern Christianity, the first time a charismatic movement had survived long enough to institutionalize and thrive. To outsiders it appeared to throw all caution to the wind about seeking the gifts of the Spirit. Beginning with what one Holiness periodical in 1908 called the "very scum of sectism,"[16] Pentecostals had traveled a long way when five decades later Bishop Lesslie Newbigin christened them as a "third stream of Christian tradition" in which the "central element is the conviction that the Christian life is a matter of the experienced power and presence of the Holy Spirit."[17] New upsurges of Pentecostal restorationism came in the 1950s and '60s with the coming of the charismatic renewal in the mainstream Protestant churches and the Roman Catholic Church. Conservative evangelicals also began to venture into the charismatic dimension of spirituality, a development labeled as the Third Wave of the Holy Spirit.[18] At the close of the century, thousands of Pentecostal and charismatic missionaries from virtually every corner of the globe were on the move to share the Gospel.

Pentecostal Spirituality

The Pentecostal movement burst on the scene with a confidence and energy that stunned observers. For the most part, "Classical Pentecostals" believed that speaking in tongues—soon understood to mean prayer in the Spirit rather than preaching—constituted the indispensable initial evidence of Spirit baptism.[19] They also tenaciously prayed for the sick long after the wider healing movement had declined.[20] Stoking the fervor, the "countdown" nature of their eschatology left them little time to complete the Great Commission.

Of course, Pentecostals were not the only evangelicals to explore the ministry of the Holy Spirit in mission; neither did they believe that they alone experienced the Spirit, as outsiders sometimes concluded. But what distinguishes Pentecostal spirituality is the emphasis placed on the affective dimension of Christian living. It is driven by an intense longing for the experiential fullness of the Spirit's power in one's life and ministry, not unlike that received by the 120 disciples on the Day of Pentecost—what New Testament scholar Robert P. Menzies describes as "a prophetic anointing which enables them to participate effectively in the missionary enterprise of the Church."[21] Where the Holiness movement had poured the foundation for the Pentecostal baptism, Pentecostals built a doctrine connecting it to the charismatic experience of speaking in tongues (glossolalia), a construct that brought a more mystical element to their spirituality. As the Singaporean theologian Simon Chan says, "Glossolalia is not just one of the concomitants of being Spirit-filled, but is the most natural and regular concomitant of Spirit-filling involving an invasive or irruptive manifestation of the Spirit in which one's relationship to Jesus Christ is radically and significantly altered." Hence, "when one experiences the coming of the Spirit in such a manner, the most natural and spontaneous response is glossolalia."[22]

Reflecting the holiness roots of the movement, one early Pentecostal explained, "The Cross is intimately and inseparably connected with Pentecost. In seeking the baptism of the Holy Ghost, the deepest crucifixion of heart is experienced as a preparation for His incoming." As a result of the surrender of the will to the Holy Spirit, "this baptism puts more love in us for God and His people and for the lost than anything that has ever come to this world. . . . His love is shed abroad in our hearts by the Holy Ghost which is given unto us."[23]

Minnie F. Abrams, a Methodist-turned-Pentecostal missionary in India who wrote the first Pentecostal theology of mission (*The Baptism of the Holy Ghost and Fire* [1906]), forged a unique adaptation of *missio Dei* when she declared, "The baptism of the Holy Ghost is the revelation of the triune God in us and through us to a lost dying world."[24] This dynamic brought an absolute certainty of the Spirit's work, leading the faithful to see their activities in mission as a restoration of New Testament Christianity—the inauguration of Acts 29 in the "last days." With this came confidence in the contemporary availability of the charismatic gifts in the life of the church and supernatural "signs and wonders" to accompany the preaching of the Good News. For this reason, the history of Pentecostal and now charismatic mission endeavors carries thousands of stories of physical healings, deliverances from chemical addictions, exorcisms, and other extraordinary happenings that have changed the lives of people.

Combined with a strong conviction about the transforming effect of the Spirit in their lives, Pentecostals took a pragmatic approach to ministry and missions. Historian Grant Wacker notes that American Pentecostals came from a cross section of society and held their restorationist and pragmatic impulses in a remarkably "productive tension" that "enabled them to capture lightning in a bottle and, more important, to keep it there, decade after decade, without stilling the fire or cracking the vessel."[25] Consequently, a certain "recklessness of faith" has characterized Pentecostals, prompting Latin American scholar Everett Wilson to say that "many of the movement's apparent successes were achieved by men and women who, on the face of it, were unlikely to realize outstanding accomplishments and whose efforts at first glance appeared futile or misdirected."[26]

This has led to unusual innovations in mission, all indicators that the practice of Pentecostal missions has involved far more than miraculous expectations. When the outcome of World War II seemed clear, the Assemblies of God (U.S.A.) recognized the need to expedite the transportation of missionaries and developed a fund-raising program for its youth known as Speed-the-Light. Two airplanes were then purchased to carry missionaries overseas before commercial air travel was fully restored.[27] Since that time millions of dollars have been raised to buy cars, trucks, bicycles, oxcarts, donkeys, motorboats, and other means of transportation. On another front, missionaries in Latin America, when lacking adequate classroom facilities for Bible institute classes, refused to be deterred and met with their students in the open air or in any facilities that could be adapted for their use.[28]

The insights of Pentecostal/charismatic spirituality, however, have sometimes been distorted. Its individualistic nature has at times bred an attitude of spiritual elitism, noncooperation, and refusal to be accountable to others. Furthermore, when the quest for spiritual power has begun to mask carnal ambitions and subsequently becomes separated from the more fundamental striving toward Christlikeness, disaster in ministry and relationships becomes inevitable. Finally, excessive literalism in biblical interpretation has occasionally reopened the debate over what may be left to restore from the life and teachings of the early church (for instance, water baptism in the name of Jesus Christ [Acts 2:38], offices of apostle and prophet [Eph. 4:11]).[29]

Women in Ministry

Phoebe Palmer, a pioneer theologian in the Holiness movement, queried in her classic *Promise of the Father* (1859), "If the Spirit of prophecy fell upon God's daughters [on the Day of Pentecost], alike as upon his sons in that day, and they spake in the midst of that assembled multitude, as the Spirit gave utterance, on what authority do the angels of the churches restrain the use of that gift now?"[30] The egalitarian concept of ministry for women within Pentecostalism can be traced to the writings of Palmer and other advocates, as well as the example of prominent Holiness women evangelists in the late nineteenth century such as Amanda Berry Smith and Maria B. Woodworth-Etter.

In early Pentecostalism, only a thin line separated professional clergy from laity; Spirit baptism equipped everyone to witness for Christ. Significant illustrations of that empowerment appear in the stories of women who were baptized in the Spirit and then felt called to ministry. Theologian Janet Everts Powers notes that "in revival, spiritual power reigns and social patterns are disrupted, so women who have spiritual power can operate autonomously. But when revival wanes, the original social and religious patterns are restored."[31] In the early years of the revival, Pentecostal women opened missionary-training institutions and also worked as the majority of missionaries for decades. Since they followed in the path of Holiness women who used the same Scripture texts to justify their ministry (Joel 2, Acts 1–2, 1 Cor. 12), where is the surprise? It stands in the persistent appearance of women around the world who have determined to minister in the power of the Spirit despite the male dominance of church organizations and continuing opposition to women serving in leadership positions.[32] From Aimee Semple McPherson, founder of the International Church of the Foursquare Gospel, to healing evangelist Kathryn Kuhlman, to Malaysian church planter Susan Tang, and to Jashil Choi, mother-in-law of David Yonggi Cho and originator of the idea of Prayer Mountain in Korea, women in the Pentecostal tradition have reached audiences far beyond ecclesiastical fence lines in ways that Phoebe Palmer could never have imagined.[33]

Though the number of women ministers in Pentecostal denominations substantially declined over the twentieth century, women in the independent sectors of the Pentecostal and charismatic movements and especially women outside of North Atlantic countries have sometimes faced fewer restrictions. For instance, during an evangelistic campaign in Kisumu, Kenya, in 1996, Bishop LaDonna Osborn of Tulsa, Oklahoma, prayed for a woman dying of AIDS. "She heard the gospel, believed in Christ, and was marvelously healed by Christ's power," Osborn remembers. "She testified publicly that she had been healed, although I could see that she was skin and bones." Returning to Kenya, Osborn again encountered the woman. Not only had she completely regained her health, but she had also planted three churches on her own initiative.[34]

More Surprises

Classical Pentecostals confidently assumed that their movement represented the "big surprise" of the Spirit and enjoyed their newfound status as the "third stream" or, as they preferred, the "third force" within Christianity.[35] The Holy Spirit, however, had a few more surprises under its feathers, notably the charismatic renewal in the mainline Protestant churches, renewal in the Roman Catholic Church, and the increasing complexity of Pentecostalism worldwide. Each would share certain spiritual commonalities with Classical Pentecostals yet differ markedly in other theological and cultural aspects.

Grassroots Pentecostals frequently applauded the charismatics from the mainline churches, not only because they perceived the same activity of the Spirit, but also for the vindication of their own spirituality that had been much maligned. American Pentecostal leaders, sensitive to the opinions of fellow leaders in the National Association of Evangelicals, approached charismatics more cautiously since the latter usually belonged to churches affiliated with the National Council of Churches. However, when many of them chose to remain within their own denominations and other troubling issues arose, the affirmation of Pentecostal leaders grew faint.[36]

No greater surprise awaited the Pentecostals than the renewal that began in the Roman Catholic Church in 1967 on the heels of the Second Vatican Council. In the years that followed, it won the endorsement of popes, bishops, theologians, and a myriad of priests and laypersons. "This is the first time in Christian history," averred Peter Hocken, "that a movement of Protestant provenance had not only entered the Roman Catholic Church, but had also been received and accepted by church authority."[37] Pentecostals who acknowledged the genuineness of the renewal recognized that where the gifts and fruit of the Holy Spirit are manifested, there one finds members of Christ's church.[38] Hence, the mutual recognition of the presence of the Spirit by Catholic charismatics, Protestant charismatics, and Pentecostals led to a groundbreaking discovery of unity in Christ, one not achieved by structure or ecumenical negotiation.

Although one of many renewal movements in the Roman church, the Catholic charismatic renewal has undeniably encouraged gospel witness and supported the "new evangelization" called for by John Paul II.[39] "The most profound signs of this renewal . . . are holiness and evangelization," wrote Archbishop Paul Josef Cordes, formerly the episcopal adviser to the International Catholic Charismatic Renewal Office in Rome. "The Holy Spirit gives gifts to the children of God, so that they might be more effective witnesses and tools in God's hand for the accomplishment of the Church's mission."[40]

Nevertheless, the stresses and strains of Pentecostal growth in nominally Catholic countries eventually produced a determination on the part of key leaders to foster good will and better understanding, most prominently through the international Roman Catholic and Classical Pentecostal Dialogue (1972–). The report of the Fourth Phase (1990–1997), which addresses important aspects of mission such as the problem of proselytism, constitutes one of the most significant ecumenical statements of the twentieth century given the worldwide size of the communities involved.[41] The events in Topeka and Rome on January 1, 1901, prefigured happenings that no one could have predicted at the time, with implications for common witness that bear further exploration.

Another surprise came unexpectedly with how readily Pentecostal spirituality was accepted on the mission fields. Early Pentecostal missionaries, though in cultural attitudes and other ways generally indistinguishable from their missionary counterparts, strongly promoted the baptism and gifts of the Holy Spirit. Since the immediate task of mission left little time for academic reflection, they sharpened their skills as practitioners. Exercising the power of the Holy Spirit held priority over involvement in discussions that examined the evangelistic pattern of the early church but doubted the possible restoration of the miraculous dimension that lay at its core. Thus, while appreciative of Roland Allen's *Missionary Methods: St. Paul's or Ours?*

(1912), Alice E. Luce, a former Anglican missionary who joined the Assemblies of God in 1915, impatiently asked, "When we go forth to preach the Full Gospel, are we going to expect an experience like that of the denominational missionaries, or shall we look for the signs to follow?"[42] In key respects, Pentecostal spirituality not only confronted non-Western peoples with the power of God in gospel proclamation but also assisted in the successful application of indigenous church principles and the training of national leaders.[43] Today an unprecedented array of missionaries pray for the sick, speak in tongues (though not necessarily accepting the Classical Pentecostal doctrine of tongues), and engage satanic forces in "power encounters."

To the dismay of Western missionaries, however, Pentecostal spirituality was sometimes contextualized in ways they had not anticipated nor would have approved. All that a believer required was the calling and infilling of the Spirit before launching out and starting his or her own congregation; this accounts for much of the church growth that has occurred outside North Atlantic countries. Yet interest in the Holy Spirit predated the arrival of Pentecostal missionaries, as illustrated by the charismatic ministry of William Wadé Harris in West Africa.[44] From the development of the True Jesus Church in China to African Initiated Churches to the myriad of independent congregations in Latin America, the varieties of theological and cultural agendas of these churches and movements have now stretched the conventional definitions of "Pentecostal" and "charismatic" to the breaking point.[45] Even national mission churches that have retained fraternal bonds with their sponsoring churches and kept their evangelical identity often have wider-ranging theological perspectives than do their mentors. The increasing numbers of so-called phenomenologically Pentecostal groups and their teachings challenge historic Protestant views on biblical authority, the nature of the church, and the parameters of evangelical belief.

A Final Reflection

Over the course of the twentieth century, Pentecostalism pressed virtually every other branch of Christianity to review its understanding of the ministry of the Holy Spirit in the mission of the church. It has thrived on an unbridled confidence that the spiritual dynamics of early Christian evangelism can be restored in the modern era. Pentecostal missions commenced prior to Edinburgh, prior to the carnage

that World War I would wreak on the mainline missions, and prior
to the issues raised by the fundamentalist-modernist controversy
that took a heavy toll on the older agencies. As with conservative
evangelical missions, Pentecostal missions remained strongly
conversionary in orientation, with their spirituality and pragmatism leading to undeniable success around the globe. Historians
George Rawlyk and Mark Noll have argued that if "the New Birth
defined the essence of evangelicalism" during the twentieth century, then "the emphases of Pentecostalism may well be the defining characteristic of evangelicals in the twenty-first century."[46]

Today vast numbers of Christians have embraced features of
Pentecostal spirituality, from charismatic Catholics in Kerala State
in India to Lutherans in Ethiopia, Baptists and Methodists in
Singapore, Presbyterians in Korea, and Moravians and Mennonites
in South America, as well as Zionists in South Africa and indigenous Christians in China. They have found a new dimension of
joyful worship, a better understanding of God's power in the preaching of the Gospel, and a faith with greater relevance to their cultural contexts.

Looking back after a hundred years, theologians may debate
whether God sovereignly outpoured the Holy Spirit in the twentieth
century or whether the Spirit's power had been available all along
but was underutilized. In either case, the prayers of earnest Christians from Jonathan Goforth and William Wadé Harris to Agnes Ozman
and Elena Guerra appear to have been answered, and the twentieth
century truly became the "century of the Holy Spirit" in mission.

Notes

1. John L. Nevius, "Historical Review of Missionary Methods—Past and
Present—in China, and How Far Satisfactory," in *Records of the General Conference of the Protestant Missionaries of China. Held at Shanghai, May 7–20, 1890,* p. 168.

2. According to the census for 1900 there were 204,672 Protestant communi-
cants and adherents out of a total population of 350 to 386 million; see Harlan P.
Beach, *A Geography and Atlas of Protestant Missions* (New York: Student Volunteer
Movement for Foreign Missions, 1906), 2:19.

3. Unnamed traveler cited in E. P. Thwing, "The Accelerated Momentum of
Truth," in *Records of the General Conference,* p. 30.

4. William R. Hutchison discusses the meager statistics in his *Errand to the
World: American Protestant Thought and Foreign Missions* (Chicago: Univ. of Chicago Press, 1987), pp. 99–100.

5. Jonathan Goforth, *By My Spirit* (Minneapolis: Bethany Fellowship, 1942), p. 137. Edinburgh, however, did issue a brief report entitled "The Superhuman Factor in Carrying the Gospel to All the Non-Christian World," in *Report of Commission I: Carrying the Gospel to All the Non-Christian World*, World Missionary Conference, 1910 (Edinburgh: Oliphant, Anderson & Ferrier, 1910), pp. 351–61.

6. "Radical evangelicals" refers to believers in the Wesleyan and Reformed "Higher Life" wings of the nineteenth-century Holiness movement; see Grant Wacker, *Heaven Below: Early Pentecostals and American Culture* (Cambridge, Mass.: Harvard Univ. Press, 2001), pp. 1–5.

7. A. J. Gordon, "The Holy Spirit in Missions," in *Student Mission Power: Report of the First International Convention of the Student Volunteer Movement for Foreign Missions, Held at Cleveland, Ohio, U.S.A., February 26, 27, 28, and March 1, 1891* (Pasadena, Calif.: William Carey Library, 1979), p. 19.

8. Peter Hocken, *The Glory and the Shame: Reflections on the Twentieth Century Outpouring of the Holy Spirit* (Guildford, Surrey, U.K.: Eagle, 1994), p. 16.

9. For information on these movements, see Donald W. Dayton, *Theological Roots of Pentecostalism* (Metuchen, N.J.: Scarecrow Press, 1987).

10. James R. Goff, Jr., *Fields White unto Harvest: Charles F. Parham and the Missionary Origins of Pentecostalism* (Fayetteville: Univ. of Arkansas Press, 1988), pp. 67–71.

11. Val Gaudet, "A Woman and the Pope," in *The Spirit and the Church*, ed. Ralph Martin (New York: Paulist Press, 1976), pp. 45, 47.

12. Gary B. McGee, "Shortcut to Language Preparation? Radical Evangelicals, Missions, and the Gift of Tongues," *International Bulletin of Missionary Research* 25, no. 3 (July 2001): 118–23.

13. See David Daniels III, "African-American Pentecostalism in the Twentieth Century," in *The Century of the Holy Spirit: One Hundred Years of Pentecostal and Charismatic Renewal*, ed. Vinson Synan (Nashville: Thomas Nelson Publishers, 2001), pp. 265–91.

14. For example, see *A Relevant Pentecostal Witness* (Chatsglen, Durban, S.A.: n.p., 1988); also, Allan H. Anderson, "Dangerous Memories for South African Pentecostals," in *Pentecostals After a Century: Global Perspectives on a Movement in Transition*, ed. Allan H. Anderson and Walter J. Hollenweger (Sheffield, U.K.: Sheffield Academic Press, 1999), pp. 89–107.

15. For a brief survey of early Pentecostal missions, see Gary B. McGee, "To the Regions Beyond: The Global Expansion of Pentecostalism," in *Century of the Holy Spirit*, pp. 69–95.

16. C. W. Naylor, cited in Grant Wacker, "Travail of a Broken Family: Radical Evangelical Responses to the Emergence of Pentecostalism in America, 1906–16," in *Pentecostal Currents in American Protestantism*, ed. E. L. Blumhofer, et al. (Chicago: Univ. of Illinois Press, 1999), p. 30.

17. Lesslie Newbigin, *The Household of God* (New York: Friendship Press, 1954), pp. 94–95.

18. See C. Peter Wagner, *The Third Wave of the Holy Spirit* (Ann Arbor, Mich.: Vine Books, 1988).

19. Kilian McDonnell coined the term "Classical Pentecostal" in "Holy Spirit and Pentecostalism," *Commonweal*, November 1968, pp. 198–204.

20. Robert Bruce Mullin, *Miracles and the Modern Religious Imagination* (New Haven, Conn.: Yale Univ. Press, 1996), pp. 237–40; also David Edwin Harrell, Jr., *All Things Are Possible: The Healing and Charismatic Revivals in Modern America* (Bloomington: Indiana Univ. Press, 1975), pp. 10–21.

21. Robert P. Menzies, "Spirit-Baptism and Spiritual Gifts," in *Pentecostalism in Context: Essays in Honor of William W. Menzies*, ed. Wonsuk Ma and Robert P. Menzies (Sheffield, U.K.: Sheffield Academic Press, 1997), pp. 53–54.

22. Simon Chan, *Pentecostal Theology and the Christian Spiritual Tradition* (Sheffield, U.K.: Sheffield Academic Press, 2000), p. 58.

23. Cited in "Some Infallible Evidences," *Cloud of Witnesses to Pentecost in India*, Pamphlet no. 2, September 1907, p. 55.

24. Minnie F. Abrams, "A New Call to Faith," *Trust*, October 1910, p. 16. On the missiological contributions of Abrams, see Dana L. Robert, *American Women in Mission: A Social History of Their Thought and Practice* (Macon, Ga.: Mercer Univ. Press, 1996), pp. 244–48.

25. Wacker, *Heaven Below*, p. 10.

26. Everett A. Wilson, *Strategy of the Spirit: J. Philip Hogan and the Growth of the Assemblies of God Worldwide, 1960–1990* (Irvine, Calif.: Regnum Books International, 1997), pp. 199–200.

27. Wayne Warner, "Flying *Ambassadors* of Good Will: The Story of Two Converted World War II Planes," *Assemblies of God Heritage* 5 (Winter 1985–86): 3–4, 13–14.

28. Gary B. McGee, *This Gospel Shall Be Preached: A History and Theology of Assemblies of God Foreign Missions Since 1959* (Springfield, Mo.: Gospel Publishing House, 1989), pp. 67–70.

29. For the emergence of "Jesus Name" or "Oneness" Pentecostalism that denied the orthodox doctrine of the Trinity, see Edith L. Blumhofer, *Restoring the Faith: The Assemblies of God, Pentecostalism, and American Culture* (Chicago: Univ. of Illinois Press, 1993), pp. 127–35; on the restoration of apostles and prophets, see C. Peter Wagner, *Apostles and Prophets: The Foundation of the Church* (Ventura, Calif.: Regal Books, 2000).

30. Phoebe Palmer, *Promise of the Father* (Boston: Henry V. Degen, 1859), p. 22.

31. Janet Everts Powers, "'Your Daughters Shall Prophesy': Pentecostal Hermeneutics and the Empowerment of Women," in *The Globalization of Pentecostalism: A Religion Made to Travel*, ed. Murray W. Dempster, Byron D. Klaus, and Douglas Petersen (Irvine, Calif.: Regnum Books International, 1999), p. 332.

32. Susan C. Hyatt, "Spirit-Filled Women," in *Century of the Holy Spirit*, pp. 233–63.

33. See Barbara Cavaness, "God Calling: Women in Assemblies of God Missions," *Pneuma: The Journal of the Society for Pentecostal Studies* 16 (Spring 1994): 49–62.

34. LaDonna C. Osborn, *Jesus and Women: Answers to Three Big Questions*, Sermon-in-Print Series (Tulsa, Okla.: OSFO Publishers, 2000), pp. 39–41.

35. Pentecostals preferred the term "third force" as used by Henry P. Van Dusen in "The Third Force in Christendom," *Life*, June 9, 1958, pp. 113–20; see Paul A. Pomerville, *The Third Force in Missions* (Peabody, Mass.: Hendrickson Publishers, 1985).

36. Ray H. Hughes, "The New Pentecostalism: Perspective of a Classical Pentecostal Administrator," in *Perspectives on the New Pentecostalism*, ed. Russell P. Spittler (Grand Rapids: Baker Book House, 1976), pp. 167–80.

37. Peter Hocken, "The Catholic Charismatic Renewal," in *Century of the Holy Spirit*, p. 211.

38. Sentiments expressed by Joseph R. Flower, former general secretary of the General Council of the Assemblies of God, in "The Charismatic Movement," in *Live in the Spirit: A Compendium of Themes on the Spiritual Life as Presented at the Council on Spiritual Life*, ed. Harris Jansen, et al. (Springfield, Mo.: Gospel Publishing House, 1972), pp. 200–15.

39. William Houck, "Introduction," in *John Paul II and the New Evangelization*, ed. Ralph Martin and Peter Williamson (San Francisco: Ignatius Press, 1995), pp. 17–21.

40. Paul Josef Cordes, *Call to Holiness: Reflections on the Catholic Charismatic Renewal* (Collegeville, Minn.: Liturgical Press, 1997), p. 70.

41. "Evangelization, Proselytism, and Common Witness: The Report from the Fourth Phase of the International Dialogue 1990–1997 Between the Roman Catholic Church and Some Classical Pentecostal Churches and Leaders"; among other periodicals, it was published in *Pneuma: The Journal of the Society for Pentecostal Studies* 21 (Spring 1999): 11–51.

42. Alice E. Luce, "Paul's Missionary Methods" (part 2), *Pentecostal Evangel*, January 22, 1921, p. 6; cf. Roland Allen, *Missionary Methods: St. Paul's or Ours?* (Grand Rapids: Eerdmans, 1962), pp. 47–48.

43. Melvin L. Hodges, *The Indigenous Church* (Springfield, Mo.: Gospel Publishing House, 1953), pp. 131–34.

44. See David A. Shank, *Prophet Harris, the "Black Elijah" of West Africa* (Leiden: E. J. Brill, 1994).

45. See Edward L. Cleary and Hannah W. Stewart-Gambino, eds., *Power, Politics, and Pentecostals in Latin America* (Boulder, Colo.: Westview Press, 1997); and Allan H. Anderson, "Types and Butterflies: African Initiated Churches and European Typologies," *International Bulletin of Missionary Research* 25, no. 3 (July 2001): 107–13; especially endnote 38.

46. George A. Rawlyk and Mark A. Noll, eds., *Amazing Grace: Evangelicalism in Australia, Britain, Canada, and the United States* (Grand Rapids: Baker Book House, 1993), p. 18.

Chapter Four

Lessons in Mission from the Twentieth Century: Conciliar Missions

Paul E. Pierson

This essay examines the missionary movement in the "mainline" or conciliar churches in the United States during the twentieth century and seeks to discover lessons we can learn from it. At the beginning of the century the mission agencies of these churches accounted for approximately 80 percent of American missionaries. By the end of the century that figure had dropped to 6 percent. The great growth of the more conservative agencies, the Southern Baptists, and the charismatic groups was an important factor in the shift. But changes in the theology of mission, the structures of mission, and the context of mission were primarily responsible for the sharp decline in the involvement in mission of the conciliar groups.

The optimism of the new century was powerfully symbolized in 1900 by the Ecumenical Mission Conference held in New York. President William McKinley of the United States, a Methodist, was a speaker, along with former president Benjamin Harrison and future president Theodore Roosevelt. The conference, with participants from 162 mission agencies and a total attendance of two hundred thousand, was a demonstration of a de facto Christendom culture that naively identified Christianity, progress, and Western civilization. Many, including McKinley, hoped to "civilize and Christianize" the peoples of Asia, Africa, and Latin America.

Despite the growing theological bifurcation in American Protestantism, the evangelical theological consensus that characterized the missionary movement remained largely intact. This consensus included four broad points: (1) the assertion that the supreme aim of missions was to make Christ known and to persuade persons to become his disciples and be gathered into churches, (2) allegiance to the unique divine nature of Jesus Christ, (3) willingness to defend the social dimensions of missions, and (4) a pragmatic ecumenism. The mission agencies of nearly all of the older "mainline" churches adhered to this consensus. The American Board of Commissioners for Foreign Missions (ABCFM), the oldest U.S. missionary agency, was an exception, having moved in a more liberal direction. At the same time the conservative "faith missions," which had begun with the formation of the China Inland Mission in 1865, were a growing phenomenon, and soon the Pentecostal movement would burst on the scene.

The Student Volunteer Movement (SVM), beginning in 1886, had played a key role. Its purpose was summed up in the slogan, "The evangelization of the world in this generation." In 1890 there were 934 American Protestant missionaries serving in foreign lands. Twenty-five years later the number had risen to 9,072, largely as a result of the SVM.[1] Most of them served under the older denominational boards. In 1910 when the Edinburgh conference was held, there were 120 American mission boards. Just over twenty of them were responsible for 65 percent of the personnel. The four largest (the ABCFM and the agencies of the northern branches of the Presbyterian, Methodist, and Baptist churches) had over 500 missionaries each. Other major agencies were those of the southern branches of the latter three denominations plus the Episcopalians and Disciples of Christ, each with between 100 and 225 missionaries.[2] Thus, at the beginning of the century the majority of personnel in the Protestant missionary movement came from the mainline churches, which would later become part of the conciliar movement. It is also safe to say that most theological reflection about mission was being done in the same groups.

Statistics for 1918 showed a total of 8,900 missionaries from the American mainline churches and only 1,900 from the Seventh-day Adventists and the newer conservative faith missions.[3]

Edinburgh 1910 and the International Missionary Council

The roots of the conciliar movement can be found in the missionary and student movements that led to the 1910 Edinburgh conference. It was chaired by the leader of the SVM, John R. Mott. Edinburgh was the most broadly based such gathering to date and included Anglo-Catholics, mainline denominational agencies, some of the newer faith missions, and seventeen representatives of the "younger churches." But Latin America was eliminated as a legitimate mission field in order to assure the participation of Anglo-Catholics and some Lutherans.

This aroused the resentment of the small but growing Latin American Protestant movement and foreshadowed antagonism to the ecumenical movement by Latin Americans in years to come.

Edinburgh conferees continued the call to world evangelization and stated that mission was the task of the whole church. They shared the general optimism regarding Western Christianity and culture but also showed concern for the indigenization of the Christian message in specific cultures and began to see the need for more appropriate church-mission relationships. They called for attitudes of sympathy and understanding toward other religions but affirmed the necessity of the "universal and emphatic witness to the absoluteness of the Christian faith."[4] However, Edinburgh's greatest contribution was in the movement toward unity and cooperation in mission, which led to the formation of the International Missionary Council (IMC) in 1921. This council included both mainline missions and many of the faith missions.

World War I shattered much of the optimism and complacency of the West, including that of the church and the missionary movement. The growing fundamentalist-modernist controversies and the growth of the social gospel movement added to the complexity of the situation. Many now questioned whether the West and its churches had anything to offer to the rest of the world; they began to turn inward, suggesting that the major task of the churches was to change their own societies. The newer generation of students in the SVM began to challenge its emphasis on world evangelization, and at the 1920 convention they revolted against the older leaders. Some wished to discuss America's domestic problems, others objected to traditional religious language, while some even questioned the missionary purpose of Christianity.[5] The questions raised in the student movement were a reflection of those being raised in the churches.

When mission leaders met at the first conference of the IMC in Jerusalem in 1928, they anticipated a number of issues that would receive greater emphasis later in the century. Mott expressed the hope that all churches would be involved in both sending and receiving missionaries. The delegates hoped the day would soon come when the indigenous churches would become the centers from which the whole missionary enterprise would be directed, "subordinating the mission to a true partnership working 'with, through, or in' the church in a particular locality."[6] There were sharp debates on the relationship of Christianity to other religions, and some feared there were hints of syncretism. The final statement spoke positively of the qualities of non-Christian persons and systems, but affirmed: "Our message is Jesus Christ. He is the revelation of what God is, and of what man through Him may become. . . . He made known to us God as our Father, in Him we find God incarnate, the final, yet ever un-folding revelation of the God in whom we live and move and have our being."[7]

But the divisive issue of Christianity and other religions was about to appear with great force. "Rethinking Missions," the report of the Laymen's Foreign Missions Inquiry, edited by William Hocking, was issued in 1932. While it made positive suggestions about the need for greater cooperation, the core of the report suggested that in place of the conversion of the world to Christian faith, a different aim should be pursued. "The Christian will therefore regard himself as a co-worker with the forces which are making for righteousness within every religious system. . . . He will therefore look forward, not to the destruc-tion of these religions, but to their continued co-existence with Chris-tianity, each stimulating the other in growth toward the ultimate goal, unity in the completest religious truth."[8] The ABCFM apparently ap-proved, and sent copies of the report to its mission stations around the world. Most other mission leaders denounced it.

The IMC commissioned Hendrik Kraemer to prepare a biblical/ theological study on the issue for its 1938 meeting at Madras, India. Kraemer, strongly influenced by Karl Barth and recent events in Ger-many, focused on Christian revelation as God's self-disclosure in Jesus Christ. Thus he stressed the discontinuity between Christian faith and other religions. Most delegates at Madras, however, took a more sym-pathetic view of other faiths, and the issue did not go away. Madras also affirmed that "the Spirit of God is guiding the various branches of His Church to seek for the realization of a visible and organic union."[9]

The Post-World-War Period and the World Council of Churches

The IMC conference at Whitby in 1947 was the first postwar reunion of the worldwide Protestant community, bringing together 112 del-egates from forty nations. With a focus on "Partners in Obedience," it called for "complete partnership in personnel, finance, policy mak-ing, and administration, in which the churches in Asia and Africa would 'put away once for all every thwarting sense of dependence on the older churches,' and stand firmly on the ground of 'absolute spiritual equality' in their witness in the world."[10] The need for

both evangelism and social involvement was stressed in its statement on Christian witness in a revolutionary world. It pledged to
support every movement for the removal of injustice and oppression but denied that such action could ever constitute the whole of
evangelism. It continued, "[W]e are convinced that the source of
the world's sorrow is spiritual, and that its healing must be spiritual, through the entry of the risen Christ into every part of the life
of the world."[11] Whitby also called for expectant evangelism to renew the missionary zeal of its members.

The concern for some form of visible unity among the churches
had its roots in the missionary movement; it had been expressed at
Edinburgh. Now, along with the IMC, two other movements arose,
also inspired in part by Edinburgh. They were the World Conference
on Faith and Order and the Council for Life and Work. In 1938 their
representatives met and drafted a constitution for a World Council of
Churches (WCC). It was described as "a fellowship of churches which
accept our Lord Jesus Christ as God and Saviour." Different from the
IMC, its members were churches that were ecclesiastical in structure
and outlook.[12] Delayed by World War II, the WCC was officially constituted in Amsterdam in 1948 with 147 different church bodies from
forty-four countries as members.

The Amsterdam meeting studied God's purpose for the world and
the church in the rapidly changing postwar context. Among the various reports was a key statement from the section "Missionary and
Evangelistic Strategy": "The whole Church should set itself to the total task of winning the whole world for Christ."[13] Naturally, the WCC
centered on the church as the agency through which God would accomplish his purpose in the world.

The Whitby meeting of the IMC had suggested that a study be
made jointly with the WCC on the nature of the missionary obligation
of the church. In 1951 the Central Committee of the WCC met at Rolle,
Switzerland, to carry the discussion further. John A. MacKay, who was
passionately committed to unity for the sake of mission, played a major
role. Rolle rejected the concept that the IMC represented the call to
evangelism and the WCC the call to unity. He insisted that world evangelism and unity must be closely related, suggesting that both the
IMC and the WCC were organs of the ecumenical movement. The theological basis for this stance was christological: "The obligation to take
the Gospel to the whole world, and the obligation to draw all Christ's
people together both rest upon Christ's whole work, and are indis-
solubly connected."[14] This concept, theologically correct, would set

the direction of the relationship of the IMC and WCC for the next decade and had significant implications for the mission movement in the conciliar churches for the rest of the century. However, as we will see later, it failed to see the basic structural issue that could be discerned all through history. This was the often difficult relationship between the centralized ecclesiastical structures, called churches, and the creative mission movements, which nearly always arose on the periphery. Indeed, it is difficult to find any new movements in mission that had not arisen on the periphery of the broader church, beginning in Antioch. That was true of the movements such as the earliest mission agencies, the YMCA, and the SVM, which led to the ecumenical movement and furnished its early leaders.

Furthermore, the worldwide context of mission was rapidly changing in the postwar period. Immediately after the war came a new period of optimism. General MacArthur asked for "missionaries and more missionaries" to be sent to Japan and wrote to the president of the Southern Baptist Convention, "Christianity now has an opportunity without counterpart in the Far East."[15] But the mood shifted quickly. There were many factors: the triumph of the Communist revolution in China, the Cold War, the Korean War, growing nationalism and the beginning of the end of colonialism, and the resurgence of non-Christian religions. Missionaries were expelled from China and would soon be asked to leave India, Burma, and other areas. Some were killed in the turmoil surrounding the end of colonialism. Where they were able to remain, their situation was vastly different from the privileged one they had often enjoyed under the rule of European governments. The perception among many was that the national churches as well as the missions could exist only under the protection of the colonial governments and that when they left, the churches would disappear as well. Increasingly, it appeared that most of the world was closed to traditional Christian missions.

Thus optimism quickly turned to extreme pessimism, especially in the conciliar groups. M. A. C. Warren of the Anglican Church Missionary Society spoke for most in 1952: "We know . . . that the most testing days of the Christian mission in our generation lie just ahead. . . . We have to be ready to see the day of missions, as we have known them, as having already come to an end."[16]

As the churches and mission agencies reached mid-century they were almost overwhelmed with crucial issues. One, as we have seen, was the need to demonstrate visibly the unity of the body of Christ as they continued to carry out their mission. Another was to formulate a theology of the church that put mission at the center instead of the periphery to which it had often been relegated. A third issue was becoming increasingly important: what should be the attitude of the Christian mission regarding the seemingly insoluble problems of poverty and the oppression of certain groups? Clearly this concern was not entirely new. Just before the turn of the century James Dennis had published *Christian Missions and Social Progress*,[17] a work that reflected the optimism of the period. The assumption of many early missionaries was that when a sufficient number of persons in a given culture became Christians, such problems would be overcome. But in the turmoil of the postwar period and the ideological struggles, it was clear that such concepts were far too simplistic. Especially after the integration of the IMC into the WCC, concern for this issue began to dominate discussions, and for many it would radically change the concept of mission.

The Integration of Missions into Churches

A fourth issue had to do with the relationship between the Western sending churches, the missionaries, and the national churches in Asia, Africa, and Latin America. The stated goal of missions was to establish churches that were self-supporting, self-governing, and self-propagating. Now the goal had been reached in many nations, but many of the national churches included only a tiny proportion of the population. Some were limited to only one or two ethnic or social groups in multicultural, multilingual nations. What would be the role of the mission and the missionary now? What relationship should they have to the national church, if indeed a national church remained? At Whitby the concern for the ecumenical church, combined with reactions against paternalism, brought a demand for the integration of missionaries into the churches. Whitby declared: "It is essential that the missionary . . . while retaining the closest relationship with the church of his origin, become in every respect a member of the church which he is to serve, and during the period of his service, joyfully give his allegiance to that church and regard himself as subject to its direction and discipline."[18] And at the Willingen meeting of the IMC in 1952, shortly after missionaries had been expelled from China, the delegates added: "We are convinced that mission work should be done through the Church. We should cease to speak of missions and churches and avoid the dichotomy, not only in our thinking, but also in our actions."[19]

Significant structural changes resulted as that ideal was implemented. The Board of Foreign Missions of the northern Presbyterian church (PCUSA) accepted the recommendation immediately. One of its secretaries said that the integration of the missions into the national churches was to begin as soon as possible. By 1956, PCUSA missions working in a number of countries were becoming part of the national churches.[20]

Thus in 1958, when the PCUSA merged with the United Presbyterian Church of North America, they dissolved their boards of foreign missions, establishing instead a Commission of Ecumenical Mission and Relations (COEMAR). This structural change symbolized an important step toward implementing the goal that missionaries in each field would be integrated into the national churches. The understanding was that the American church would now relate to those churches as equals. At the same time, the mission institutions, including schools and medical facilities, would gradually be turned over, with their properties, to the churches. And, of course, the missionaries would work under the churches' direction.

But the concepts embodied in new structure raised serious questions. To many, the new structure seemed to say that the major focus was now church-to-church relationships instead of mission to the unreached. Would the role of the missionary change, and if so, how? Who would make decisions about how funds from the Western churches would be used? Historically, the missionaries had determined the use of funds from outside. Often this resulted in pioneering new ventures, reaching out to new areas and peoples. Sometimes it led to the establishment of institutions, such as schools and hospitals, which made great contributions, especially in the early period. At times it led to paternalism and "empire building" by missionaries or to projects which a missionary controlled but which were not seen as necessary by the national churches. In the new situation the use of funds would be determined by board executives in the home country in consultation with national church leaders. But if the missionary's voice was too powerful earlier, now there was danger that leaders of a national church, which often represented a tiny minority of the population, would also be shortsighted and even self-serving.

Two examples from Brazil illustrate the dilemma. In 1954, Presbyterian missionaries who labored in the interior sought a loan fund to help construct new church buildings. At the same time their New York board received two requests from two Brazilian congregations, each for a $100,000 loan. They came from the First Presbyterian Church of Rio de Janeiro and the largest Presbyterian church in São Paulo, the two wealthiest congregations in the denomination. The pastors of the two churches were the executive secretary and the president of the denomination respectively.[21] The loan was granted to the church in Rio but never paid back. On the other hand, one Presbyterian mission in Brazil allocated more funds each year to its primary schools in the interior than it did to aid the theological seminaries of the national church. Clearly a better balance in decision making was needed.

The question of missionary assignments was also crucial. Historically, many missionaries have been highly motivated to take risks, to move out into uncharted territories, motivated by the conviction of a strong call from God. They have felt the need for freedom to pursue that call. More often than not they have lived in some tension with their boards, and even more tension with traditional ecclesiastical structures, which have focused more on orderly processes than on spontaneity. This has been the case since Carey went to India. Integration into the national churches often robbed missionaries of a key component in their personalities, the desire to take new initiatives, to push out the edges. The positive value of working under national churches was often offset by this negative aspect that obstructed ministries to neglected groups that were not seen as priorities by the church. There was often undue optimism about the fact that the Christian church existed in nearly every nation on earth, as stated by Archbishop Temple in 1942. Some even had the impression that the task of Western missionaries was nearly complete. Bishop Stephen Neill wrote: "The myth of the nineteenth century church was the myth of the 'Christian West'; the myth of the twentieth century is the myth of the younger churches."[22] He suggested that it was essential to remember that, for the most part, the "younger churches" exist as tiny minority communities and that often the great needs existing within such churches would lead them to use expatriate missionaries and their resources to meet those needs instead of reaching out to new areas and peoples.

A related problem was the maintenance of medical and educational institutions established by the missions. In almost every case they required support in personnel and funds far beyond the ability of the national church. As the contribution of the American missions decreased, the tendency was for such institutions to become secularized and lose much of their Christian witness.

The Integration of the IMC into the WCC, 1961

In 1961 at New Delhi the IMC was integrated into the WCC as its Division of World Mission and Evangelism, later the Commission on World Mission and Evangelism (CWME). This step was a logical consequence of the concept that church and mission should be one. MacKay strongly favored the step, asserting that it would put mission at the very heart of the WCC.[23] Two Anglicans disagreed. Max Warren feared that the unfinished missionary task would suffer as a consequence. He pointed out that mission had often been pursued in disunity, citing the Pentecostals and Roman Catholics as examples.[24] Stephen Neill was even more blunt, saying, "The present attitude of the World Council . . . is that the IMC is simply an anachronistic nuisance, and the sooner it is liquidated by becoming a part of the World Council, the better." He added that the WCC did not show "signs of any strong missionary passion" and predicted that "the IMC would simply become one department of the WCC among ten or twelve, and by no means the most important."[25]

Mackay, Warren, and Neill were all passionately committed to mission, but there is little doubt that Neill and Warren were correct. In 1977 Warren expressed his conviction more strongly: "Mission, understood as evangelization (the IMC definition), calls for almost infinite flexibility, because no two situations are alike. And flexibility demands, in practice, specialist organs for action and . . . a readiness to take initiatives which may be mistaken. Official bodies have an inbuilt hesitation about ever taking risks. . . . This is where, as I see it, the Voluntary Principle bcomes important. . . . The role of the voluntary society within the Church is to serve as a spiritual vanguard, as regards mission. Now it was this role of 'spiritual vanguard,' as regards world evangelization, which the IMC was discharging."[26]

One consequence of the merger was that a number of evangelical missionary leaders left the IMC, depriving it of much of its energy and commitment to world mission.

Fear had also been expressed that with the integration of the IMC into the WCC, member churches would cease to see the need for agencies devoted specifically to the missionary task. This soon happened in some of the conciliar churches. In 1968 the Reformed Church of America formed its General Program Council, an agency that integrated all denominational programs into one structure.[27] A few years later the PCUSA disbanded its COEMAR and formed a "Program Agency" in which mission was simply one department. Thus mission, which for well over a century had been carried out through focused structures within the churches led by deeply committed persons, now became simply one program among many, just as Neill had predicted regarding the WCC.

Along with the structural changes came a new theological direction. The key concept here was *missio Dei*, articulated and popularized by George Vicedom in 1965. It "affirmed that mission is in the final analysis, God's mission. It derives from the trinitarian being and action of God." The decision of God to use human agencies is secondary.[28] This concept was embraced by virtually all branches of the church. In addition, a series of study groups was set up to examine the missionary structure of the congregation. Van Engen asserts that these three factors—the integration of the IMC into the WCC, the concept of *missio Dei*, and the studies on the missionary nature of the church—shaped a consensus that "the church is mission." Before long it was often affirmed that everything the church did was mission.[29] This resulted in the loss of mission as historically defined. As Stephen Neill often said, "When everything is mission, nothing is mission."[30]

At the heart of the problem was a major theological shift, as the understanding of *missio Dei* changed radically in conciliar circles. Van Engen added, "Almost as soon as the three major factors had an appreciable impact, they began to undergo radical reconceptualization. The primary source of this change was the influence of Johannes Hoekendijk on ecumenical mission thinking."[31] In 1950 Hoekendijk was in charge of the WCC's study department on mission and evangelism and had strong influence on the preparatory documents for Willingen in 1952. He began to move ecumenical missiology away from church-centered to world-centered mission. His influence was evident in the meetings of the CWME in Mexico in 1963 and Bangkok in 1973 and at the Uppsala meeting of the WCC in 1966. His thought "reinterpreted the meaning of *missio Dei*, it reoriented the results of integration, and it redefined the mission of the congregation."[32] Rather than remaining faithful to a biblical concept of mission and church, ecumenical theology was pulled in a direction in which both got lost. Hoekendijk was extremely pessimistic about the church. He asserted that "a church-centric missionary thinking is bound to go astray . . . because it revolves around an illegitimate center." His influence brought about a change in the mission order, from God-church-world to God-world-church. He wanted "the Kingdom of God, shalom, and service in the world to replace the Church as the central locus of mission and evangelization,"[33] a concept that implied a latent universalism.

In the turmoil of the sixties the younger generation in the West and many leaders in the Two-Thirds World paid special heed to Hoekendijk. They were disillusioned with the failure of much of the church to speak out against the Vietnam War and pervasive poverty in Asia, Africa, and Latin America. When the new concept of mission saw the church primarily in terms of its usefulness in producing social and even political revolution, it found a positive response. But as Van Engen observed, "The church (as the unique company of believers in Jesus Christ) gets lost in the jungle of sociopolitical and economic agendas."[34] Although some in the CWME still advocated the goal of world evangelization, the momentum was now in a very different direction.

The 1963 meeting of the CWME in Mexico spoke of "Mission on Six Continents." By implication this minimized the necessity of taking the Gospel to peoples and areas of the world where the church did not yet exist. The 1966 WCC meeting at Uppsala lifted up humanization as the goal of mission. Canon Douglas Webster, deeply committed to the ecumenical movement, voiced one of the strongest criticisms of Uppsala: "It is high time to draw attention to the increasing secularization of the Christian concept of mission, which is in danger of being divorced from its roots in the Bible. Should this continue unchallenged and unchecked, the Church cannot expect to have much of a future. . . . The world's agenda is being allowed to take precedence over the Bible's message. . . . I would hazard a guess that the time will come . . . when those with the most knowledge and experience of real mission will consider the Uppsala report on mission little short of a sell-out to the diseased and confused spirit of our age."[35] On an earlier occasion Webster charged that the directors of the WCC "assume that mission has nothing to do with winning converts or planting churches."[36] A 1968 WCC-sponsored conference on development concluded, "The missionary societies should be encouraged to place the work for justice and development in the center of their activity."[37]

The 1973 meeting of the CWME in Bangkok on "Salvation Today" showed continued ambivalence in defining mission. While evangelicals such as Arthur Glasser called for evangelism, others, including M. M. Thomas, chairman of the WCC's Central Committee, and Philip Potter, WCC general secretary, concluded that salvation in Christ was "concerned with the liberation of persons and societies from all that prevents them from living an authentic existence in justice and a shared community."[38] The issue of a moratorium also arose at Bangkok. It was suggested there that in some cases it would be better to withdraw all missionaries in order that the national church could discover its own identity, set its own priorities, and find within itself the resources necessary to carry out its mission.[39]

The 1975 Nairobi meeting of the WCC continued the ambivalence of Bangkok. Of the six study sections, one focused on "Confessing Christ Today," but three were concerned with the struggle for liberation and justice. Even so, there was an attempt to move toward a more balanced view of the relationship between evangelism and social action. On the one hand, Bishop Mortimer Arias of Bolivia gave a strong call for evangelism. On the other, a play was presented that linked Christian missions with the evils of colonialism and gave the impression that many African problems were the result of the coming of Christianity.[40]

Some Results

Without carrying the analysis further, it is clear that from Edinburgh to Uppsala and beyond there was a massive theological shift in the understanding of mission, a shift that was embraced by much of the leadership in the conciliar churches. This change radically undercut the traditional goal of mission as world evangelization. And as the mission agencies of those churches, which had previously enjoyed a degree of autonomy, were absorbed into the ecclesiastical structures, decline in personnel and financial resources assigned to mission and confusion about the missionary task were inevitable.

The exclusive focus on church-to-church relationships had other unfortunate consequences. For a time, a policy of the Program Agency of the PCUSA decreed that missionary personnel would be sent out only in response to a request from a national church. This eliminated areas and people groups where no national church existed. This writer knew two Presbyterian couples who felt called to work among the Kurds in Iraq. Their request was refused by the Presbyterian agency because there was no Kurdish church to call them. They eventually served under a nondenominational group. Fortunately, the PCUSA has formed a new structure, and its current World-Wide Ministries Division (WMD) has changed that policy.

It appears that the changing context of mission, the ideological struggles, and the pervasive poverty and oppression in much of the world transformed the naïve optimism of the West to doubt and confusion about the nature of Christian mission.

One result of these changes can be seen in the great decrease in the number of missionaries sent by the conciliar churches. In 1952 they numbered 8,800; by 1996 there were only 2,900.[41] A list follows showing changes in the number of missionary personnel from 1964 to 2000 for several churches. Note that in four cases the first number represents the total missionary force of churches or agencies that merged before 2000. These include the Methodists and Evangelical United Brethren, the Lutheran churches, the northern and southern branches of the Presbyterians, and the merger of the ABCFM, the board of the United Church of Christ, with that of the Disciples of Christ. The numbers represent personnel serving four years or more.

	1964	2000
American Baptists	363	120
United Methodists (UMC)	1,655	413
Evangelical Lutheran Church	1,168	163
Presbyterian Church USA	1,722	368
Reformed Church of America	158	51
Protestant Episcopal Church	456	21
United Church of Christ and Disciples of Christ	826	None listed in 2000[42]

The numbers do not tell the whole story. In several cases conservative groups left their parent bodies and formed new denominations with their own mission agencies, or remained but formed alternative mission structures. In 2000 the Conservative Baptist board, formed in 1943, had 480 workers. Two groups that left the PCUSA, the Presbyterian Church of America (1973), and the Evangelical Presbyterian Church (1981) had between them 506 missionaries. The Mission Society for United Methodists, sponsored by a group that remained in the UMC, numbered 55 workers.[43] Also, a significant number of members of conciliar churches serve through multidenominational agencies.

One encouraging new model is the Presbyterian Frontier Fellowship (PFF), formed by Harold Kurtz, a retired missionary to Ethiopia. It has worked successfully with the WMD of the PCUSA to encourage greater focus on unreached peoples. It is active in recruiting, raising funds, educating churches about the unfinished task, and calling them to prayer. The WMD is the only conciliar mission agency in the United States that affirmed the goals of the AD2000 movement.

The Lessons

What can we learn from this history? First, it is clear that mission can go forward only if based on an adequate biblical and theological foundation. This foundation certainly will include an analysis of the human condition that recognizes the social as well as the personal aspects of human sin, high Christology, and a deep understanding of repentance and discipleship. I am convinced that the center, though not the totality, of mission must always involve calling men and women to faith in Jesus Christ, gathering them into worshiping and witnessing communities. Here it is helpful to quote John Stott. In his response to the call to evangelism given by Mortimer Arias at the Nairobi WCC meeting, Stott listed five things he felt the WCC needed to recover:

1. The doctrine of man's lostness (over against the popular universalism of the day)
2. Confidence in the truth, relevance, and power of the biblical Gospel (without which evangelism is impossible)
3. The uniqueness of Jesus Christ (over against all syncretism)
4. The urgency of evangelism (alongside the urgent demands for social justice)
5. A personal experience of Jesus Christ (without which we cannot introduce others to him)[44]

In addition, the Pentecostal/charismatic movement has much to teach us about the role of the Holy Spirit in mission. Perhaps most important of all, we are called to reformulate our theology of the church and put mission at its very heart.

This brings up the question of mission structures, a second area in which we can learn from the history of conciliar missions. Ecumenical documents have stated that the church exists for mission, but ecclesiastical structures have too often betrayed the concept. I believe the problem lies in the fact that the church is still seen primarily as an institution, structured around the clergy and its functions, with maintenance as its primary goal. Warren believed that the voluntary, specialized, flexible mission agencies, which have normally arisen on the periphery, were essential if the missionary calling was to be fulfilled. History confirms this belief. For two thousand years such groups have taken the Gospel to new places and peoples. Too often church leaders have disdained them, and they have gradually been absorbed into the churchly structures, losing their freedom to act. Yet the people of God have existed in many different structures through history, from apostolic missionary bands to Moravian communities to house fellowships in China, often led by laywomen. If we begin to think of the church as the people of God instead of as an institution, perhaps we can affirm the validity of the great variety of mission and church structures that the Holy Spirit has created and used throughout history. This variety also implies a more lay oriented, flat, horizontal view of the church in place of the traditional hierarchical models.

It is clear that Western missions are called to partnerships with the national churches wherever they go—a third lesson. To their credit, conciliar missions recognized this before most others. While such partnerships will involve different forms, depending on the various traditions, they should exhibit willingness to explore new initiatives that may not be on the agenda of the existing church. Neither the church nor the mission should be idealized. Both are called to listen honestly to each other and to challenge each other. In addition, we need to recognize that we have moved into a postdenominational era. So while it will not be easy, I believe the conciliar churches are called to enter into relationships with the rapidly growing newer movements, Pentecostal, charismatic, and independent, both to learn from them and to contribute to them. There is also the issue of relationships with the growing missionary movement from the Two-Thirds World. Thus, the conciliar movement is called to become more, not less, ecumenical.

A fourth lesson is the need to inform Western Christians about the remarkable growth of the church in many parts of the world. Conciliar churches contain much ignorance and unwarranted pessimism about the missionary movement. Accurate information can become a powerful motivation to greater and more effective missionary participation by local congregations.

Finally, it is essential to note that mission has always come as a result of a new and profound work of the Holy Spirit. This is true whether we are speaking of the haystack prayer meeting, the

Moravian Pentecost, Azusa Street, or the SVM. If the conciliar churches, or any other churches, are to renew their commitment to mission, they (and we) are called to seek personal and corporate renewal. This will begin with a new vision of God, a deeper understanding of our human condition, and a renewed touch of grace that enable us to hear again the call, "Whom shall I send, and who will go for us?" (Isa. 6:8).

Notes

1. W. Richie Hogg, "The Role of American Protestantism in World Mission," in *American Missions in Bicentennial Perspective*, ed. R. Pierce Beaver (Pasadena, Calif.: William Carey Library, 1976), p. 374.

2. William R. Hutchison, *Errand to the World: American Protestant Thought and Foreign Missions* (Chicago: Univ. of Chicago Press, 1987) p. 127.

3. Robert T. Coote, "Twentieth-Century Shifts in the North American Protestant Missionary Community," *International Bulletin of Missionary Research* 22, no. 4 (October 1998): 152.

4. Rodger C. Bassham, *Mission Theology, 1948–1975: Years of Worldwide Creative Tension, Ecumenical, Evangelical, and Roman Catholic* (Pasadena, Calif.: William Carey Library, 1979), p. 19.

5. Michael Parker, *The Kingdom of Character: The Student Volunteer Movement for Foreign Missions (1886–1926)* (Lanham, Md.: Univ. Press of America, 1998), p. 148.

6. Bassham, *Mission Theology*, p. 21.

7. Harvey T. Hoekstra, *Evangelism in Eclipse: World Mission and the World Council of Churches* (Exeter: Paternoster Press, 1949), p. 32.

8. Bassham, *Mission Theology*, pp. 24f.

9. Ibid., pp. 25f.

10. Ibid., p. 26.

11. Ibid.

12. Kenneth Scott Latourette, *A History of Christianity* (New York: Harper & Row, 1975), p. 1378.

13. Bassham, *Mission Theology*, p. 29.

14. Ibid., p. 32.

15. Richard V. Pierard, "Pax Americana and the Evangelical Missionary Advance," in *Earthen Vessels: American Evangelicals and Foreign Missions, 1880–1980*, ed. Joel A. Carpenter and Wilbert R. Shenk (Grand Rapids: Eerdmans, 1990), pp. 174f.

16. Ibid., p. 156.

17. James S. Dennis, *Christian Missions and Social Progress: A Sociological Study of Foreign Missions*, 3 vols. (New York: Revell, 1897, 1899, 1906).

18. Paul E. Pierson, *A Younger Church in Search of Maturity: Presbyterianism in Brazil, 1910–1959* (San Antonio, Tex.: Trinity Univ. Press, 1974), p. 226.

19. Ibid., p. 227.

20. Ibid.

21. Ibid., p. 228.

22. C. W. Ranson, "Younger Churches and New Nations," in *The Christian Mission Today*, ed. Methodist Church (US) Board of Missions (New York: Abingdon Press, 1960), p. 217.

23. The author often heard him say this in class at Princeton Theological Seminary.

24. Hoekstra, *Evangelism in Eclipse*, p. 43.

25. Ibid., p. 37.

26. Ibid., pp. 44f.

27. Charles Van Engen, *Mission on the Way: Issues in Mission Theology* (Grand Rapids: Baker Books, 1996), p. 151.

28. Ibid.

29. Ibid., pp. 152f.

30. Ibid., p. 147.

31. Ibid., p. 153.

32. Ibid., p. 154.

33. Ibid., pp. 154f.

34. Ibid., p. 155.

35. Hoekstra, *Evangelism in Eclipse*, pp. 83f.

36. Ibid., p. 85.

37. Ibid., p. 69.

38. D. Hoke, "Salvation Isn't the Same Today," in *The Evangelical Response to Bangkok*, ed. Ralph D. Winter (South Pasadena, Calif.: William Carey Library, 1973), pp. 83f.

39. Bassham, *Mission Theology*, p. 97.

40. Hoekstra, *Evangelism in Eclipse*, pp. 127f.

41. Coote, "Twentieth Century Shifts," pp. 152–53.

42. The figures are from *Statistics of North American Missionary Personnel* (New York: Missionary Research Library, 1964) and John A. Siewart and Dotsey Welliver, eds., *Mission Handbook: U.S. and Canadian Ministries Overseas, 2001–2003*, 18th ed. (Wheaton, Ill.: Billy Graham Center, 2000).

43. Siewart and Welliver, eds., *Mission Handbook*.

44. Timothy Dudley-Smith and John Stott, *The Later Years* (Downers Grove, Ill.: InterVarsity, 2001), p. 206.

Chapter Five

Baptist Missions in the Twentieth Century

John Mark Terry

This essay sketches the history of Baptist missions during the twentieth century, focusing primarily on the development of missions among Baptists in North America. At the beginning of the century Baptists were active in missions, but the number of missionaries deployed was small in comparison to that of other mission boards such as the China Inland Mission. During the century the Southern Baptist Convention grew dramatically, and this growth fostered the growth of the Foreign Mission Board of the SBC (now International Mission Board). The essay assesses the effects of the world wars, the Great Depression, and the fundamentalist-modernist controversy on Baptist missions. The origin and ministry of the Baptist World Alliance are examined and evaluated. The internalization of Baptist missions is mentioned, and statistics are provided showing the growth of Baptist unions and conventions around the world. A list of Baptist mission boards in North America and the number of missionaries they have under appointment is provided. The essay concludes with a list of factors that have influenced the growth of Baptist missions in North America.

If the nineteenth century was the "great century" for Protestant missions, then the twentieth century was the great century for Baptist missions. When the century dawned, only four Baptist international mission boards were functioning in the United States. Two small boards served African-American churches. The two large boards were the Foreign Mission Board of the Southern Baptist Convention (SBC) and the American Baptist Missionary Union, which served Northern Baptists. The missionaries of the two boards combined totaled only 568.[1] At the end of the twentieth century there were sixty-five Baptist missions agencies, and the International Mission Board of the SBC alone had almost five thousand missionaries under appointment.[2]

The Situation in 1900

Baptists in the United States once carried out their missions mandate through a single society, the General Convention of the Baptist Denomination in the United States for Foreign Missions, founded in 1814. Most people referred to this convention as the Triennial Convention because its members met every three years. In 1845 Southern Baptists withdrew from the Triennial Convention and organized the Southern Baptist Convention. In its first two actions the SBC created the Foreign Mission Board and the Domestic Mission Board (later called the Home Mission Board and now the North American Mission Board). Southern Baptists wished to follow a "convention" pattern of work in which the denomination owned and controlled its institutions through convention-elected trustees. Northern Baptists preferred to continue with the "society" approach, with semiautonomous societies for home missions, foreign missions, and church literature.

In 1900 the American Baptist Missionary Union was by far the stronger of the two boards. According to its annual report that year the Union had 474 missionaries under appointment, serving in Burma, China, Assam, India, Japan, and the Philippines. The Foreign Mission Board (now International Mission Board) reported 94 missionaries, who served in Brazil, China, Italy, Japan, Mexico, and Nigeria.[3] Brazil, China, and Nigeria were the predominant fields of service for Southern Baptists.

Twentieth-Century Developments

The Baptist World Alliance (BWA) was founded in 1905 in London, England. Three thousand Baptists from twenty-one countries participated in the first meeting. In 1940 the Alliance moved its offices to Washington, D.C., because of the war in Europe. The BWA has provided a forum for fellowship and encouragement for new Baptist bodies and Baptists who struggle in difficult areas. The BWA had a particularly effective ministry to Baptists who lived behind the Iron Curtain during the cold war.[4]

World War I

World War I affected Baptist missions by giving Baptists in the United States an expanded understanding of world geography.

Baptists serving in the military traveled all over the world, and their increased knowledge led to an increased concern for the peoples of the lands they visited. The demand for cotton, the South's main crop, also provided badly needed funds for Southern Baptist missions.

The 1920s

During the 1920s the Northern Baptist Convention experienced fierce doctrinal discord due to the modernist controversy. The controversy affected Southern Baptists to a lesser degree.

In 1919 Southern Baptists embarked on the Seventy-Five Million Campaign, an effort to raise $75 million for Baptist agencies and institutions. Southern Baptists pledged $92 million, but due to falling cotton prices only $58 million was actually collected. This campaign affected Southern Baptists both negatively and positively. Negatively, the Foreign Mission Board went into debt. It borrowed money, assuming that all the pledges would be redeemed. When they were not, the board was left with a significant debt. Positively, the Southern Baptist Convention learned the value of united giving. This paved the way for the adoption of the Cooperative Program in 1925. Through the Cooperative Program, Southern Baptist churches voluntarily give a percentage of their church income to the denomination. Historically, about 50 percent of Cooperative Program receipts go to foreign missions and about 20 percent to missions in North America. The advent of the Cooperative Program helped the mission boards to do proper financial planning.

The Great Depression

The Great Depression, which began in October 1929 and continued in North America until the beginning of World War II, had a negative impact on missions. The economic downturn meant that both individuals and churches gave less to missions. For example, in 1930 the budget of the SBC's Foreign Mission Board was $1,390,000. In 1932 the Foreign Mission Board received only $691,302, and in 1933 it had to reduce its budget even further to $605,575. More than 10 percent of that reduced budget had to be designated for repayment of the board's indebtedness, which had soared to $1,349,000 in 1932.[5]

The financial shortfalls dramatically affected missionary appointments. The Foreign Mission Board reported in 1932 that it had lost

127 missionaries in the period 1926–1932. It appointed three missionaries in 1932 and only one in 1933. In 1932 Foreign Mission Board officials detained thirty missionaries on furlough in the United States and asked them to find other jobs until they could be salaried again and sent back to their fields of service. The FMB's financial situation gradually improved, but the board did not become debt-free until 1943.[6]

Northern Baptist Missions

After their split with Southern Baptists, the Baptists in the North continued to do missions through the American Baptist Home Mission Society and the American Baptist Missionary Union. The Home Mission Society developed significant ministries among African-Americans in the South and among immigrants in the North. The American Baptist Missionary Union later changed its name to the Northern Baptist Foreign Missions Society after the Northern Baptist Convention was organized in 1908. In 1949 Northern Baptists renamed their convention the American Baptist Convention.

The fundamentalist-modernist controversy of the 1920s and '30s affected the Northern Baptist Convention much more than it did the Southern Baptist Convention. Due to doctrinal issues in the Northern Baptist Convention, the Association of Baptists for World Evangelization (ABWE) was organized in 1927. This group has done a strong work in the Philippines since that year. A group of churches withdrew from the Northern convention in 1933 to form the General Association of Regular Baptists. In 1943, concerns over the doctrinal beliefs expected of missionaries led to another withdrawal and the formation of the Conservative Baptist Foreign Mission Society (now CBInternational).

American Baptists carried out admirable missions work in Burma, India, and China. In Burma (now Myanmar) they enjoyed their greatest success. The hill tribes such as the Karen, Kachin, and Chin have been remarkably responsive to the Gospel. American Baptists gradually shifted from a society approach to the convention approach. The number of American Baptist missionaries has declined in recent years, due primarily to theological changes in the denomination and a shift in missions emphasis from evangelism to social ministries. Nevertheless, they continue their missions work through their Board of International Missions and Board of National Mission.[7]

World War II

World War II had a much greater impact on Baptist missions than did World War I. The first war lasted about four years; World War II began in 1937 in China and continued until 1945. When the Japanese launched their full-scale attack on China in 1937, the Foreign Mission Board of the SBC faced the problem of evacuating 178 missionaries and 84 children. The other mission agencies struggled with a similar problem. Further, the displacement of millions of persons in China created the need for a massive relief effort. Both Northern and Southern Baptists participated in the effort, principally through the Church Committee of China Relief.[8]

Some missionaries chose not to leave their places of service, and some had no opportunity to do so. Caught up in the winds of war, many missionaries were interned in Japanese prison camps in China, Japan, and the Philippines. Several Northern Baptist missionaries were killed by the Japanese in the central Philippines. A few missionaries were able to escape into "Free China," where they continued their missionary labors. One of these was Baker James Cauthen, who later served as executive secretary of the Foreign Mission Board.[9]

While World War II adversely affected the missionaries in Asia, it brought prosperity to the United States. The need for trucks, jeeps, planes, and tanks prompted nationwide industrial development. With full employment came prosperity and an end to the debts that crippled the mission agencies. In 1943 the Foreign Mission Board celebrated becoming debt-free. Relief from debt combined with growing budgets enabled administrators to look to new fields for missionary work, such as South America.

The war also gave millions of young American servicemen and women an opportunity to travel around the world. The needs they saw prompted them to pursue theological education back in the United States and to return eventually to those faraway places as missionaries.

The Communist Takeover in China

The 1949 victory of the Communists under Mao Tse Tung in the Chinese Civil War created a tidal wave of change in Baptist missions. China had been the premier mission field for both Northern and

Southern Baptists. The civil war and the Communist takeover presented the missionaries with a dilemma. They had to decide whether to remain at their posts during the fighting or to withdraw ahead of the Communist advance. The missionaries were allowed to choose their courses of action. Many tried to stay, but this option did not prove fruitful. Winston Crawley describes the situation: "Missionaries who remained after the Communist take-over hoped that they could continue their ministries in spite of expected limitations. Communist policy, however, followed the usual pattern: 'first toleration with freedom, then toleration with control, and finally active opposition.' The opposition became especially severe after China entered the Korea war in late 1950. In the meantime, missionaries had gradually realized that their presence brought embarrassment and even danger to Chinese Christians. They began to withdraw as exit visas became available."[10] Bill Wallace, a missionary surgeon, was one of those who chose to remain. In December 1950 the Chinese authorities arrested him on trumped-up charges, and he died under torture in prison in February 1951. By the end of 1951 no Baptist missionaries remained in China.[11]

The closing of China became something of an Acts 8 experience for Baptist missions. When Saul persecuted the church in Jerusalem, the believers were scattered all over the eastern portion of the Roman Empire. When the Communists expelled the missionaries from China, they relocated to countries all over Asia: the Philippines, Indonesia, Hong Kong, Taiwan, Hawaii, Singapore, Malaysia, and Thailand. These displaced missionaries opened Baptist work in these countries, and Baptist churches have multiplied rapidly, especially in the Philippines and Indonesia.

The 1950s: A Period of Advancement

During the 1950s the Baptist Missionary Society in Great Britain enlarged its missions program, deploying missionaries to India, Bangladesh, Sri Lanka, Zaire, Angola, Tanzania, Jamaica, Trinidad, Brazil, and Hong Kong. The largest number of missionaries served in African countries and Brazil. The British Baptists have engaged in planting churches as well as in education, pastoral training, medical work, agricultural work, and other types of social ministries. Baptists in Commonwealth nations, such as Australia, South Africa, Canada, and New Zealand, have also sent many missionaries.[12]

The 1950s were a period of rapid church growth for the churches in North America. The postwar baby boom and economic prosperity provided Baptists in North America with more missionary candidates and more money for their support. The Southern Baptist Convention in 1948 adopted the Program of Advance, a program that called for an increase in missionaries from 600 to 1,750 and a budget increase from $4.7 million to $10 million. In addition, a large portion of Cooperative Program surplus funds were designated for the Advance Program; in 1950 this "over and above money" amounted to $675,044 and provided a great boost to the work of the Foreign Mission Board.[13]

During the 1950s many nondenominational and parachurch agencies were founded or expanded greatly. These included Wycliffe Bible Translators, Missionary Aviation Fellowship, and Campus Crusade for Christ. Many Baptists served in those agencies.[14]

The 1960s and 1970s

The period of the 1960s and '70s was a time of turmoil and cultural change in the United States. The American Baptist Church (formerly Northern Baptist Convention) participated in the World Council of Churches, and that body's theological shifts negatively affected the motivation of American Baptists to send missionaries.

Southern Baptists did not join the World Council, and the Foreign Mission Board of the SBC continued to grow both in number of missionaries and in countries entered. Two conservative Baptist mission boards were founded during this period, Baptist International Missions (1960) and Baptist World Mission (1961). The conservative Baptist missions agencies have opposed the ecumenical movement and refused to enter into comity agreements. The situation in recent years has been something of an ecclesiastical "free-for-all." In fact, Albert Wardin writes that "[t]oday no Baptist mission agency can even stake out a country for itself or even a field, expecting other Baptists to stay out. There may be some mutual consideration and even some cooperation with other Baptists or even non-Baptists, but each mission develops its own program."[15] What Wardin states has been generally true, but in recent years Southern Baptists have shown more willingness to cooperate with other groups. In 1995 the Foreign Mission Board joined the Evangelical Foreign Missions Association and also committed to working with other "Great Commission Christians" to evangelize unreached people groups around the world.

Entering the Twenty-first Century

The most significant trend in evangelical missions and especially in Baptist missions is the increase in missionaries coming from the Two-Thirds World. Baptists in countries that formerly received missionaries are now sending their own missionaries. They wish to participate actively in missions. Baptists in Brazil, Nigeria, Korea, Taiwan, the Philippines, Japan, Argentina, and elsewhere are sending missionaries to serve in cross-cultural settings. They are concentrating on unreached people groups in the 10/40 Window. Baptists in Brazil support more than five hundred home missionaries who work within Brazil and more than one hundred foreign missionaries who serve in nineteen other countries.[16]

Baptist Missions in 2001

The following is a list of the largest Baptist missions agencies in North America. The statistics come from the *Mission Handbook, 2001–2003*. All the numbers are taken from this one valuable resource, though one recognizes that the numbers change daily and are out of date even when they are printed.

Association of Baptists for World Evangelization (founded 1927)
    761 missionaries in 38 countries
American Baptist Churches (1814)
    126 missionaries in 23 countries
Baptist Bible Fellowship (1950)
    822 missionaries in 77 countries
Baptist General Conference (1944)
    115 missionaries in 15 countries
Baptist International Missions (1960)
    529 missionaries in 63 countries
Baptist Mid-Missions (1920)
    612 missionaries in 42 countries
CBInternational (Conservative Baptist) (1943)
    550 missionaries in 46 countries
Lott Carey Baptist Mission (African-American agency) (1897)
    Primarily supports national workers

National Baptist Convention, USA (1880)
   27 missionaries in 11 countries
International Mission Board of the Southern Baptist Convention (1845)
   4,570 missionaries in 154 countries

According to the *Mission Handbook* a total of sixty-five Baptist mission agencies have headquarters in North America.

Baptists Around the World

According to the Baptist World Alliance, there were 44,077,715 Baptists in 118 countries around the world in the year 2000. Of course, some countries, such as the United States, have multiple Baptist conventions or unions. Countries with large populations of Baptists are Korea (680,000), Nigeria (1,026,000), Democratic Republic of the Congo (1,007,987), India (1,788,434), and Myanmar/Burma (662,834).[17]

Factors Affecting Baptist Growth

Baptists have grown significantly around the world due to their aggressive missions efforts. The number of Baptist missions increased almost twentyfold during the century. Many factors influenced this growth. First, Baptists have a strong emphasis on evangelism. Their conversionist theology prompts them to carry the Gospel around the world. Second, Baptists place great importance on the local church. This church-centeredness has lent itself to intense church planting efforts, both in the United States and around the world. Third, Baptists adopted the church growth philosophy of Donald McGavran. This philosophy moved them to concentrate on methods that produced masses of new converts and new churches. Fourth, Baptists stress the doctrine of the priesthood of all believers. This has led them to emphasize the role of volunteers in missions. In 2000 more than thirty thousand Southern Baptists traveled overseas to do volunteer missions work, and more than a hundred thousand did volunteer missions projects in North America. Fifth, Baptists have adopted a holistic approach to missions. Baptist missionaries have done medical, agricultural, social, and community development work around the world. From agricultural stations in the Philippines to well drilling in Brazil, Baptists have sought to bring both eternal life and abundant life to the peoples of the world.

Conclusion

During the twentieth century Baptists became "one of the major Protestant bodies in the world." The only other significant free church movement in the world whose growth outstripped Baptists was the Pentecostal movement.[18] Baptists can be justly proud of their progress; however, the remaining task of evangelizing the unreached people groups of the world should move them to prayer and redoubled efforts.

Notes

1. "Eighty-sixth Annual Report," *Baptist Missionary Magazine* 80 (July 1900): 455; and "Fifty-fifth Annual Report of the Foreign Missions Board," *Annual of the Southern Baptist Convention, 1900*, Appendix A.

2. John A. Siewert and Dotsey Welliver, eds., *Mission Handbook 2001–2003* (Wheaton, Ill.: Evangelism and Missions Information Service, 2000), p. 41.

3. "Eighty-sixth Annual Report," p. 455, and "Fifty-fifth Annual Report," Appendix A.

4. "BWA Facts," from http://www.bwanet.org/fellowship/stats.html; Internet; accessed 9 April 2001.

5. William R. Estep, *Whole Gospel: Whole World* (Nashville: Broadman & Holman, 1994), p. 213.

6. Baker J. Cauthen, *Advance: A History of Southern Baptist Foreign Missions* (Nashville: Broadman Press, 1970), p. 41.

7. Justice Anderson, "Baptist Missions," in *Evangelical Dictionary of World Missions*, ed. A. Scott Moreau (Grand Rapids: Baker Books, 2000), pp. 110–14.

8. Estep, *Whole Gospel*, p. 241.

9. Ibid., p. 243.

10. Cauthen, *Advance*, p. 102.

11. Ibid.

12. Anderson, "Baptist Missions."

13. Cauthen, *Advance*, pp. 52–53.

14. Albert W. Wardin, ed., *Baptists Around the World* (Nashville: Broadman & Holman, 1995), p. 9.

15. Ibid.

16. Anderson, "Baptist Missions."

17. Baptist World Alliance, available at www.bwanet.org.

18. Wardin, *Baptists Around the World*, p. 8.

Chapter Six

The Near Demise of the Domestic Mission in America in the Twentieth Century: Can We Learn Anything from It?

Charles L. Chaney

In 1901 the American domestic mission was at its zenith; by 2001 it was almost forgotten. Between 1886 and 1920, home mission leaders embraced the view that Anglo-Saxon America was the New Israel destined to *democratize* and *Christianize* the world. Home missions for majority Protestants switched from *evangelization* to *socialization*. Systemic evangelism progressively replaced personal evangelism, and church merging and closing replaced church planting. Eventually, home missions was replaced by social activism. After 1925, home missions' fragile consensus was fissured. Fundamentalists gave themselves to building training institutions and "great" churches and calling America back to God through city crusades and radio. Meanwhile, black Protestants, Pentecostals, and some Southern white Protestants continued to grow through classical home mission strategies. The story provides serious lessons for missions today.

In 1900 the home mission movement had reached the acme of its prestige and influence in American Christianity. The full measure of monetary support for the domestic mission would go higher, but by 1920 the home mission was already in serious trouble. In the next decade there was massive disruption from many directions. The Inter-church World Movement collapsed. The fundamentalist-modernist controversy erupted. Overextension brought on crippling debt to all missionary agencies. The great social unrest that followed the First World War cast a pall over American mainline religion. Racial and labor injustice exploded in strikes, riots, and lynchings. The Ku Klux Klan was reborn in both South and North. The Great Depression dawned.

The social gospel had arisen by 1900 and by 1920 was fully identified with *modern thought* and the *new theology*. Lyman Abbott, writing

in 1915, boasted of his role, during the decade 1886–1896, in opening up the American Board of Commissioners for Foreign Missions
(ABCFM) to candidates who believed in future probation for the
heathen. He reported that in 1901 he was the preacher at the dia-
mond jubilee of the Congregational Home Missionary Society. His
sermonic proposition was "that it is the function of the Christian
Church to establish the kingdom of God here and now on this earth,
not to save men, few or many, from a world given over and abandoned as a wreck and lost, but to save the world itself by transforming it, translating it, transfusing it with new life."[1]

Between 1900 and 1920 nearly every major denominational
group had someone writing a history of home missions for its group,
and, as the century turned, Joseph B. Clark wrote *Leavening the
Nation: The Story of American [Protestant] Home Missions*, which, with
characteristic arrogance, is principally the story of the American
Home Missionary Society and its successor, the Congregational
Home Missionary Society. He did give considerable attention to
Presbyterians (before 1852), some less to Northern Baptists, almost
none to Methodists, Episcopalians, and the Reformed churches. The
domestic missionary achievements of the Southern denominations
were hardly considered. The South still remained "missionary
ground." The attitude expressed in 1864 had hardly been revised
in a generation: "We have not only to conquer the South—we have
also to convert it. We have not only to occupy it by bayonets and
bullets—but also by ideas and institutions. We have not only to
destroy slavery,—we must also organize freedom. . . . [E]ven the
older slave States have ever been as truly missionary ground as the
newly settled regions of the West. In these [Southern] churches,
too, such as they have been, a full and free gospel has never been
preached. . . . For years a great population, white and colored, possessing neither education nor a full and free gospel, have been right
across our borders, awaiting the day of their redemption. But we
have never been able to reach them. . . . Now the trumpet of God
has been sounding . . . and the heretofore impregnable Jericho is
impregnable no longer, and . . . God speaks clear and loud . . . to
the American churches, 'Go ye in and possess the land.'"[2]

The tremendous growth of American Protestant Christianity,
Clark averred, was due to the home mission effort. Most of the
existing churches had been planted as a result of home mission work.
The institutions of Christian higher education then existing had their
stimulus from the work of the domestic mission. Quoting Richard

S. Storrs, a prominent pastor in Brooklyn, Clark insisted that the domestic mission was primarily responsible for the patriotism and manpower that won the Civil War. Storrs had said, "Home Missions saved this country once and will save it again if necessary."[3]

For Clark, the leavening of the nation had one primary source, New England. He defined the domestic mission as primarily devoted to evangelism and church planting. For two generations the Congregationalists had viewed the home missionary as more a state builder and a nation builder than an evangelist and church planter. Thus, Clark described the home missionary as one whose task was to create a Christian civilization: "Plant a . . . church in any community and it becomes at once the nucleus of law, order, moral living, and civic virtue. Such communities multiplied across the State give character to a commonwealth, and such multiplied commonwealths make a nation strong by making it righteous."[4] Further, "in government by the people and for the people nothing counts so much as high ideals of duty. With these enthroned in the thought and life of its citizens, a nation may meet almost any shock . . . and nothing has yet been discovered . . . that has power to create higher ideals of duty than Christianity. . . . It is thus that missionary societies, whose sole function is the planting of churches, enter into the *hidden life of a nation* in ways that political parties cannot enter, and which . . . men are sometimes slow to appreciate. Not only law, order, . . . and the claims of humanity are thus conserved . . . , but the instinct of patriotism itself, in which the very life of the nation consists, finds its nursing mother in the Church of Christ."[5]

Penetration of the "hidden life of the nation," as then perceived, made the domestic mission supremely important. Long before 1900 the American nation had already been identified as a Christian nation and as the hope of world redemption. Both Lyman Beecher and Horace Bushnell had so identified it and made America the key to the ultimate divine objective, the evangelization of the world. In 1876 Cyrus D. Foss, the president of Wesleyan University, Middletown, New York, and later bishop of the Methodist Church, proclaimed the truth that "God has a plan for nations as well as for men. He assigns to each nation the part for which it is especially fitted in working out the grand problem of the civilization, the enlightenment, the Christianization of the world. . . . The August Ruler of all the nations designed the United States of America as the grand depository and evangelist of civil liberty and of a pure religious faith. And these two are one."[6]

In 1881 Austin Phelps contended that the domestic mission (to the Occidental nations) had priority over the foreign mission (to the Oriental nations): "Those whose *speedy* conversion is most vital to the conversion of the rest are the nations of the Occident. The pioneer stock of mind must be the Occidental stock. The pioneer races must be the Western races. And of all the Western races, who that can read . . . the providence of God . . . can hesitate in affirming that the signs of divine decree point to this land of ours as the one which must take the lead in the final conflicts of Christianity for the possession of the world. Ours is the elect nation for the ages to come. We are the chosen people . . . the emergency is great. We cannot wait. The plan of God . . . [has] brought us to one of the closing stages of this world's career, in which we can no longer *drift* with safety to our destiny. . . . Such . . . is the central fact in the philosophy of American Home Missions."[7]

Clark completed his book with renewed "faith in the final triumph of American Home Missions." Religious forces were never stronger, consecrated wealth never larger and more freely given, Christian workers never more numerous and willing, and the spirit of mutual cooperation between denominations never greater for the leavening of the nation than at the turn of the century. "The twentieth century opens with auguries for our country a thousand times brighter than our home-missionary fathers had at the time of the nineteenth century."[8] This period is well named the Progressive era in American history. The year before, President Theodore Roosevelt had spoken at the Presbyterian centennial of home missions. "It would be difficult to overestimate the value of the [home] missionary work," he said. "They [the home missionaries] bore the burden and the heat of the day, they toiled obscurely and died unknown, that we might come to a glorious heritage."[9]

Such was the perception of many of the most prominent Americans at the turn of the twentieth century. The home mission movement, Clark insisted, had begun with the formation of the Missionary Society of Connecticut in 1798. The movement's progress and effectiveness in a century had been amazing.

Today, one hundred years after Clark's book, the domestic mission in America is at its nadir.[10] For many conciliar Protestant leaders evangelism is a dirty word that receives little program support, and church planting is nothing less than denominational aggrandizement that must be supported in an effort to staunch the loss of members and churches. For many evangelical leaders the domestic mission is the stepchild of their denominations. The commitment to church planting is more talk than reality. With rare exceptions the denominations look to parachurch groups to create and coordinate their evangelism and church planting. Most of the myriad of evangelical parachurch agencies look on America as a Christian nation that needs to be repaired, if necessary by wielding political power. American churches are seen as the primary source for funding international mission projects.[11]

Fragmentation of the Domestic Mission

Many forces have contributed to the present situation. The seeds of fragmentation were sown in the growing identification of this nation as a Christian empire raised up by God to be the agent not only of world redemption but also of worldwide civil liberty. The mission of the church was passed to the nation.[12]

The actual fragmentation of the domestic mission, however, began in the 1880s while the first significant steps were being taken toward enhancing cooperative missionary efforts. The following events all combined to contribute to the fragmentation:

1. The Niagara Bible Conference, refounded in 1875, had settled down in 1883 at Niagara-on-the-Lake and by 1885 had begun its most influential decade. Rejecting the postmillennial optimism common in the previous 150 years, its teachers denied that a spiritual millennium would be in existence, that an actual thousand years of peace and prosperity would have arisen, or that the nations would have been converted at the time of Christ's return. After 1884 there was a strong emphasis on the "any-moment" return of Christ.[13] Before World War I the principal teachers of this conference also denied that the kingdom of God would be realized first in America. Jerusalem was to be the seat of kingdom government. The new perspective on Christ's coming added a new level of urgency to the world mission. Contrary to many critics, the nerve of missionary commitment to evangelism and church planting in foreign or home missions was not sundered by premillennialism.[14] The new perspective did foster a strategy for broadcast evangelism: in home missions it tended toward citywide evangelistic campaigns and radio evangelism, when that medium became viable after World War I. New churches were planted by the process of building Holiness and Pentecostal denominations before and after World War I and the separation process after the fundamentalist controversy in the

twenties. *Urgency,* in light of the any-moment return of Christ, was always a key factor. The proliferation of Bible institutes was intended essentially to train laymen and -women for spiritual ministries in the cities, to prepare persons for the mission fields without the long multiyear seminary process, and to train leadership designed to reach the immigrant groups that were pouring into America before 1920.

2. Josiah Strong's book, *Our Country: Its Possible Future and Its Present Crises,* published in 1886, was a bestseller on anyone's list. Nothing like it had come along since *Uncle Tom's Cabin* in 1852. Its ultimate impact was divisive, contributing significantly to the rising social gospel; but it was successful in switching the focus of the domestic mission from the frontier. Strong identified eight perils, some closely interrelated, that threatened America and had the potential of keeping America from fulfilling its destiny to evangelize and democratize the world. Of the eight perils he identified (Romanism, religion [or the lack of it] in the public schools, Mormonism, intemperance, socialism, amassed wealth, and the new commercial and industrial cities), only Mormonism and intemperance had direct relationships with the vanishing western frontier. The eastern seaboard and the mushrooming midwestern cities were the new frontiers.

3. The rebirth of D. L. Moody's Northfield conference for YMCA workers took place in 1885. In 1886 this conference launched what became the Student Volunteer Movement for Foreign Missions. A vast second wave of American foreign missionaries was soon on its way overseas.[15] Since that date American Christians have suffered from what I have called the Babylonian captivity of the Great Commission.[16] When Matthew 28:18–20 is mentioned, the average American Christian has an automatic flashing light in his or her brain that illuminates the words "foreign missions . . . foreign missions." Though John R. Mott insisted otherwise at the first North American Missions Congress in 1930,[17] the domestic mission indeed ceased to be part and parcel of the world mission of the church.

4. The Evangelical Alliance of the United States took on a new direction and a new and dynamic leader in 1886, when Josiah Strong became the general secretary. The focus of the American Alliance for the next fifteen years was on national, not international, problems. The goal was to eliminate, by concerted, concentrated, and practical activities, the threats to a truly Christian nation, all those things that hindered the realization of the kingdom of God on earth.

Strong led the Evangelical Alliance to expand its circle of participants, reaching out even to some leaders of southern churches. He conducted three great conferences in 1887, 1889, and 1893 that tremendously impacted almost all stripes of Protestants. His books laid the foundation for the social gospel movement. Sidney Ahlstrom asserts that Strong's views "constituted the core program of the Social Gospel movement."[18]

5. Holiness groups were finally pushed out of the Methodist Church, North and South, after 1893. Before 1880 there was positive support for the Holiness movement in the Methodist Church, but in 1885, at the General Holiness Assembly in Chicago, a creedal definition of entire sanctification was adopted that defined the process of sanctification as an instantaneous second work of grace in which the heart is entirely cleansed from corruption and filled with perfect love for God.[19] Warm support soon turned to cold detente.

Actions were taken by the Methodist Episcopal Church in 1893 and the Methodist Episcopal Church South in 1894 that guaranteed that many advocates of the Holiness movement would leave. Holiness churches had already begun to form. In 1901 the *Pentecostal Holiness* movement was born, and in 1907 the Azusa Street revival in Los Angeles became the fountain for a nationwide and, indeed, a worldwide movement. Contrary to the assessment of some Methodist scholars, this movement was a natural development for people in the search of sure evidence of a second work of grace leading to true holiness.

6. The American National Baptist Convention met for the first time in August 1886, in St. Louis, with the express purpose of bringing together three different regional conventions of African-American Baptists in the United States. Three events helped to make this possible. In 1889 Emanuel Love, president of the all-black Baptist Foreign Missionary Convention and pastor of the First African Baptist Church, Savannah, was on his way to Indianapolis with a large entourage for the annual convention. He and his group, having paid for first-class tickets, were assaulted and driven from the train. This rallied black Baptists to consider a national organization to strengthen their political resistance to the Jim Crowism and segregation then developing in the South, with acquiescence if not endorsement in the North.

At the same meeting, black Baptist leaders met with officials of the American Baptist Publication Society and negotiated an arrangement in which the society would use African-American authors.

The outcry from Southern Baptists, who did not have their own publishing board, was so severe that the publication society reneged on the agreement.

The final straw came in 1894. Leaders from the Southern Baptist Convention, including Isaac T. Tichnor, corresponding secretary of the Home Mission Board, met with leaders of the American Baptist Home Missionary Society (ABHMS), including Henry L. Morehouse, corresponding secretary of that society, in Fortress Monroe, Virginia. The primary subject of discussion was a plan of comity and cooperation concerning the black population of the South. No African-American was present, nor were African-American leaders consulted. The decision was made to attempt to pull Southern Baptist churches into the support of ABHMS schools for freedmen. Further, they agreed to appoint missionaries cooperatively to work among the freedmen through the white and black state conventions.[20] These actions, when they were known, tended to divide the black Baptist forces in some states. Those who leaned toward cooperation supported these plans; the growing number of black separatists seized the opportunity to move toward united national organization.

In 1895, three national conventions came together in a structure much like the Southern Baptist Convention. The three conventions became the Boards of Education, Foreign Missions, and Home Missions of the National Baptist Convention of the United States of America. Though plagued with controversy and eventual division in 1915, African-American Baptists were to become a major force in both evangelism and church extension in the twentieth century.[21]

7. The rise of the social gospel and the movement toward inter-denominational cooperation and organization had a pervasive impact on the domestic mission. With roots deep in the nineteenth century, the social gospel was flourishing by 1900. Walter Rauschenbusch's blockbuster, *Christianity and the Social Crises,* though only one of several books published in 1907 on the subject, summed up the essence of the movement.[22] The social gospel, in spite of all that was done to minister to the poverty-stricken and working classes, remained a middle-class movement among both white and black Protestants. Black Protestants who adopted social gospel ideas, like their white cohorts, were the better educated and more elite members of African-American society. Whether black or white, they were intent on social salvation, the Christianization of society in *all* of its various dimensions. However, in spite of the best efforts of recent historians, it still is obvious that the most prominent

Northern leaders of the social gospel, with few exceptions, came late to address the racial issue in America.[23]

The social gospel was successful in penetrating the core of the Home Missions Council (HMC) and the Council of Women for Home Missions (CWHM). Both were formed by denominational boards and societies in 1908. In a report to the HMC in 1912, H. P. Swartz asseverated that there were "two types of missionary mind." The first, "more or less consciously *individualistic*," was designed to "save souls," add them to local churches, and teach them to live and give for Christ. The second type of missionary understanding was often called the "Social Spirit." It aimed at nothing less than the establishment "here and now of the Kingdom of God." While the evangelistic goal was not to be ignored, the trend must be to move toward the social emphasis. That was the direction of the two national home mission councils.[24]

8. The U.S. census of 1890 declared that the frontier was closed. American civilization was no longer ever moving westward. The flood of European immigrants, the rise of industrial cities, problems between labor and management, and the success of the Roman Catholic Church in America made this announcement stand in bold relief. The domestic mission for most leaders of the most politically influential denominations required a new direction.

Home Mission in the Twentieth Century

Because of these events and movements, the domestic mission has severely fragmented in the twentieth century. That movement so highly favored in 1900 has fissured into at least five distinct movements, and the status of Protestant home missions has been greatly diminished, although, in my opinion, the fissures have *not* been the primary contributing factors in the diminution of the domestic mission. In fact, the union of most denominational home mission agencies, culminating in the Home Mission Council of North America becoming a constituent agency of the National Council of Churches in 1950, has been a major factor in the decline. The reasons for deterioration are complex, but in some circles the home mission is all but dead or has been redirected primarily into liberal politics.

The conciliar Protestant faction of American Christianity has members from North and South, both black and white, of English- and non-English-speaking backgrounds, but it continues to reflect the mentality of the Northeastern Protestant establishment. In the twentieth century its concept of the domestic mission has been characterized more by cooperation and social action than by evangelism and church planting. Though the naïveté of the social gospel was abandoned in the 1920s, the concern to actualize the kingdom of God in America persisted. Paul A. Carter has asserted that the social gospel was under fire if not dead by the end of the twenties and was reborn in the political philosophy and social legislation of the New Deal.[25]

The ideal of a Christianized social order arose while the vision of America as the great Christian empire of destiny was most visible and while progressive postmillennialism was most immoderate. This definition of the domestic mission still tends to reflect the presuppositions and goals of that era. The primary architect of this understanding of the domestic mission was Josiah Strong. Strong was "the dynamo, the revivalist, the organizer, and altogether the most irrepressible spirit of the Social Gospel movement."[26] Most historians discuss only his first book, *Our Country*. He turned out a series of books, however, that continued, after his break in 1899 with the Evangelical Alliance, until his death in 1916. All his books pursued the literal application of the teaching of Jesus to the social situation in America. He perceived, correctly, the rising social potential and peril concentrated in the cities. The kingdom of God, he believed, would be actualized in American society and then spread to the world. At his death he was working on the third volume of a four-volume work entitled *Our World*.[27]

Buoyed up on the swells of scientific and cultural racism and militant nationalism and imperialism, Strong predicted that Anglo-Saxons would spread over the earth. The Anglo-Saxon, the true American, has, according to Strong, two traits of genius: "self government" and "pure *spiritual* Christianity." These two traits constitute the great needs of mankind. God had prepared in Anglo-Saxon civilization "the die with which to stamp the peoples of the earth." "The Anglo-Saxon holds in his hands the destinies of mankind for ages to come."[28]

But "the Anglo-Saxon race would speedily decay but for the salt of Christianity." This is precisely the role of home missions. The churches must Christianize immigrants so they can be "Anglo-Saxonized." The Christians of the United States have the prerogative to hasten or retard "the coming of Christ's Kingdom to the world" by hundreds or thousands of years. "We of this generation and nation," Strong said, "occupy the Gibraltar of the ages which commands the world's future."[29]

The mission *to* America, from Strong's perspective, was no longer integral to the world mission of the church. The domestic mission was subservient to the *mission of the nation*. The *national* mission had become identical with the mission of God. America was, indeed, the New Israel.

In *The New Era, or The Coming Kingdom*, published at the threshhold of the twentieth century, Strong continued to exalt the role of America, especially white, English-speaking America, in the evangelization of the world. He found that the Hebrew genius for religion, the Roman genius for conquest and organization, and the Greek genius for individualism and freedom had all been combined in the Anglo-Saxon race. As those three civilizations had prepared mankind for the first coming of Christ, so the Anglo-Saxon race was "especially commissioned to prepare the way for the coming Kingdom on earth."[30] He wrote: "[N]ow for the first time . . . these three great strands pass through the fingers of one predominant race to be braided into a single supreme civilization in the new era, the perfection of which will be the Kingdom fully come. . . . North America, the future home of this great race, is . . . thrice fitted to prepare the way for . . . the Kingdom [and] must, under God, control the world's future. . . . Is it not reasonable to believe that this race is destined to dispossess many weaker ones, assimilate others, and mould [sic] the remainder, until . . . it has Anglo-Saxonized mankind?"[31]

This purpose was right at the heart of the domestic mission. "He does most," Strong said, "to Christianize the world and to hasten the coming of the Kingdom who does most to make thoroughly Christian the United States." He insisted that he harbored no thought that God loved Anglo-Saxons more than Africans or Orientals. "My plea," he said, "is not, Save America for America's sake, but, Save America for the world's sake."[32]

The mission of the church is to complete the mission of Jesus. Jesus came to inaugurate the kingdom of God on earth. By "Kingdom of heaven," Strong said over and over again, Jesus did not mean the abode of the dead, "but a Kingdom of righteousness which he came to establish on the earth, of which he is the King, and whose fundamental law is love." It was Jesus' "great mission to inaugurate the Kingdom of God on earth and ours to extend it." "It is, therefore, the mission of the church to accomplish the purposes of Christ, to complete the work he began. . . . It is . . . the mission of the church to extend it until the Kingdoms of this world are become the Kingdoms of our Lord, and the prophetic prayer of

Christ that God's will might be done on earth as in heaven has found its fulfilling answer."[33]

All this is not to suggest that Strong had given up on personal and public evangelism, and embraced social action as the only form of Christian ministry. True, he did have little good to say about church planting. Mergers of small churches in small towns were a greater need. However, he proposed in *The New Era* an extensive plan, already introduced in the 1889 meeting of the Evangelical Alliance, to sustain by cooperative efforts a monthly visitation to every household in America. This monthly visitation focused on evangelism, meeting human needs, and bridging the gap between the rising middle-class churches of Protestantism and the working-class families of the cities.

For Strong, the kingdom of God preached by the Old Testament prophets was a "worldwide society in which universal obedience to the divine law, administered by the Lord's anointed, would bring universal blessings, spiritual and temporal; or in one word, the Kingdom of God realized would be an ideal world." The kingdom that Jesus preached was the fulfillment of Old Testament prophecies; it was the "perfected world-society, the social ideal, which the . . . prophets had heralded and . . . that the messiah would inaugurate." This correct understanding of the kingdom reveals the true mission of the church. When the church accepts that doctrine, "she will move out upon the highway of progress to the fulfillment of her mission. Failing to recognize the physical element in the Kingdom, she has failed in her duty to the physical needs of humanity."[34]

When these neglected truths about the teachings of Jesus are preached in the churches, then church members will take their stand for Christian service, sacrifice, and love; the ideal human society will be realized; the kingdom of God will be fully come; and the next great awakening will take place.

Twelve years later H. Paul Douglass wrote more about the new day, made an assessment of the domestic mission and its work of the past, and spelled out the new social perspective that home missions had to assume. But his vision was essentially the same: the realization of the social ideal of Jesus in human society, the kingdom of God fully come. He said that home missions had "overspread the continent with the hearthstone and the spire." "They have visioned in beauty and order a Paradise Redeemed . . . the most perfect reflection of the World that Shall Be." He continued, "Now home missions must undertake the final phase of their task, namely the combination of these fragments of success into a more perfect realization of Christianity in America worthy to be presented to God for ultimate completion."[35]

Douglass celebrated the passing of the old home missions and welcomed the birth of the new. "The last quarter century," he said, "has seen the gradual transformation of home missionary aims and methods until their social aspects are now the dominant ones." The domestic mission was being redirected. This redirection tended not to destroy but to fulfill the missionary activities of the older type. Yet there were distinct differences. Among those differences was a change in the church's focus from individual salvation to social redemption. In essence the switch was from the missionary as evangelist to the missionary as "social engineer."[36]

Throughout the twentieth century, with only brief relapses into realism in the Niebuhrian period, into evangelism and church planting in the revival of the 1950s, and again in the panic over runaway decline in the 1970s and '80s, conciliar Protestants pursued the "final phase" of the mission to America, attempting to actualize the kingdom of God in the social fabric of the nation.

There was real achievement. Not only were dramatic steps made in social and racial justice in America in the twentieth century, but the social consciousness of other Christians was aroused. Conciliar Protestants, primarily through the leadership of the black denominations, played a vital part in this achievement.

The identification of the domestic mission with the social involvement of the churches has stressed ministry and presence as essential missionary actions. Involvement in political issues is preferred to personal evangelism. Systemic evangelism, not individual conversion, will change the world. There is little place for a sovereign God who made the world or a Christ crucified for our sins and raised for our justification. These seek a city of man, made with human hands, where men are just and God is unnecessary. But in doing this, it is affirmed, the church has found what God is doing in the world and has joined him in his work. The home mission is more closely related to racial and social justice than to evangelism and church planting. Political action is seen as a part of the mission of God. Humanization, gender correctness, reproductive freedom, and the elimination of poverty are equally the objectives of the domestic mission. Indeed, these objectives rise above making disciples and gathering churches.

At least four other segments of American Christianity must be considered in this analysis. Time and space will not permit a full discussion for these remaining. Though the twentieth century saw the rise of ecumenical Christianity, the vision of the domestic mission has become not only fragmented, but also myopic. Views of the domestic mission have been defined most often in reaction— positive or negative—to the most imposing view of the nineteenth century that America, not the church, is the New Israel.

Serious disruption came to American Christianity, though primarily in the North, after 1910. In the fundamentalist-modernist controversy of the 1920s, that disruption became violently visible. Fundamentalists/evangelicals came out of the controversy with major emphasis on the overseas mission. They, too, have viewed America as essentially a Christian nation and have lamented the lack of fervent evangelism, sound biblical doctrine, and separated living that have been evidenced in many denominational churches. Joel Carpenter, George Marsden, Leonard Sweet, and others helped secular and church historians escape the clichés about fundamentalism in the era between World War I and the Vietnam War.[37] These years were spent in building new denominational organizations, creating new institutions, regaining respectability, restating in more current and popular fashion the fundamentals of the historic Christian faith, and forming new channels of cooperation and work. After World War I the commitment of conservative Christians to patriotism and other factors helped to reshape their view of the importance of America in God's divine plan for the ages. "They were convinced that at heart America was a Christian nation, both a recipient and a channel of divine blessing."[38] They were, and continue to be, a vital part of the third and fourth great waves of overseas missionary endeavor from America after World War II.

The aversion to social ministries that developed among Northern evangelicals was a reaction to the identification of the domestic mission with social issues and took place gradually.[39] After 1910 and by 1930, Northern evangelicals responded to human need by helping individuals and by shunning political activity. Northern evangelicals have hardly developed a domestic mission. In their denominational structures they have, indeed, created home missionary societies, boards, or departments. These are sometimes combined with, a part of, or distinct from a department or division of evangelism. Few groups until 1975 had a concerted strategy for church planting in the United States. Influenced by the moderate wing of the nineteenth-century Holiness movement, especially Keswick theology, they hoped to see the kingdom of God actualized in the lives of *individual* Christians. They have been quick to meet individual human needs, to develop rescue missions, to found children's homes, and, of late, to raise up crisis pregnancy centers, but have despaired of social actions as the solution to the problems of mankind or as an essential expression of obedience to Christ's missionary command. Evangelism as an expression of their hope of a national revival has been their overarching concern, but this evangelism has had its foundation on a conception that America was essentially Christian and adequately churched. The nation, like Israel of old, only waited for a national revival.[40]

A major segment of Northern evangelicalism has held firmly to a premillennial view of Christ's coming. Despite charges to the contrary, this belief has not deterred from the commitment to make disciples and gather churches through foreign missions.[41]

The vision of these Northern evangelicals for the ultimate victory of Christ and a literal reign of peace and prosperity over the earth was not much different from the vision of the conciliar Protestants at the turn of the twentieth century. Christ would reign over the earth. The big difference was in the way that reign would be actualized. The conciliar Protestants said that it would come by preaching the Gospel, human progress, and the gradual realization of an ideal society. For that larger segment of Northern evangelicals who embraced premillennialism, the kingdom would be realized only by the sudden return of Christ from heaven. The time was short; the Gospel must be preached to the nations. Believers must be gathered from every tribe and tongue. The Great Commission must be fulfilled, and then Christ would come. That same missionary motive is strong today, but it has seldom been directed toward North America. North American churches needed to be purified and revived. Although since 1975 there has been a new surge in church planting and church growth among evangelicals, this new surge is seldom expressed in terms of a domestic mission. The title of a recent book by George Barna illustrates the point: *Re-churching the Unchurched*. The two or three generational cohorts that are most unchurched have never been "churched."

A third segment of the fragmentation of the domestic mission is the African-American churches, especially black Baptist churches. These groups in the main affiliated with conciliar Protestantism in the twentieth century. But black churches did not shape conciliar Protestantism, and they exercised little influence until the civil rights movement and its aftermath.

The National Baptist Convention, organized in 1895, was plagued by dissension and in 1915 divided into two "national" Baptist conventions. During the century there were other divisions. Each of the three major denominational bodies has a functioning home mission board, society, or department; but their dynamism has not been in the various domestic mission structures.

The fantastic record of National Baptist churches in evangelism and church planting in the twentieth century, especially in the inner cities of this nation, has been ignored in most discussions of the mission of the American churches on this continent. Invariably, stories of the home missionary enterprise have told about evangelistic, educational, and social ministries of white churches to black people, but no word is said of the multiplication of Christians and churches by black Christians in the black communities.[42] The numbers and broad base of the black churches made black leadership in the civil rights movement a possibility. Seldom, except by that relentless researcher John N. Vaughan, has there been recognition that a large number of African-American churches are megachurches.

The primary mission of the black churches to America has been confined to the black community. Only in the civil rights movement did they assume a national dimension. For most black churches—though identified with the social and political goals of the black community, and even with articulations of black theology—the major emphasis continues to be on warm and personal church-centered evangelism.

While white Protestants of all types have lamented their loss of the inner city in the twentieth century, African-American churches gained the city. Their participation in any effort to evangelize and adequately church the North American cities is an absolute necessity. Yet these groups continue to be ignored or avoided, or, when invited, to refuse to participate in much of the domestic mission strategy focused today on urban areas. Their achievement was spontaneous rather than a planned and executed strategy from a missionary perspective.

A fourth significant segment of American Protestantism that demands attention is a group that might be classified as Southern Biblicists. The Southern Baptist Convention and the Churches of Christ are the best examples of this classification. Both have been, through the twentieth century, oriented toward Southern culture, and during the last half century have moved out of the South and Southwest into all parts of America.

I will not speak of the Churches of Christ, but I can speak with some authority about Southern Baptists. Southern Baptists struggle to actualize a national strategy. They struggle constantly with the conflict between evangelism and culture. In the South and Southwest, where they often constitute a cultural establishment, it is difficult to be prophetic, and they have become middle class. Outside the traditional areas of the convention they are often considered a sect. But the presence of multiple churches in most communities means that they have effectively addressed all segments of society—except the black community. Since 1970, two thousand African-American churches have been added to the fellowship, about half of them started by missionary activities, and there are now about nine thousand black and ethnic churches affiliated with Southern Baptists. This has been a result of the domestic mission activities of state and national convention agencies.

Northern evangelicals have tended toward premillennialism. Southern Biblicists have, until recent years, tended to be amillennialists. The emphasis has been on personal salvation with no real expectation that this world and human society would be actually renovated, either by the evolution of human society or by the direct intervention of God.[43] Rather, Christ would return, the resurrection and judgment would occur, and the saints would go to heaven.

Bible-centered personal evangelism and a strong emphasis on local churches have made the Southern Biblicists avid and successful church planters. They do give offense to many, but, seeing all men in need of Christ, since they escaped the boundaries of the old South after World War II, they have viewed America as a mission field on a par with other nations of the world. For them the domestic mission is part of the world mission of the church.

Finally, a fifth segment of American Protestantism that shares the fractured condition of the domestic mission is the Pentecostal churches. At the time when a large portion of the Protestant establishment in the North was moving away from individual salvation and church planting to a social mission aimed toward the alienated of America, and while the Protestant establishment in the South was developing its rationale for evangelizing whites only, there was an explosion of spiritual faith—largely among the poorer people of this country—that majored on the conversion of individuals and (in its early stages, at least) crossed racial barriers in North and South.

All the growth of Pentecostal churches has taken place since 1901. The most significant thing that happened in the twentieth century in reference to the world mission of the church was not the ecumenical movement, but the birth of Pentecostalism and the multiplication of Pentecostal churches across the world. I graduated from a respectable Christian college, had two degrees from one of the largest theological seminaries in the world, and had just about finished a graduate program in the field of church history at a major university before I ever heard about the great Azusa Street revival of 1906 and the effect of that revival in raising up men and women who would win others to Christ and gather churches all over the world. The equal place of women in the churches that evangelicals passionately debate today was settled at the beginning of that century for Pentecostals. No twentieth-century group has more effectively mobilized the laity or penetrated the lower classes of American society than the Pentecostals.

They, too, give offense to many. Many of these churches are rapidly becoming middle class. Nevertheless, even though Pentecostalism, like the rest of American Protestantism, is splintered into many groups, their churches provide an exciting option for many Americans; they are found in all parts of the nation, and they now penetrate—to a degree—all the social levels of American society.

Lessons to Be Learned

With all the diffusion, what can evangelicals learn from the near demise of the home mission in North America in the twentieth century? First, the North American domestic mission should be reinstated as a vital part of the world mission of the church. North American foreign missions emerged out of the blossoming domestic mission. Long before the first overseas societies were formed as part of the institutionalization of the Second Great Awakening (1812, 1814, 1817, 1821, and following), hundreds of American missionary committees, societies, and conferences prayed, raised funds, and commissioned evangelists and church planters for the domestic mission. Before the Connecticut Missionary Society was formed, associations of Standing Order ministers and churches were commissioning missionaries. Fifteen years before the Society for Propagating the Gospel among the Indians and Others in North America (SPGNA) was created by an act of the General Court of Massachusetts in 1787, the Eastern Association of Ministers, located on the edge of New England's northeastern wilderness, sent Daniel Little of Wells to the frontier and Indian settlements in Maine. The Philadelphia Baptist Association had an extensive mission to the South and West by 1760. The Charleston Baptist Association already had itinerant missionaries at work on the southern frontier by that time. The Sandy Creek Baptist Association in western North Carolina was itself a missionary venture of New England Separatists-become-Baptists and a domestic missionary agency sending missionaries north and south across the southern frontier. The Warren Baptist Association ordained its first itinerant evangelist at its second meeting in 1768. When aging Daniel Little, sent by the SPGNA, arrived in the district of Maine in 1791, he found that Warren Baptist missionaries had already gathered churches and had organized the Bowdoinham Association in 1787. By 1810 nearly all Baptist associations had a missionary committee or missionary society that managed their various domestic mission projects. The late-arriving Methodists had circuits all over the new nation by 1784, except in New England. Jason Lee began his work in that region in 1789. Each circuit rider was a domestic missionary, and each annual conference as they developed after 1796 was a home missionary agency. Quakers, Moravians, Presbyterians, and others were all involved in the domestic mission before the first overseas missionary societies came into being.

At about the turn of the twentieth century, the domestic and foreign mission were divided. The home mission became the instrument for perfecting the new Christian empire. The churches of North America provided the chief source of money and personnel for the church's mission around the world. This dichotomy should be abolished. Any distinction between the missionary task of the Church in America and Canada and the missionary task of the church in the rest of the world is delusive and postulated on a lingering myth of Christendom. The mission to North America and the international mission are one.

A second lesson from the story of domestic mission is that all remnants of the concept of America as the *New Israel*, God's chosen nation to redeem the world, or of Canada as *His Dominion*, a nation of divine destiny, must be jettisoned from our missionary thinking. America, and I could speak of Canada as well, is not and has never been a Christian nation. The risen Christ has not shifted his missionary commission to the nation instead of the church. Making America the "redeemer nation" contaminates, compromises, and denigrates the role of the churches in global missions. Identifying America as the New Israel (of course, no one would use that term today), with its own special covenant with God, makes the church unnecessary and irrelevant.

Evangelicals have not as yet recovered from this nineteenth- and early-twentieth-century myth. In fact, the last quarter century has seen a resurrection of this idea. The cultural war that currently rages around us in politics, education, and the media is largely motivated by this vision. At the time this vision was receiving its most vociferous expression, racism reigned supreme among white churches, except the newborn Pentecostal groups, and Anglo-Saxon ethnocentrism was most extreme.

The local church in America and Canada is too often a mixed multitude in a mess, not a company of obedient disciples on a mission. In the meantime, the nation is deluded by allegiance to civil religion and ensnared by militant hedonism, secular humanism, and a new and exotic paganism, caught in the volcanic upheaval created by the crash of two cultural tectonic plates: modernity and post-modernity. Evangelical Christians assume that America is already thoroughly churched. We do not live in the post-Christian era in North America. America and Canada have never reflected the mind of Christ. The reign of Christ over these geopolitical nations has not yet dawned. I do not expect it by human effort.

Secularism and pluralism are not new things in North America. They are just more acceptable options today. Since the Declaration of Independence the United States has been moving, as Franklin Littell has said, from state church to pluralism.[44] There was a period when a certain brand of evangelical Protestantism, primarily from New England, had tremendous influence on those who molded American culture. But that was almost as oppressive to other evangelical Protestants as it was to Roman Catholics and Latter-day Saints.

The churches in North America are young churches. North America is a mission field where there are multitudes to be discipled, baptized, and taught to be responsible members of responsible churches.

A third lesson from the domestic mission is that we should learn to hold tightly and execute single-mindedly the chief and primary tasks of the redemptive mission of the church. For the overseas mission and the domestic mission in North America, evangelism and church planting must hold the central place. "Missions" today— for many American Protestants, including evangelicals—is anything a church, parachurch or denominational agency, or Christian does that is good, that improves the human condition. The mission of the church must be more strictly defined. The mission of the church is essentially to make disciples and gather them into churches. True, we cannot remain silent before social and racial injustice. We are sent to minister as well as to witness. But we cannot overlook the intention of God to take out of the nations a people for his name (Acts 15:14), and the commission of the churches is to carry the good news that Jesus, who was crucified, God has raised from the dead and made both Lord and Christ (Acts 2:32, 36). He alone can give life that is both abundant and eternal. To follow the New Testament pattern, those who receive the Good News should be gathered into churches.

There are more than 300 million people in the United States and Canada. George Barna recently said that 100 million unchurched people are in the United States alone, a very conservative figure in my opinion.[45] In terms of warm bodies, the American church is in the midst of one of the largest mission fields in the world today. And the population is basically responsive.

North America must be viewed like the rest of the world. To use a term Donald A. McGavran made famous, these nations must be viewed as a vast mosaic. Just because a city of ten thousand has thirty churches, this fact does not mean that the city is adequately churched. There may be numerous churches, but the majority address the Gospel to only the middle classes of the black and white communities. Among Protestants, only Pentecostals, black churches, and a few others address themselves to the poor folks. Most evangelicals, from my observation, are in the upper middle classes and aspire to the upper classes.

Competition exists between churches, but they compete for the people in one class, usually the recently unchurched of that class. Little competition exists for the never-churched, the pagans and neo-pagans all around us. They are forgotten or ignored. Most church planting strategies today are aimed at the upwardly mobile middle classes or at picking up unchurched people of their own denominations. The making of disciples and multiplying of churches among all segments of human society is the essential mission of the church in the world. The mission to North America is not different.

Finally, from the North American domestic mission of the twentieth century we should learn to avoid and eschew plans of comity and plans for mergers of churches or church planting movements.

These two strategies were characteristic of conciliar home missions during the twentieth century.[46] These strategies were also massive failures.[47] Evangelicals are deeply engrossed today in discussions of partnership, cooperation, and a united front in missions. I am deeply committed to those ideals myself. However, I choose to raise a caution flag and to wave it vigorously. Much that I read today about cooperation among evangelicals sounds strangely familiar. It is remarkably like the rhetoric of the first decade of the twentieth century that led to the formation of the HMC and the CWHM and the creation of the Federal Council of Churches. The rhetoric continued for the first six decades of the century. Political issues related to racial and economic concerns have ruled since that time. Much of the material I read today concerning mission and community development sounds like the passionate logic of the advocates of the social gospel after 1900.

Christians should lead the way in community development. Yet this must not be confused with the essential redemptive mission of the church. Educational institutions continue to be an important part of the world mission. Some of the most significant evangelical educational institutions in North America today were begun to provide workers for the domestic mission. However, William Rainey Harper insisted that the University of Chicago was a home mission effort.[48] All of these random statements are just to warn of potential dangers of consolidation, comity and contraction in North America's domestic mission field and the global task.

In Conclusion

In conclusion, North American evangelicals should awaken to the need to address the classic domestic mission with vigor and urgency. The mission to North America must be moved from a focus on ministries at the periphery of middle and upper class churches to the heart of the redemptive mission: making disciples of the multiplied segments of North American society and gathering them into churches with leaders indigenous to those groups. This should be done from at least three perspectives. First, the mission to North America should become a field for more intense and expansive academic research, analysis, and explanation by missiologists, historians, anthropologists, and sociologists. At the turn of the twentieth century, home missions studies were multiplied. Has anyone read a full-scale analysis or history of the domestic mission in North America at the turn of the twenty-first century? Second, the mission to North America should be executed with wisdom, with zeal, and in the power or the Holy Spirit by all church and mission structures in North America today, and the missionary forces from outside the continent should be urged to engage in that mission—not just bankroll their varied ministries elsewhere. Third, all those who think, act, and pray toward the fulfillment of the world mission of Jesus Christ should learn from both the successes and the failures of the mission in North America.

Notes

1. Lyman Abbott, *Reminiscences* (Boston: Houghton Mifflin, 1915), pp. 472–79.

2. Lyman Abbott, "Southern Evangelization," *New Englander* 89 (October 1864): 699–708.

3. Quoted in Joseph B. Clark, *Leavening the Nation: The Story of American [Protestant] Home Missions* (New York: Baker & Taylor, 1903), p. 343.

4. Ibid., p. v.

5. Ibid., p. 342.

6. Cyrus D. Foss, "The Mission of Our Country," *Christian Advocate: New York*, July 6, 1876, p. 1. This article is an abstract of a baccalaureate sermon preached at the Methodist Church, Middletown, N.Y., Sunday morning, June 25, 1876.

7. Quoted in Clark, *Leavening the Nation*, p. 350.

8. Ibid., p. 351.

9. Colin B. Goodykoontz, *Home Missions on the American Frontier* (Caldwell, Idaho: Caxton Printers, 1939), pp. 406, 426.

10. The domestic mission did not have its rise in 1798 with the Connecticut Missionary Society, nor was that society created from a strong missionary passion. The primary concern of most of those who were finally moved to action in 1798 was how to block the growth of Methodists and Baptists on the New England frontiers. See Charles L. Chaney, *The Birth of Missions in America* (South Pasadena, Calif.: William Carey Library, 1976), pp. 101–49.

11. George B. Hunsberger and Craig Van Gelder, eds., *Church Between Gospel and Culture* (Grand Rapids: Eerdmans, 1996), p. 3.

12. Sidney Mead, *The Nation with the Soul of a Church* (New York: Harper & Row, 1975), pp. 48–77.

13. Ernest R. Sandeen, *The Roots of Fundamentalism: British and American Millennialism, 1800–1930* (Chicago: Univ. of Chicago Press, 1970), pp. 139–40.

14. Timothy P. Weber, *Living in the Shadow of the Second Coming* (Grand Rapids: Academie Books of Zondervan, 1983), pp. 65–81.

15. R. Pierce Beaver, *Ecumenical Beginnings in Protestant World Mission* (New York: Thomas Nelson & Sons, 1962), pp. 294–95.

16. Charles L. Chaney, "The Babylonian Captivity of the Great Commission," *The Home Missions Magazine*, June 1967, pp. 13–14.

17. Quoted in Robert T. Handy, *We Witness Together* (New York: Friendship Press, 1957), p. 127. The North American Home Missions Congress was held in Washington, D.C., December 1–5, 1930.

18. Sydney E. Ahlstrom, *A Religious History of the American People* (New Haven: Yale Univ. Press, 1972), p. 799.

19. John L. Peters, *Christian Perfection and American Methodism* (Nashville: Abingdon, 1956), p. 162.

20. Southern Baptist Convention, *Proceedings of the Southern Baptist Convention Held at Washington, D.C., May 10–14, 1895* (Atlanta: Franklin Printing & Publishing, 1895), p. 15.

21. James M. Washington, *Fractured Fellowship: The Black Baptist Quest for Social Power* (Macon, Ga.: Mercer Univ. Press, 1986), pp. 135–57.

22. Other books published in the same year include Edwin C. Dargan, *Society, Kingdom, and Church* (Philadelphia: American Baptist Publication Society, 1907); Shailer Mathews, *The Church and the Changing Order* (New York: Macmillan, 1907); and Josiah Strong, *The Challenge of the City* (New York: Young People's Missionary Movement of the United States and Canada, 1907). However, clusters of books were published on Christianity and social issues in 1903 and 1910 as well.

23. See Donald K. Gorrell, *The Age of Social Responsibility: The Social Gospel in the Progressive Era, 1900–1920* (Macon, Ga.: Mercer Univ. Press, 1988); Ronald C. White, *Liberty and Justice for All: Racial Reform and the Social Gospel* (San Francisco: Harper & Row, 1990).

24. Handy, *We Witness Together*, p. 31.

25. Paul A. Carter, *The Decline and Revival of the Social Gospel: Social and Political Liberalism in American Protestant Churches, 1920–1940* (Ithaca, N.Y.: Cornell Univ. Press, 1954), pp. 121, 140.

26. Ahlstrom, *Religious History*, p. 798.

27. Strong's books come in this order:

      1886 *Our Country*
      1891 *Our Country* (updated with 1890 census)
      1893 *The New Era, or The Coming Kingdom*
      1898 *The Twentieth Century City*
      1900 *Expansion Under New World-Conditions*
      1900 *Religious Movements for Social Betterment*
      1901 *The Times and Young Men*
      1902 *The Next Great Awakening*
      1907 *The Challenge of the City*
      1907 *My Religion in Every Day Life*
      1913 *Our World: The New World—Life*
      1915 *Our World: The New World—Religion*

28. Josiah Strong, *Our Country: Its Possible Future and Its Present Crises*, rev. ed. (New York: Baker & Taylor, 1891), pp. 200–201, 205, 217.

29. Ibid., p. 218.

30. Josiah Strong, *The New Era, or The Coming Kingdom* (New York: Baker & Taylor, 1893), p. 69.

31. Ibid., pp. 69, 75, 80.

32. Ibid., p. 80.

33. Ibid., pp. 231, 233.

34. Josiah Strong, *The Next Great Awakening* (New York: Baker & Taylor, 1902), pp. 70–71, 217.

35. H. Paul Douglass, *The New Home Missions: An Account of Their Social Redirection* (New York: Missionary Education Movement, 1914), p. 227.

36. Ibid., pp. 54, 57.

37. Joel A. Carpenter, *Revive Us Again: The Reawakening of American Fundamentalism* (New York: Oxford Univ. Press, 1997); George M. Marsden, ed., *Evangelicalism and Modern America* (Grand Rapids: Eerdmans, 1984); George M. Marsden, *Reforming Fundamentalism: Fuller Seminary and the New Evangelicalism* (Grand Rapids: Eerdmans, 1987); Leonard I. Sweet, ed., *The Evangelical Tradition in America* (Macon, Ga.: Mercer Univ. Press, 1984).

38. Robert E. Wenger, "Social Thought in American Fundamentalism" (Ph.D. diss., Univ. of Nebraska, 1973), p. 120.

39. George M. Marsden, *Fundamentalism and American Culture* (New York: Oxford Univ. Press, 1980), pp. 124–38.

40. Northern evangelicals (and Southern Biblicists and Pentecostals discussed below) through most of the twentieth century placed a major portion of their domestic mission strategy into citywide evangelistic or "revival" campaigns (designed to call backsliding America back to God); the development of "great" churches (by this was meant very large and evangelistically-active local congregations, more or less independent of denominations, the forerunners of, but not identical with, today's megachurches); the utilization of radio, television, and other technologies as extensively and effectively as possible; the multiplication of parachurch mission structures to win, train, and mobilize high school and college students and lay persons for evangelism; the creation of rescue missions and Bible institutes; and the proliferation of innumerable regional and national conferences. See Carpenter, *Revive Us Again*, pp. 110–210; "The Fundamentalist Leaven and the Rise of an Evangelical United Front," in Sweet, *The Evangelical Tradition*, pp. 257–88; "From Fundamentalism to the New Evangelical Coalition," in Marsden, *Evangelicalism and Modern America*, pp. 3–16; Richard N. Ostling, "Evangelical Publishing and Broadcasting," in Marsden, *Evangelicalism and Modern America*, pp. 46–55; Leonard I. Sweet, ed., *Communication and Change in American Religious History* (Grand Rapids: Eerdmans, 1993), especially chapters by Leonard Sweet, James H. Moorhead, and David Edwin Harrell, Jr.; Quentin J. Schultze, ed., *American Evangelicals and the Mass Media* (Grand Rapids: Zondervan, 1990); and Mark Ellingsen, *The Evangelical Movement* (Minneapolis: Augsburg Publishing, 1988), pp. 179–96. For a different perspective on radio/television see Dennis N. Voskuil, "Reaching Out: Mainline Protestantism and the Media," in *Between the Times: The Travail of the Protestantism Establishment in America, 1900–*

1960, ed. William R. Hutchison (New York: Cambridge Univ. Press, 1989), pp. 72–94. The evangelistic campaign as a missionary strategy is well illustrated in Lyle W. Dorsett, *Billy Sunday and the Redemption of Urban America* (Grand Rapids: Eerdmans, 1990), and Edith L. Blumhofer, *Aimee Semple McPherson: Everybody's Sister* (Grand Rapids: Eerdmans, 1993). By mid-century Southern Baptists had institutionalized this strategy in a local church format. See Charles E. Matthews, *The Southern Baptist Program of Evangelism* (Atlanta: Home Mission Board of the Southern Baptist Convention, 1949), and Charles S. Kelley, Jr., *How Did They Do It: The Story of Southern Baptist Evangelism* ([New Orleans:] Insight Press, 1993).

41. Timothy Weber, *Living in the Shadow of the Second Coming,* pp. 65–81.

42. Charles L. Chaney, *Church Planting at the End of the Twentieth Century,* rev. ed. (Wheaton, Ill.: Tyndale House, 1991), pp. 213–34.

43. This paragraph deserves several pages. Most of the Reformed wing of the fundamentalist movement of the 1920s and 1930s has not tended toward premillennialism. Some Southern Baptists held premillennial views throughout the twentieth century and many hold these views today. The Churches of Christ emerged at the end of the nineteenth century out of complex eschatological views, and nothing has been more divisive among them. See Marsden, *Fundamentalism and American Culture,* pp. 124–38; George Beasley-Murray, *Revelation: Three Views* (Nashville: Broadman Press, 1977); and Richard T. Hughes, *Reviving the Ancient Faith* (Grand Rapids: Eerdmans, 1996), pp. 117–67.

44. Franklin H. Littell, *From State Church to Pluralism* (Garden City, N.Y.: Doubleday Anchor Books, 1962), pp. 167–68.

45. George Barna, *Re-churching the Unchurched* (Ventura, Calif.: Issachar Resources, 2000), back cover.

46. Handy, 1957, pp. 75–82, 99–103.

47. Roger Finke and Rodney Stark, *The Churching of America, 1776–1990* (New Brunswick, N.J.: Rutgers Univ. Press, 1992), pp. 199–236.

48. George M. Marsden, *The Soul of the American University* (New York: Oxford Univ. Press, 1994), pp. 248–50.

Chapter Seven

Between Past and Future: Non-Western Theological Education Entering the Twenty-first Century

Jonathan J. Bonk

Laying its eggs in the nest of smaller birds of another species, the cuckoo then flies away, leaving the responsibility of raising its offspring in the hands of these unsuspecting dupes. Responding to the big cuckoo chick's desperate cries for food, the befuddled adoptive parents stuff it full of worms at the expense of their own offspring. When they turn their backs, the cuckoo hatchling shoves another of their own flesh and blood overboard. The smaller birds never seem to notice. Is there an analogy to Western mission societies and denominations that establish theological seminaries for training church leaders and missionaries in impoverished countries? Can North American models of theological education and mission, once transplanted, and then bereft of the support of those whose cultural DNA they bear, similarly survive only at the expense of the species indigenous to the nest? What can be done about this situation?

"The past is never dead, it is not even past."[1]

The Past

The missiological DNA peculiar to Western evangelical Christian missions may be traced to forebears who, scarcely two hundred years ago, set forth confidently to employ means to bring to the world their evangelical understanding of Christianity,[2] Western commerce, and European civilization (though not always in that order). These blessings were grafted into the richly diverse soils of thousands of distinct peoples by means of such Western cultural institutions as churches, schools, and hospitals. A quick perusal of the figures indicates that the results of missionary activity have been impressive. According to Barrett and Johnson's "Annual Statistical Table on Global Mission:

2001," between 1900 and 2000 the number of self-confessed Christians increased from 558,132,000 to 1,999,564,000. Of these, "Great Commission Christians" (defined as "active church members of all traditions who take Christ's Great Commission seriously") increased from 77,931,000 to 647,821,000. Such figures are truly impressive until one looks at the percentages they represent, for it then becomes clear that missionary efforts have barely kept pace with population growth. Whereas in 1900 Christians represented 34.5 percent of the total population, by 2000 their proportional numbers had slipped to 33 percent.[3] Nevertheless, the value ascribed to even one soul by our Lord should elicit from us heartfelt praise for what God has accomplished through the sometimes dismayingly human instrumentality of Christian missions!

We are properly humbled, furthermore, by the dawning awareness that we (the Western mission establishment) have tended to attribute too much of the success to our missiological strategies and expatriate personnel. We have overlooked the fact that it has been the evangelists and catechists who have actually produced the fruit. While they have borne the lion's share of the incarnational work of establishing new churches, their names are scarcely mentioned in our official histories, and their stories are almost never told. We are like the fly on the back of the elephant who remarked, as his lumbering host crossed a swinging bridge and clambered heavily up the opposite bank, "Whew! We sure did shake that bridge!" Too often, the story of the church outside of Europe and North America is told as though it were simply a footnote to the story of European tribes.[4]

Nevertheless, as we contemplate the century past, we can surely add our hearty "Amen!" to A. T. Pierson's words as he concluded his speech at the New York Ecumenical Missionary Conference in 1900: "The ideal missionary must have four passions: A passion for the truth; a passion for Christ; a passion for the souls of men, and a passion for self-sacrificing. And I may say that the history of missions in the last century has shown not one, nor fifty, nor one hundred, but thousands of men and women that have filled out the grand ideals of the mission service in the mission life."[5]

The Present

Lest the Evangelical Missiological Society indulge in similarly uncritical self-congratulation, against the impressive growth of the church we do well to juxtapose some less edifying figures. The Western missionary endeavor now finds itself at the end of a century marked by unparalleled prodigies of destructiveness—with much of the blame to be placed at the feet of our own civilizations. In one hundred years the world's population has quadrupled, but more people than ever before in human history have been slaughtered, starved, and driven into exile. While human collective wealth has risen astronomically, the distinction between rich and poor countries, and rich and poor individuals, is more skewed in 2001 than it was in 1901 or 1801, and Herculean efforts to create equity have fostered megalomaniac tyrants, horrific genocides, and entrenched injustice.[6]

One-third of the world's population uses and wastes three-quarters of the world's food and not less than 83 percent of all other resources. Two-thirds of the world's population must make do with one-quarter of the world's food and 17 percent of other resources. As a result, 1.2 billion people live in absolute poverty, having an income of less than $100 per year. Half of these have nothing, and an estimated 38 million people are literally starving to death. Every 2.4 seconds a child in the Third World dies of starvation, while at the same time a 10 percent per capita surplus of food is rotting away in the storehouses of the West. Clearly, the prospect of material and economic and technological progress—once thought to be an inevitable outcome of social and economic organization along capitalist lines—has proven to be an illusory and fundamentally false dream. The relative proportion of impoverished people around the world is increasing, not diminishing. At the same time, the relative proportion of very rich persons is diminishing while the percentage of the planet's material resources they control is increasing. This is the global context within which members of the body of Christ, a majority of whom are poor, must live out their faith and engage in their mission.[7]

According to Robert Conquest, the twentieth century's uniquely memorable contributions to human history are threefold: total war, totalitarianism, and terror.[8] The century past has been convulsed by ideological frenzies that have resulted in the extermination of some 170 million civilians, massacred by their own states, in the name of tribe, nation, race, class, religion, and ideology. Some 30 millions—mostly civilians—have likewise perished by war. All of this has been made possible by modern science and productive industry—largely Western, and highly profitable—together conceiving and building the instruments of mayhem: airplanes, tanks, missiles, bombs, trains, roads, submarines, machine guns, poison gases, and biological weapons.[9]

The unspeakably horrifying destruction of the universally recognized symbols of Western fiscal confidence and domination, together with approximately 2,800 civilians, on September 11, 2001, simply reinforces Conquest's thesis and reminds us that the affluent and powerful United States is not regarded with universal approbation and that its vision for humanity is not shared by all. As John Burns aptly noted in the Sunday, September 16, 2001, edition of the *New York Times*:

> Of all of history's great powers, from Athens and Rome to Byzantium and imperial Britain, perhaps none has ever so dominated the globe as America does now. Nor has any of these powers aroused such a complex of feelings, positive and negative, that could go some way toward explaining how extremists from a distant world could mount an attack of the unfathomable hatred seen this week in New York and Washington, followed by the unrestrained outpouring of sadness and support from some of the very peoples that America's terrorist enemies claim to represent.
>
> America, with its daunting economic, political and military power, its pervasive popular culture, and its instinct to spread the freewheeling, secularist ways of American life—even to those who may prefer to shun them—has an impact on peoples' lives to the farthest corners of the earth.
>
> Americans, with the richness of intermingling cultures, can find it difficult to grasp how vulnerable other societies can feel as their own cultures begin to erode.
>
> . . . Islamic . . . groups have their own ideology rooted in a deeply conservative reading . . . of the Koran. . . . They reject American values . . . then rouse their followers by arguing that the United States violates [its own principles of democracy, tolerance and respect for individual rights] in its support for Israel, and with the sanctions that stifle Iraq.
>
> . . . Often the suffering of Muslim civilians in conflicts around the world—in Afghanistan, Chechnya, Iraq, Lebanon, Kashmir, Somalia, and, above all, Palestine is evoked.
>
> . . . In recent years . . . even more moderate Muslims have been swept by an ascent of anger against the United States, particularly over Israel and Iraq, and . . . for the sense that . . . America . . . was indifferent to the causes of their rage.[10]

In a perceptive analysis of the difficulties of coming to grips with the still shadowy and elusive terrorists and their supporters responsible for the apocalyptic destruction of the World Trade Center towers, Serge Schmemann points out that the perpetrators issued neither demands nor ultimatums:

> They did it solely out of grievance and hatred—hatred for the values cherished in the West as freedom, tolerance, prosperity, religious pluralism and universal suffrage, but abhorred by religious fundamentalists (and not only Muslim fundamentalists) as licentiousness, corruption, greed and apostasy. The attack . . . was . . . against a symbol—the twin towers of Sodom and mammon.
>
> That [is] the problem for a nation marching off to war: that the enemy was not a government, gang or despot, but hatred. And a hatred powerful enough to motivate a person to live for years among his victims while preparing their common death is a form of madness, a disease.
>
> . . . And dealing with terrorism rather than just terrorists requires not only stamping out cells, but understanding the poverty and hopelessness in which recruits are found, as well as the conflicts that, left unresolved too long, foster deep and lasting hatreds.[11]

Given the encouraging spread of Christianity over the last one hundred years, and given the correspondingly depressing state of the world just described, missiologists must surely ask themselves how the church can be so numerically impressive and yet make so little difference, either inside or outside of North America. I leave the perennial quest for a satisfactory answer to this question to theologians, and move on to a less speculative sphere of missionary interest.

Not even a multivolume encyclopedia, let alone a single article or presentation, could begin to catalogue the evil outcomes of many well-intentioned efforts by Westerners, including missionaries, to find ways and means of bringing the rest of the globe's population to see things as we do. But I have time and space to explore only one example of an institution, the school—introduced by well-intentioned missionaries throughout the world—that shows increasing signs of producing effects that are exactly the opposite of those intended or foreseen. I choose this example because I believe that, given an adjustment of our ecclesiology, we will be permitted to see the day when the things hoped for will in fact be forthcoming. I speak of that education that has come to be associated with theological colleges and seminaries around the world.

A distressing example of the mixed outcomes of well-intentioned missionary endeavor may be found in the schools established across

Canada as far as the Mackenzie River Delta where Inuit and northern Indian children were sent to board away from their families.
Education, for long regarded as the engine of social and ecclesiastical progress, has been a significant part of what Western missionaries have offered to the "uttermost parts" of the earth. These Canadian schools, founded and staffed by Christian missionaries of admirable dedication and lofty ideals, "raised a level of bitterness
among the students who attended them that is hard to imagine,"
James Houston[12] relates, continuing:

> Yet it is so universally agreed by former students as having been a
> horrible experience that one has to wonder at the methods. The use of
> their native language by the children was absolutely outlawed in school,
> in favor of French and English, and the message was reinforced by
> beatings. Sadly, this was a method that did great harm to the ongoing
> cohesion of family groups, as kids returned home barely able to speak
> their parents' language. The underlying idea seemed to be to change
> hunters, trappers, and fishermen into farmers or business folk, even
> where the lands were unsuitable and few real business opportunities
> were likely to occur for perhaps half a century.
>
> To add insult to injury, the mission schools sometimes held on to
> money they were supposed to spend on the children: I know this be-
> cause I did the school inspection for the old Department of Mines and
> Resources. In the cases I remember the boarding schools not only took
> the government money to spend on feeding and clothing the kids, they
> demanded that the father of each child forced into school supply the
> mission with enough caribou meat and hides to completely feed and
> clothe the child. This amounted to . . . about forty caribou per child
> per year, and the parents naturally set out hunting to make sure that
> their kids were fed. . . .
>
> It is hard to believe, but the mission schools, financed by the gov-
> ernment, set about [thoughtlessly] destroying a culture that had sur-
> vived on its own for thousands of years.[13]

But allow me to edge a little closer to home for those of us
involved in international theological education. Ever since the most
populous portion of the North American continent achieved political
and economic independence from Great Britain over two hundred
years ago, we Canadians have grumbled about the endemic insensitivity and parochialism of our powerful neighbor to the south, the
United States. In our better moments we have conceded that U.S. mis-
understanding and disregard of other peoples is not so much a
matter of ill will as it is the inevitable by-product of power. What

little thought the powerful *do* give to those who are weaker and poorer is typically utilitarian, frequently patronizing, and sometimes mildly contemptuous. For as Canadian-born Harvard economist Kenneth Galbraith once wryly observed, "Nothing so gives the illusion of intelligence as personal association with large sums of money."[14] The fact is, there appears to be a perception on the part of the United States that it does not "need" anybody, whereas almost everybody "needs" the United States.[15]

En route to my son's graduation in Winnipeg some time ago, I picked up an old issue of *MacLean's*, Canada's answer to *Time* and *Newsweek*. Inside the back cover was columnist Allan Fotheringham's typically cranky regular feature, in this instance titled "Learning to Love the American Bully Next Door." He was commenting on a letter appearing in a Toronto newspaper by a writer who identified herself as an American living in Canada, and who was fed up with what she referred to as all the "anti-American" ranting in the press and media of my homeland. And it is true: Canadians do tend to criticize the United States. But Fotheringham makes the point that Canadians, being Americans themselves, are not "anti-American." They are anti–United States. What is the difference? "Americans as individuals are wonderful," declares Fotheringham, but "the United States, as a nation, is a bully [and] people generally don't like bullies."[16]

When Canada attempted to make and enforce laws that would enable the country (as opposed to Hollywood) to control its own film distribution system a few years ago, Jack Valenti, then a presidential aide and now the highest paid lobbyist in Washington for Hollywood movies, warned that if Canadians achieved their goal this would be a "virus" that could spread to Europe. No country likes to be described, even respectfully, as a "virus"! "We don't dislike Americans," Fotheringham concludes. "We just fear the United States."

Lest I convey the impression that the United States is a uniquely sinister empire, bent on controlling the world no matter how evil the means, let me hasten to add that what is often perceived as American "bullying" is usually little more than a natural consequence of relative scale . . . of disparate entities in close proximity. *The United States is very* big—in every way, whereas *most other nation-state entities* are *very* small—in every way. As a Canadian prime minister once observed, "Living next to you is in some ways like sleeping with an elephant. No matter how friendly and even-tempered the beast, one is affected by every twitch and grunt."[17]

Since the most powerful engine driving the globalization juggernaut is the United States, few parts of the human enterprise
today are unaffected by the social, economic, political and religious
energies and agendas of that great nation. It should come as no
surprise, then, that theological education and mission around the
world should likewise be in unwitting thrall to the multifaceted
expressions of its power.

As a twenty-four-year veteran of theological education at Providence College and Seminary, an interdenominational evangelical seminary located in Manitoba, the heartland of Canada, and as one who—
by virtue of having missionary parents—has spent a goodly part of
his life in Ethiopia, I have personally witnessed and experienced the
inevitability, the peril, and the promise of globalization. This irresist-
ibly destructive juggernaut is well illustrated in the case study below,
from which may be extrapolated lessons for non-Western theological
education entering the twenty-first century.

The story related by Helena Norberg-Hodge is the familiar
chronicle of a people's two-generation descent, via the Western en-
gines of progress, from cultural integration and vigor into social dis-
sonance and decay.[18] Since we human beings have no identity apart
from culture, it is within and by means of culture that each of us must
make his or her journey through life. What happens, then, when tourism, media images, Western education, and the global economy combine to undermine the integrity of an indigenous culture? For the
Ladakhis, as with thousands of other aboriginal peoples, "In the space
of little more than a decade, feelings of pride [gave] way to . . . a cultural inferiority complex. In the modern sector today, most young
Ladakhis—the teenage boys in particular—are ashamed of their cultural roots and desperate to appear modern."[19] The creation of artifi-
cial needs, the division of a once unified people, the emergence of
generational rifts, and endemic violence have been the all too predictable results of "development."

It is, I believe, both theologically and missiologically instructive
to reflect briefly on the deleterious influences and effects identified by
Ms. Norberg-Hodge, to see whether they have their counterparts in
those enculturation processes and institutions that we have come to
associate with Christian missions, and then to draw some tentative
conclusions from the exercise.

Ladakh ("Little Tibet") was virtually untouched by modernization until 1962, when the Indian army built a road to link the region

with the rest of the country. With the road came "development"—government bureaucracy, traders with new consumer items, tourists—and the makings of a fragmentary and essentially false impression of what life was like in the outside world.

Tourism

When tourists began visiting Ladakh in 1975, they seemed to come from another planet, sometimes spending as much as $100 in one day—a situation roughly equivalent to someone's going to a small country village in rural Kentucky and spending $50,000 per day. When the first tourists arrived, money played only a minor role in Ladakhi society, being used only for luxuries such as jewelry. The intricate web of human relationships had always provided for necessities such as food, clothing, and shelter free of charge. Ladakhis were not aware that tourists came from cultures in which money, and plenty of it, was absolutely essential even for necessities.

This was, in effect, their "tree of good and evil," and once they had tasted its fruit, innocent self-confidence surrendered to a shameful awareness that they were wretched. When asked in 1975 to identify the poor among his people, a young Ladakhi, after a moment of perplexity, had responded, "We don't have any poor people here." Eight years later the same man was begging tourists for money because he and his people were so poor. Not his circumstances, but his perceptions, had changed.

There are parallels to this tourist phenomenon in Western mission and theological education around the world. Earnest young missionaries come from North America in the knowledge that they are just passing through. Financial support, agendas, and modus operandi all come from North America. Most have virtually no experience as founders or leaders of congregations, and few know what it is to suffer for their faith. Their chief qualifications include a combination of intelligence, educational opportunities, a range of career options, idealism, and financial means. Most, even if they remain for many years, will one day retire to their homelands, taking their budgets with them but leaving their ideas and institutions behind.

These theological and missiological tourists—superbly trained, well funded, and well equipped—can often make local teachers and indigenous missionaries feel tawdry, poorly provided for, and backward. Since human beings are imitators, the predictable result is scores of young men and women around the world who likewise aspire to become teachers and missionaries—on those terms that they have observed in their North American mentors. Ideally, this requires making the pilgrimage to North America to earn their credentials. If this is not possible, the second-best option is to gain membership in a school or mission (modeled on North American lines with some North American personnel) within the country. While the multifaceted impact of such a process is not entirely without merit, the resulting theological and missiological infrastructures do not always serve non-Americans well in non-American contexts, any more than did Saul's armor—as finely fashioned and as well intentioned as it might well have been—serve David's particular mission.[20]

Media Images

Concurrently and perhaps more insidiously, Ladakhi "development" included exposure to Western and Indian media, with its unrelenting siren portrayal of the glamorous lives of the rich, the beautiful, and the mobile. Films and television provided the Ladakhis with mesmerizing images of luxury, idleness and power. Progress was implicitly defined by monodimensional, fantastic images of youthfulness, beauty, super-cleanliness, fashion, competitiveness, speed, and technological gadgetry. By comparison, Ladakhi village life seemed absurdly primitive. Young people became ashamed of their parents' traditional way of life, involving as it did hard, dirty physical work in the fields, with little or no financial remuneration. Ladakhi youths thus joined millions of other young people around the world who, having been convinced of the superiority of Western culture, reject their cultures wholesale. Eagerly embracing the global consumer monoculture, they began to sport sunglasses, Walkmans, blue jeans, cigarettes, and violence as symbols of progressive life.

As a close observation of domesticated animals has taught us, the grass is always greener on the other side of the fence! In the realm of theological education, North American money has produced buildings, libraries, programs, and curricula that are the envy of the world. Seminaries vie with one another to add to their faculties men and women who are both well educated and well publicized. Presidents, chancellors, and provosts comb the lists of alumni and constituents to ferret out those with the potential to increase endowments and add to both the glory and the stability of the institution. On the missiological side, mission agencies compete with the best when it comes to fund-raising and big budgets. Persons who have earned exclusive right to call themselves "missionaries"—by simple virtue of the fact that they make their living as members of mission societies—tend to be adequately supported, by North American standards. Indeed, in many so-called "faith" missions, membership is finally determined on the basis of financial criteria. Those who can raise the stipulated adequate amount of personal support gain admission; those who do not are denied membership. This ensures that "mission," as conceived on this model, remains the prerogative of those fortunate enough to have plenty of this world's goods.

What is wrong with this picture? It seems far removed from New Testament models of theological education and mission, a picture whose details are modeled by the apostle Paul and outlined by him in some graphic detail in 2 Corinthians 4 and Philippians 2. Can "end of the procession" missionaries and servant leaders be the natural fruit of institutions whose chief purpose appears to be perilously close to self-aggrandizement? Can incarnational missionaries be nurtured in settings of ease where every whim and comfort is pandered to and where care is taken to generate a sense of entitlement to "all these things"? Both scripture and experience tell us no.[21]

If theological educators and mission agencies outside of this continent wish to address the spiritual condition of their worlds, they must tether themselves to biblical rather than American models.

Western-style Education

Also arriving in Ladakh was modern "education" . . . training children for local irrelevance. Education, in its broadest sense, is the complex process whereby a people or a society ensures its own survival across generations. As creatures whose primary identity (language, values, behavior) is culturally derived, we humans are compelled to imitate other human beings. Our survival as individuals and as communities depends upon this ability. We call the process *enculturation* . . . of which education is simply an element.

Credited with being the single most important key to all known human aspirations—from health and wealth to politics and power—education in much of the non-Western world today has become a profoundly alienating force in the lives of millions of people, isolating children from their culture and families and denying them the skills needed to survive in their traditional communities. Most of what passes today for "education" is not local-context-specific, with the result that children leave school unable to use their own resources or even function skillfully in their own world. Sometimes if they have become sufficiently "well educated," they have lost the capacity to use their mother tongue. "School is a place to forget traditional skills, and worse, to look down on them," Helena Norberg-Hodge comments sadly.[22]

Western education came to the Ladakhis just over twenty-five years ago; today there are approximately two hundred schools. The basic curriculum is, in Helena Norberg-Hodge's words, "a poor imitation of that taught in other parts of India, which itself is an imitation of British education. There is almost nothing Ladakhi about it."[23] Most of the skills taught in these schools are of no real use to the students who master them. In effect, Ladakhi children receive an inferior version of an education that might be appropriate for a resident of New York. "They learn from books written by people who have never set foot in Ladakh, who know nothing about growing barley at 12,000 feet or about making houses out of sun-dried bricks."[24]

Throughout the world this is now what is called *education*, a process of enculturation that focuses on faraway facts and figures based on Eurocentric assumptions. Typically, such education both ignores local resources and robs the community of its self-esteem. Everything in the school promotes the Western view of life, and as a direct consequence, children learn to think of themselves and their traditions as inferior.

Does this phenomenon have a counterpart in theological education and mission? Theological educators in other parts of the world must answer this question for themselves. Speaking as a Canadian and as a minister in a Mennonite church, I would have to say that the people who really drive the content, design, standards, and accreditation of Canadian curricula are not Canadians. Those charged with overseeing the Association of Theological Schools in the United States and Canada (ATS) are mostly Americans, and diligent stewards of what they have received. But what they have received is not local-context-specific; it assumes that legitimate theological education everywhere will follow certain predictable, procrustean, essentially American guidelines, which they as officers of the organization are charged with refereeing and enforcing. As a result, graduates of these institutions, whether they become pastors, teachers, or missionaries, are often so out of touch with local realities that they of necessity gravitate to ministry in institutional settings somewhat congruent with those which have formed and influenced them back in North America.

Creation of Artificial Needs

Before the arrival of the leaven of tourism and modernization, the Ladakhis were socially, psychologically, and economically self-sufficient. The "luxuries" associated with "development" had not mutated into "needs." Before the undermining of their psychological and cultural self-respect, Ladakhis did not *need* electricity, plastic, wristwatches, and designer jeans to prove that they were "civilized" and, hence, of value. But now, overwhelmed by the young people's need to appear modern, traditional culture has been rejected. Cultural self-confidence has been displaced by acute self-consciousness and insecurity as the youth feel pressure to live up to the idealized images of the American Dream.

Are there theological and missiological counterparts to this sad phenomenon? In September, 2001, I listened to the heartbreaking story of a young mother who was to be the first of her people to earn a Ph.D. in New Testament. To do so, she had had to spend years away from her husband and her two children. She wept as she spoke of her feelings of deep guilt and excruciating anguish at the price she and they were paying so that she could properly imitate her Western mentors. Her six-year-old son hardly knew her; her sixteen-year-old daughter had recently been sexually molested. She was stuck in North America, deeply immersed in mastering skills and a body of knowledge that would be of doubtful use to her own people but which were a necessary part of satisfying the appetite of our Western educational Molech.

Division Based on Irrelevance

A final troubling effect of modernization as observed among the Ladakhi is the weakening of family and community ties along intergenerational lines. Enculturation to consumerism breeds hunger for material status symbols, and this in turn engenders emotional and social insecurity. As the Ladakhi increasingly come to regard the acquisition of manufactured consumer goods as the true path to admiration and respect, new divisions between young and old, male and female, rich and poor are created. The modern, educated "experts" have little respect for those who have remained on the land, and tend to look down on those less modern as country bumpkins, to be ridiculed.

Theological education based on the academic prestige models imported from North America rather than on the humble servant model of our Lord can likewise stress degrees, diplomas, awards, and status. Those who have not had the benefits of such education are often not taken seriously in the theological and ecclesiastical discourse of the national church. They are too easily marginalized and rendered voiceless, silent before their eloquent and impressively credentialed brothers and sisters who have studied abroad. Western missionaries often show the way, and an entire market has responded to the demand in the form of advanced mission-studies-related degrees. Whether such degrees have produced better missionaries or more impressive results is not known.

The Future

What lies ahead? Here I tread with great trepidation a path strewn with the wreckage of prognostications, including those of missiological soothsayers, from the beginning of human time until the present.[25]

I return once again to my experience as an Ethiopian-grown Canadian, engaged for most of my adult life in the preparation of men and women for ministry in Canadian or other non–U.S. contexts. It is clear that even in the benign world of seminary education the globalization juggernaut has its counterpart. Theological schools around the world, aware of their relatively meager instructional and material resources, and insecure about their institutional impressiveness when compared with their counterparts in the Western world, are caught up in the desire to emulate "the best." Imitation—the sincerest form of flattery—takes many forms. Nor—even in designing curricula and assembling faculties on the basis of models and criteria that have evolved as a part of another people's history, and which have been reified in the accrediting associations created by these institutions— are the results necessarily culturally irrelevant or ecclesiastically harmful. Curricula designed in faraway places may be good or bad, appropriate or inappropriate, relevant or irrelevant, benign or harmful, even in cultural contexts that closely approximate the source culture. Where, then, should we educators begin in addressing the issues flowing from the globalization of theological education outside the United States?

To ensure that our best efforts at "discipling all nations" in the coming century do more good than harm, avoiding or at least ameliorating the deleterious theological and ecclesiastical counterparts to the sad effects witnessed by Norberg-Hodge among the Ladakhi, let me conclude by articulating several challenges that will constitute a complex part of our Western evangelical missiological agendas into the foreseeable future.

The Cuckoo Phenomenon

Could it be that those institutions, facilities, faculties, and libraries characterizing North American theological training are the unwitting cuckoos of theological and missiological education in other poorer parts of the world? If so, what can be done about this situation?

As Stephen Budiansky once reminded readers of the *Atlantic Monthly*, "the cuckoo . . . lays its eggs in the nest of some poor unsuspecting dupe of a bird of another species. The befuddled parents see a big mouth crying out for food and stuff it full of worms at the expense of their own offspring. Every time they turn their backs, the cuckoo hatchling shoves another of their own flesh and blood overboard. The parents never seem to notice."[26]

The analogy to Western mission societies or denominations—that establish theological seminaries for training church leaders and missionaries in impoverished countries, staffing these initially with North American faculty whose support comes entirely from that continent and at North American levels—is obvious.[27] North American models of theological education and mission, once transplanted and then bereft of the support of those who conceived and evolved them, can similarly survive only at the expense of the species indigenous to the nest. What can be done about it? We need to begin with our theological foundations. Only a biblically rigorous ecclesiology of *interdependence* can ensure the credibility of the church globally and the ongoing viability of such institutions particularly. But this ecclesiology of interdependence is precisely what evangelical missiologies have historically lacked. The language of the church in its Western missionary cross-cultural usage is largely managerial, drawn from the corporate business world rather than from the Bible. Thus mission agencies strive mightily to fashion "partnerships" with their economic inferiors, but the outcome is almost always disappointingly predictable. Language that reifies the *otherness* of the non-mission entity such as a school provides too easy an escape from the ideal embedded in New Testament metaphors for the church. Our Scriptures use the organic language of "body" and body "members" . . . implying that there will never be a healthy church so long as some members are detached or "independent" from other members. This brings me to my second question.

The Partnership Challenge

Can evangelical seminaries and mission societies construct a more rigorously biblical ecclesiology? Addressing the frustrating anomalies of materially unequal partnerships will require that we evangelicals refashion our ecclesiologies to conform more to the true nature of the church as understood in our Scriptures. It is important to recognize that no matter where local expressions of the body of Christ be found, believers around the world are in the most profound sense members of the same body. We need each other. Lest we be tempted to go our own way and too quickly embrace the missiological ideal (but theological heresy!) of "independence," we need to remind ourselves constantly that our Scriptures do not ever speak of the "bodies" of Christ, only of the body; that there is, furthermore, no acknowledgment of the three-self *independence* of the several members of this body one from another, but an insistence on our mutual *interdependence* (Eph. 4; Rom. 12; 1 Cor. 12). The interdependence described and advocated in our Scriptures has not only mystical but also practical dimensions, including economic ones.

The Conversion Challenge

Is it possible for North American models for theological education and mission to be converted? This is, of course, a rhetorical question, since personal conversion is such an integral part of the Good News that we experience, model, and proclaim. In most instances, training and support models remain implicitly predicated on the assumption that mission moves *from* contexts of power and relative affluence *to* the uttermost parts of the earth, and that the *uttermost parts* of the earth are those regions whose economic and social conditions least resemble those in North America. Mission is thus treated as a unidirectional process, with a stress on three-self models of ecclesiology, as though the chief end of mission were to produce independent churches and independent church-related institutions.[28]

These may be admirable goals, but they fall short of the New Testament vision of the church, Christ's body, and they tempt us to model a selective obedience . . . teaching all things without obeying all things, on the grounds that our culture of plenty exempts us from obedience to pervasive biblical teaching to the righteous rich about sharing.

We must resist the comfortable but heretical dichotomy between social gospel and evangelism, a dichotomy that seemingly treats biblical ethical teaching as a buffet, with diners selecting only those portions that they find palatable or attractive, so that one half of the church chooses to obey the practical injunctions of Scripture while the other half obeys the proclamation parts. Holistic obedience is essential if we evangelicals are to maintain our reputation for personal and corporate integrity into the dawning century.

The Relevance Challenge

Can Western good intentions be translated into contextual relevance? I believe that it can. It is important to recollect that we teachers and missionaries—even those of us trained in the United States—mean well, although both our training and our perspectives must inevitably bear the marks of human deficiency. Since we understand conversion to be a lifelong process, consummated only when we see Christ face to face, a humble awareness of our own inadequacies, our cultural "thorns in the flesh," is not a bad thing. My own seminary training was at Trinity Evangelical Divinity School in Deerfield, Illinois. No seminary options were open to me in Canada at the time, and in any event, the luster of a degree taken at a faraway institution was irresistible. Most of my colleagues, likewise, studied at seminaries in the United States—Baptist, Free Church, or nondenominational, and usually dispensational. There was little awareness on our part that Canadian ecclesiastical contexts might require different tools and unique emphases. It was not until 1981 when I was elected as a minister in my local church, eventually serving in the leadership of my denomination, that I became sufficiently aware of such issues as to be able to articulate them.

I began to realize that my colleagues who had been teaching ecclesiology and practical theology had little practical understanding of the way a local church actually functioned at the congregational level. Few of them had ever been intimately involved in a Canadian church, apart from pulpit supply on Sundays. What they had been teaching had been garnered from books written by seminary-based authors in the United States—often men and women who, like those they mentored, had little or no grassroots church experience. As a result, our graduates were being sent out with practical skills and understanding that were frequently at odds with local contexts.

Are there discernible reasons for the diminishing effectiveness of the Western missionary enterprise as a vital force in the global expansion of the church—quite apart from demographics? Pondering this question is uncomfortable but essential, and reasons may not be very difficult to discern. From a missiological perspective it is possible to trace at least part of the blame to the missiological training dispensed in our seminaries. So prolonged and rigorous is this formal enculturation process that the graduate, once the course is finished, finds himself or herself saddled with both family and debt, ensuring postponement of any anticipated venture into missionary work. By the time would-be missionaries from North America arrive at their appointed places of service, they are beyond the age when humans can be expected to learn another language fluently and must necessarily be caught up in the implicit social imperative to enculturate their children as North American consumers, regardless of where they are. Yet this model is being embraced in non–North American schools as the last word in missiology, despite the fact that most of the actual expansion of the faith around the world is the by-product of incarnational indigenous missionaries.

In retrospect, it is difficult to see how biblical exegesis, or counseling, or missiology, or practical theology, or Christian education, could have been adequately taught by instructors who themselves had no experience apart from books and exposure to other instructors whose experience was, likewise, restricted to books. There *is* a cerebral element to theological education and mission, that is true. But since Christianity is not simply mental assent to a series of correct propositions about God and related subjects, so training for ministry is not simply the by-product of orderly lectures. Modeling is essential. The Christian instructor or missionary not only talks but also shows the way (Matt. 23:2–3).

The Modeling Challenge

Is it possible for Western evangelical missiology to adopt an "end of the procession" model for mission in its training and operations? All human beings must by nature, by inclination, and by necessity imitate other human beings. Indeed, everything that we call "education" is in fact "imitation." While there is much in North American theological education and mission that can and should be imitated, global distribution of economic resources and the widening gap between rich and poor make it clear that Western-style institutions will not thrive in non-Western contexts without sustained assistance. A rigorous theology of interdependence would provide us with the necessary biblical foundation for struggling with the complicated and controversial practical issues arising from fidelity to this vision of the church. But I wonder whether there is not also room for repentance in our modi operandi themselves? Can imitation of St. Paul's "end of the procession" model of mission (2 Cor. 4) become a personal and institutional objective? The alternative seems to be acquiescence to the more comfortable but essentially impotent model depicted in Revelation 3, and no church or mission society, no matter how well equipped and comfortable, has any prospect of spiritual vitality so long as its Lord is kept safely outside the door! This brings me to my final challenge.

Conclusion

With some notable exceptions—a burning bush, lice, flies, frogs, hail, smoke, plagues, a donkey, a whale, and so on—God has generally preferred to proclaim and model his message in word and deed *to* and *through* those created in his own image. It is to *humans* that he delegates the responsibility for fulfilling his will on earth.

We have tended to stress the more quantifiable and measurable entities of *what* and *how* and *when*, and have frequently simply assumed the *who*. The scriptural stress, on the other hand, has ever been on the *who*. And God's preferred *who* have never been the wise or the eminent. Yet there is little evident stress on the character of those who bear the tidings to every land. Of course, there is screening, candidating, and deputation. But in missiology the overt stress continues to be, in sharp contrast to the Scriptures, on how and where and how much . . . on technique and results rather than on person and character. These two are not, of course, mutually incompatible. But in an age of technique and computers and mass communication, it is increasingly evident that where the Gospel moves forward, it does so via the humble channels of more incarnational catechists and evangelists rather than the salaried professionals that we have come to recognize as missionaries.

I believe that the way forward is to get back to our Bibles. The Gospel we proclaim need not be a mere prisoner of our culture; as the power of God unto salvation, it is also the liberator of culture. As the evangelical missions from the West move into the twenty-first century, we must struggle for a more Christlike model for mission, a missiology of *interruptions*, of *servanthood*, and of *neighbor*. In other words, we must aspire to a missiology of fewer a priori agendas and to a modus operandi that reflects greater trust in the ability of God to work through our faithfulness to his microinterpersonal agendas.

Jesus, who came to save the whole world, lived an extremely parochial life. Furthermore, he does not seem to have been upset by the fact that most of what subsequent generations of his followers would know about him was the interruptions to his schedule by ordinary men and women who had intensely personal needs . . . for healing, for feeding, for forgiving, for friendship. This was his agenda, and it should be ours, too. What could be more missiologically potent than living life as Jesus did wherever we find ourselves? His example should be the standard, not our institutional programs and agendas or our susceptibility to the procrustean pressures embedded in all religious franchises that we have come to know by their denominational or mission agency names whose will can be best exerted and sustained by means of managerial principles. We still find it difficult to practice the golden rule, instead working with predetermined agendas that we bring with us to "the field." We need to be reminded that Jesus, despite his mandate to save the entire world, is known chiefly as one who responded to the interruptions occasioned by the petty, intensely personal agendas of ordinary people. His was a missiology of interruptions, sanctified and blessed by the Holy Spirit to multiply and now bless millions. And thanks to the seemingly cataclysmic interruption to his life just when he was in his prime, we today can proclaim the good news that Jesus is the power of God unto salvation!

Notes

1. Hannah Arendt, *Between Past and Future: Six Exercises in Political Thought* (New York: Viking, 1961), p. 9. Quoting Faulkner's wry observation, Arendt draws attention to something that is routinely forgotten, overlooked, or denied by those of us whose social conditioning has caused us to be—at the functional level—highly critical of the past.

2. William Carey, *An Enquiry into the Obligations of Christians, to Use Means for the Conversion of the Heathens. In which the religious state of the different nations of the world, the success of former undertakings, and the practicability of further undertakings, are considered* (Leicester: Printed and fold by Ann Ireland, and the other Booksellers in Leicester; J. Johnson, St. Paul's Church yard; T. Knott, Lombard Street; R. Dilly, in the Poultry, London; and Smith, at Sheffield, 1792).

3. David B. Barrett and Todd M. Johnson, "Annual Statistical Table on Global Mission: 2001," *International Bulletin of Missionary Research* 25, no. 1 (January 2001): 24–25.

4. Attempts to redress this distortion are being made. In Africa, my own *Dictionary of African Christian Biography* is attempting to provide an information base for utilization by future African historians who tell the story of the church in that continent. In 1999 *A World History of Christianity*, edited by Adrian Hastings, was published by William B. Eerdmans as "the first genuinely global one-volume study of the rise, development, and impact of the Christian faith." In 2001 Orbis Books announced the release of the first volume of what is billed in its fall 2001/ winter 2002 trade catalogue as "the first comprehensive account of Christianity as a world religion from its origins to the present": *History of the World Christian Movement*, vol. 1: *Earliest Christianity to 1453*, by Dale T. Irvin and Scott W. Sunquist.

5. Rev. A. T. Pierson, Editor-in-Chief of the *Missionary Review of the World*, uttered these words in Carnegie Hall on April 23, 1900, in his address entitled "Proofs of God's Favor and Blessing" before delegates to "the largest sustained formal religious event in the history of the [American] republic to that date and the best attended international missionary conference ever." This ten-day super mission conference attracted an estimated 200,000 attendees, including such political luminaries as former president Benjamin Harrison, sitting president William McKinley, and New York governor Theodore Roosevelt. A. T. Pierson's address is found in the official published records of the conference, *Ecumenical Missionary Conference, New York, 1900: Report of the Ecumenical Conference on Foreign Missions, Held in Carnegie Hall and Neighboring Churches, April 21–May 1*, 2 vols. (New York: American Tract Society, 1900). Pierson's address is part of a chapter entitled "The Irresistible Plea for Advance" (2:325–47; for the Pierson quotation see p. 328). Thomas A. Askew has provided a very useful review of this event in his article, "The New York 1900 Ecumenical Missionary Conference: A Centennial Reflection," *International Bulletin of Missionary Research* 24, no. 4 (October 2000): 146–54.

We do well to remember that Pierson was but echoing a significant body of published testimonials and research appearing at that time, all calculated to demonstrate that missionaries were in the forefront of advancing science and civilization. Ten years earlier Robert Young, F.R.S.G.S., author of several mission-related volumes, had published a documented assessment of missionary accomplishments in a book entitled *The Success of Christian Missions: Testimonies to the Beneficent Results* (London: Hodder & Stoughton, 1890). Only one chapter of his 278-page volume touched on "unfavorable opinions" (pp. 13–46). The rest was eulogistic. *Are Foreign Missions Doing Any Good?* queried the title of a small volume appearing in 1894 and dedicated to W. W. Peel, then speaker of the House of Commons. Only 124 pages in length, the book is comprised of twelve short chapters, six reviewing "The *Social* Results of Foreign Missions" and six their "*Spiritual* Results." Among those bearing tribute to the social consequences of missionary work were such well-known luminaries as Charles Darwin, Captain J. Hannington Speke, Sir Harry H. Johnston, Lord Rosebery, and Sir Bartle Frere. The spiritual transformation wrought by missionaries was attested to by similarly reputable public figures and high-ranking civil servants. Similarly impressive sappearing in 1902, *Official and Lay Witness to the Value of Foreign Missions.* But by far the most thoroughly researched and comprehensive registry of missionary accomplishments was James S. Dennis's three-volume (plus statistical atlas) *Christian Missions and Social Progress: A Sociological Study of Foreign Missions,* published by Fleming H. Revell in 1897. This encyclopedic work was designed to dispel all doubt and to reassure agnostics both within and outside of the church as to the profound and far-reaching impact of missionary activities on human well-being around the world. The massive encyclopedia edited by David Barrett and Todd Johnson attests to the fact that not all of this optimism was misguided. The church in one form or another is now truly universal.

6. See J. M. Roberts, *Twentieth Century: The History of the World, 1901 to 2000* (New York: Viking, 2001), reviewed by Paul Kennedy in the January 2, 2000, *New York Times Book Review,* pp. 4–5. Roberts lays out the large context in which we live and move: human numbers, the world's wealth, structures, wars, etc. For an attempt to understand how "civilized" humans can and do perpetrate great evil, see Jonathan Glover's deeply troubling work, *Humanity: A Moral History of the Twentieth Century* (London: J. Cape, 1999).

7. From *Maitreya's Mission,* vol. 2, by Benjamin Creme, the chief British editor for *Share International.* A *United Nations Human Development Report,* summarized in section 4, page 16, of the September 27, 1998, issue of the *New York Times,* provides some perspective on just what this means:

- The world's 225 richest individuals, of whom 60 are Americans with total assets of $311 billion, have a combined wealth of over $1 trillion—equal to the combined wealth of the poorest 47 percent of the entire world's population.
- The three richest people in the world have assets that exceed the combined gross domestic product of the forty-eight poorest countries.

- The average African household is some 20 percent poorer today than it was twenty-five years ago.
- The richest fifth of the world's people consumes 86 percent (more than four-fifths) of all goods and services. The poorest fifth consumes 1.3 percent.
- Americans and Europeans spend $17 billion a year on pet food—$4 billion more than the estimated additional annual total needed to provide basic health and nutrition for everyone in the world.
- Americans spend $8 billion a year on cosmetics—$2 billion more than the estimated annual total needed to provide basic education for everyone in the world.

8. Robert Conquest, *Reflections on a Ravaged Century* (New York: W. W. Norton & Company, 1999).

9. See Paul Schrag, "Tight Budget, Loose Spending," *Mennonite Weekly Review*, August 23, 2001, p. 4. In this editorial Paul Schrag comments on the National Defense Authorization Bill passed by the House Armed Services Committee on August 1 by a vote of 58 to 1. The bill called for a 2002 defense budget of $343.5 billion—a $33 billion increase over the 2001 figure. The proposed increase alone was almost three times the combined defense budgets of the seven countries identified as "states of concern." The total military expenditures of Iran, Iraq, Libya, North Korea, Cuba, Sudan, and Syria amounted to $12.8 billion. It was more than the federal government was spending on higher education ($13.8 billion) and law enforcement ($13.6 billion) combined. The proposed increase alone was more than the GDP of seventy of the world's poorest nations. Woe is us!

Figures provided by Eric Schmitt several years ago in his article, "It Costs a Lot More to Kill Fewer People" (*New York Times*, May 2, 1999, p. 5), provide a glimpse into the enormous cost of satisfying the national paranoia. The hourly cost of flying the various aircraft that NATO used in its war against Yugoslavia and the cost of the missiles fired is staggering:

Plane	Per hour cost
B-52	$8,300
C-17	6,789
F-15E	6,167
F-14	6,112
U-2	6,000

Missile	Per launch
Cruise	$2,000,000
Tomahawk	1,000,000
Hellfire	$42,700
Laser guided bomb	$26,200
Satellite guided bomb	$23,200

10. John F. Burns, "America Inspires Both Longing and Loathing in Arab World," *New York Times*, September 16, 2001, Travel sec., p. 17.

11. Serge Schmemann, "What Would 'Victory' Mean?" *New York Times: Week in Review*, September 16, 2001, pp. 1–2.

12. James Houston is the well-known Canadian author-artist widely acknowledged to be "the prime force in the development of Inuit art" (James Houston, *Zigzag: A Life on the Move* [Toronto: McClelland & Stewart, 1998], cover). He spent twelve years among the Inuit of the Canadian Arctic as a northern service officer and as the first administrator of west Baffin Island, a territory of 65,000 square miles.

13. See the chapter "Mission Schools" in James Houston's *Zigzag: A Life on the Move*, pp. 233–34.

14. John Kenneth Galbraith, "The 1929 Parallel," *The Atlantics* 259, no. 1 (January 1987): 62.

15. What follows is an edited and somewhat expanded version of my chapter, "Contextualizing Theological Education and Mission Outside the United States," in Jose Varickasseril and Matthew Kariapuram, eds., *Be My Witnesses: Essays in Honour of Dr. Sebastian Karotemprel SDB* (Shillong: Vendrame Institute Publications & Don Bosco Centre for Indigenous Cultures, Sacred Heart Theological College, 2001), pp. 79–87.

16. Allan Fotheringham, "Learning to Love the American Bully Next Door," *MacLean's*, April 13, 1998, p. 68.

17. Pierre Elliot Trudeau (1919–2000) was prime minister of Canada from 1968 to 1979 and from 1980 to 1984. He secured Canada's final constitutional independence from the British Parliament in 1982. This offhand remark (on the occasion of a speech to the Washington Press Club in 1969) was in response to a reporter's request that he comment on the always incipient and sometimes aggressive, U.S. domination of Canada's cultural and economic institutions.

18. Helena Norberg-Hodge is a native of Sweden who has for over thirty years observed and analyzed the effects of contemporary models of development upon peoples of three continents. She was the first foreigner to make her home in the Himalayan province of Ladakh (Kashmir), where she lived for thirty years, observing the gradual disintegration of the society as it was overwhelmed by the modernizing forces of globalization. See her chapter, "The Pressure to Modernize and Globalize," in *The Case Against the Global Economy and for a Turn Toward the Local*, ed. Jerry Mander and Edward Goldsmith (San Francisco: Sierra Book Club, 1996), pp. 34–46.

19. Ibid., p. 34.

20. Paul Borthwick's observation, following his participation in YWAM's School of Frontier Missions in Barbados in the summer of 2001, is an apt articulation of the challenge faced by emerging mission agencies and would-be missionaries attempting to emulate the only model of mission to which they have thus far been exposed, the Western model: "We confronted one of the greatest challenges in world missions—mobilizing missionaries from 'new'

sending countries. We listened to the realities that these folks face as they return home to the insurmountable task of raising support from countries and churches for which 'missions-sending' is outside their world-view. As the missions enterprise moves to being truly 'Global,' we recognize that developing effective sending structures from cultures of economic scarcity will present great challenges." From an e-mail dated July 5, 2001.

21. This question is explored in my book, now in its seventh printing, *Missions and Money: Affluence as a Western Missionary Problem* (Maryknoll, N.Y.: Orbis Books, 1991).

22. Norberg-Hodge, p. 37.

23. Ibid.

24. Ibid.

25. See William A. Sherden, *Fortune Sellers: The Big Business of Buying and Selling Predictions* (New York: Chichester John Wiley & Sons, 1998). The author takes an unsentimental look at the modern prophecy industry and at modern soothsayers who make a handsome living out of human anxiety about the future. Sherden refers to the prediction business as "the world's second-oldest profession." The desire to predict the future lies at the foundation of virtually every religion devised by humankind. Despite the fact that future predictors are almost always wrong in their long-term predictions, they persist and thrive as a part of the long train of false prophets dating from the beginning of human time, parasites on the deep insecurity that we naturally feel about what lies ahead. In North America an estimated $200 billion is paid each year to various kinds of experts who claim to be able to predict the future: meteorologists, economic forecasters, stock market gurus, demographers, technology assessors, and, of course, prophecy buffs. Of the fourteen different kinds of forecasting identified by Sherden, only two—one-day-ahead weather forecasting and that demography that specializes in predicting that the population is aging—only these two can be relied on. And only one—weather forecasting—has any scientific foundation or rigor. All other forecasters have about as much chance of being correct as you would if you flipped a coin to determine what lay ahead.

The catalogue of their inaccuracies and failed predictions is so striking that one wonders how the prediction industry can possibly survive. Our predictors have missed all the major turning points in history . . . even recent history: the destruction of the World Trade Center towers, the stock market crash of 1987, the implosion of Communism, the collapse of the USSR, Saddam Hussein's invasion of Kuwait, the crash of the Asian economy, computers, the light bulb, the telephone, and so on. Another iconoclast, Steven Schnaars, conducted a detailed study of technology forecasts published between 1959 and 1989 in seven of America's most prestigious publications: *Wall Street Journal, New York Times, Business Week, Fortune, Forbes, Time,* and *Newsweek.* He discovered that nearly every prediction (85 percent) was dead wrong. One of the more startling predictions was that by the year 1979 human life expectancy would average between 150 and 200 years. Another was that by 1990 we would all be using nuclear powered cars, trains, planes, homes, refrigerators, and wristwatches! See Schnaars's book, *Megamistakes: Forecasting and the Myth of Rapid Technological Change* (New York: Free Press, 1989).

26. Stephen Budiansky, "The Truth About Dogs," *Atlantic Monthly* 284, no. 1 (July 1999): 39.

27. Canada, at least, has an economy strong enough to sustain theological education done in the way of the rich and the powerful. But when this educational model is transplanted, say, to Ethiopia, there are problems. Western teachers bring their salaries and benefits and education with them. They are transplants who, when they return to their own country, will take that salary and those credentials with them, leaving an impoverished church to try to sustain an educational infrastructure that presumes money, and plenty of it.

28. There has for many years been sharp criticism, for often justifiable reasons, of the missiology of financially subsidized churches and institutions. It is worth reflecting, however, that all of mission is, in some ways, "subsidy" . . . personnel, ideas, technologies, and cultural forms brought in from the outside by foreign missionaries. Financial subsidy is just one dimension of a much larger and exceedingly complex package. It captures our attention because its effects for good and for ill are most measurable, perhaps, but its effects can be no more or no less significant than all of the other kinds of subsidy which are a part and parcel of this era of Christian mission.

But here the question of integrity must be raised. Christians—in this instance, foreign missionaries—who are themselves not only "rich" by local standards but also usually heavily subsidized by numerous churches other than the one in which they might hold membership, and whose missionary presence and ministry, furthermore, would be withdrawn were the financial subsidies ever to cease, cannot command the moral high ground in their refusal to subsidize brothers and sisters in dire need.

There is a continued need for a thoroughly biblical theology of the righteous rich and for a concomitant missiology out of affluence. Western missiology has a well-developed and highly functional doctrine of ecclesiastical independence, but its exegetical and theological foundations are somewhat shaky. Its roots are pragmatic rather than biblical. There is a desperate need for a rigorous ecclesiology of interdependence. The church is, after all, the body—not the bodies—of Christ. What does this mean, practically?

Chapter Eight

Changing the Face of World Missions in the Twenty-first Century: A Fervent Appeal to the African-American Community for Effective Partnership in World Missions

John Moldovan

The completion of the missionary mandate calls for serious mobilization efforts on the part of twenty-first-century believers, churches, agencies, and missionaries. The global interdependence and mutual participation of the entire church is required. Yet some significant groups, such as the African-American Christian community, are seriously underrepresented in missions. Can this be changed? How? How soon? What will it take to accomplish this goal?

The African-American Christian community could get ready to be significant globally, find its specific niche in the missionary enterprise, intercede for the people of every nation of the world, serve and minister to them, and play its strategic role in the kingdom of God. This essay is an earnest appeal to our African-American brothers and sisters to link up with the evangelical community in an effective partnership in world missions. This is the most appropriate time for strategic action, fervent prayer, reconciliation, and unity.

One could offer good grounds for the ardent appeal to partnership. Historical precedents are compelling, missiological and biblical factors call for urgent action, and the unique "manifest destiny" of the African-American Christian community and its unique practical qualities and resources substantiate this appeal.

The task of Christian mission appears dauntingly immense in the face of current global trends. We are facing serious challenges in several areas. David Larsen has identified in North America a trend called "the Europeanization of the church."[1] The disunity in the body of Christ leads to anemic, comatose Christians and churches. In the meantime, the North American mission force is aging and diminishing.

Regardless of how discouraged we may feel about these developments, God still reigns. He is using even ordinary people to expand his kingdom. Still, the demands on twenty-first-century missionaries, churches, and agencies will be heavier than ever. William H. Smallman is, therefore, accurate in his perception of missions as not "a solo work but a symphony, demanding the harmonious creativity of many players," requiring "input from people of many nations and several generations."[2] The global interdependence and mutual participation of the entire church is required.

A careful observer of recent developments in global evangelism would soon realize that some significant groups such as the African-American Christian community are seriously underrepresented in missions. Can this be changed? How? How soon? What will it take to accomplish this goal?

The African-American Christian community should get ready to be significant globally, to find its specific niche in the missionary enterprise, to intercede for the people of every nation of the world, to serve and minister to them, and to play its strategic role in the kingdom of God. This essay is an earnest appeal to our African-American brothers and sisters to link up with us in an effective partnership in world missions.

Effective Partnership

Partnership has become a buzzword recently. Luis Bush defines partnership as "an association of two or more Christian autonomous bodies who have formed a trusting relationship and fulfill agreed-upon expectations by sharing complementary strengths and resources to reach their mutual goal."[3]

Several passages delineate the biblical basis for partnership. Ecclesiastes 4:9, 12 shows that two can accomplish more than twice as much as one, and three is even better. In Philippians the goal of Christian partnership was the advance of the Gospel (Phil. 1:12; 1:5). Jesus taught, in John 17, that sanctification and unity are prerequisites for missions. The essence of Christ's prayer is not "unity *for* mission, but unity *in* mission."[4]

Three developmental stages of partnership have been identified. The *consultative* partnership model has various agencies consult with one another to achieve an ultimate goal. In *consensus* partnership, agencies go beyond consultation and agree to work together to achieve a common goal or goals. A deeper level occurs in *constitutional* partnership, in which agencies enter into a formal contractual relationship.[5]

An effective partnership includes compatible vision, structure, and attitudes; commitment relationships based on equality and mutual respect; and clearly defined expectations. Healthy partnerships are characterized by common vision, demonstrable servanthood, dependability, commitment, honesty, maturity, mutual respect and trust, integrity, adequate communication, acceptance of cultural differences, flexibility, patience, willingness to forgive, humility, prayer, sacrifice, results, theological compatibility, and accountability.[6]

The Rationale for the Appeal

One could offer good grounds for the ardent appeal to partnership. Historical precedents are compelling, missiological and biblical factors call for urgent action, and the unique "manifest destiny" of the African-American Christian community and its unique practical qualities and resources support this appeal.

Historical Rationale

African-American individuals who served and now serve as missionaries have made important contributions. Some of them, such as David Cornelius, have reached strategic positions of leadership within respected missionary organizations. Cornelius is the director of African-American church relations and co-director of the International Volunteer Fellowship of the International Mission Board of the Southern Baptist Convention. He served for nine years as a missionary in Nigeria.[7]

Ambassador Fellowship's founder and director, Rev. Virgil Lee Amos, served as a missionary with Operation Mobilization for ten years in Mexico, India, Sri Lanka, and Iran. Ambassador Fellowship (AF), an international, interdenominational mission organization, has ministries in Mexico, Spain, Kenya, Nigeria, Puerto Rico, Benin, the United States, and other nations. In 1997 AF began focusing its attention on mobilizing African-American churches by encouraging them to adopt unreached people groups.[8]

The early period of African-American missionary initiatives, before Emancipation, reveals the sacrifices made and the sincere desire on the part of the missionary pioneers to obey the Great Commission.

In the late 1700s John Stewart, a freeborn mulatto addicted to alcohol who was converted at a Methodist service, became a missionary to the Wyandotte Indians in the Ohio territory.[9]

Leroy Fitts maintains that the foreign mission movement of the independent black Baptist churches predated the home missions movement. David George went as a missionary to Sierra Leone, where he established the first Baptist church on the continent. Having been emancipated, George Liele worked tirelessly to establish a Baptist presence in Jamaica.[10]

Many African-American Christians, according to James Stallings, "felt stifled and neglected in most mixed or white-controlled churches." As a result, leaders such as David George, George Liele, Andrew Bryan, Richard Allen, and James Varick formed separate structures for black worship, evangelism, and fellowship. In these settings (racially separated congregations) worshipers "could express themselves more forcefully against slavery."[11]

The African Methodist Episcopal Church (A.M.E.), formed in 1816, organized missions as early as 1844. William Paul Quinn was officially commissioned by the Parent Home and Foreign Missionary Society of the A.M.E. Church as its first missionary. L. L. Berry indicates that Quinn "had established forty-seven churches with a combined membership of two thousand, had seven traveling preachers and twenty-seven local preachers. He had organized fifty Sunday Schools . . . and had held seventeen camp meetings."[12] Assisted by the white deacon William Crane, two black Baptists, Lott Carey and Colin Teague, organized the Richmond African Missionary Society in 1815. Carey and Teague sailed for Africa in 1821 under the auspices of the Triennial Convention and the American Colonization Society (organized in 1814) and supported in part by the Richmond Society.[13] Daniel Coker, an American Methodist Episcopalian, preceded the black Baptists by one year. He resettled, in 1820, in Sierra Leone.[14]

During the pre–Civil War years some of the evangelistic outreach was characterized by a combination of missionary activity with African colonization. Black religious and secular leaders advocated that individual blacks should be free to emigrate. However, "the claim made by black and white religious persons, such as Lott Carey, that the repatriation of blacks in Africa would support the development of a Christian civilization," according to Stallings, "sounded unconvincing to many black church people."[15]

Stallings also questions the validity and appropriateness of foreign mission activity by whites in all non-Christian lands: "How could whites expect the world to take them seriously as missionaries of the Christian gospel if they did not practice it at home?" They should have "first reconciled themselves with and done justice to the blacks."[16]

Southern blacks also played a crucial role in black foreign mission programs. Their prime concern was to evangelize areas with predominantly black populations such as Africa and the Caribbean. The Baptists pioneered the work in Africa. The most influential development in African missions occurred in 1875 when William W. Colley traveled to Africa, supported by the black Virginia Baptist State Convention and the white Southern Baptist Convention. In 1880 Colley spearheaded the formation of the Baptist Foreign Mission Convention, which first commissioned missionaries in 1883. Later, in 1895, this convention merged with two other groups to become the National Baptist Convention. In 1902 Lewis G. Jordan, now the leader of the National Baptist Convention foreign mission program, spoke of the responsibility of African-Americans to evangelize Africa: "God calls you to duty; He calls you to service and He calls you now."[17] The African Methodist Episcopal Zion Church joined the post–Civil War efforts to evangelize Africa. Their representative, Andrew Cartwright, journeyed to Liberia in 1876 and organized churches. Bishop John Bryan Small also developed interest in the new African mission.[18]

Unfortunately, most African-American pastors are not aware of this rich heritage of African-Americans in missions. They should seek to educate themselves and their congregations about missions. The time for catching a vision of God's love for every people is now.

Missiological Rationale

African-American churches are searching for models of missionary involvement and organizational structures that facilitate missionary deployment. Rapid changes in the world are impacting the way we do missions. Missiologists need to make every effort to analyze fresh data, reevaluate positions taken earlier, and disseminate their findings to church leaders and various agencies.

Priority should also be given to developing "missions-minded" pastors. In his book *Missionary Administration in the Local Church*, Reginald L. Matthews expects a "missions-minded" pastor to "(1) face the issue of God's call in his own life; (2) study missionary passages in Scripture and preach on them; (3) read missionary books, literature and history; (4) become acquainted with missionary personnel and agencies; (5) pray that his church will become a missionary-minded church; (6) possess a knowledge of missionary principles in the light of God's Word and seek to implement them."[19] In order for any missionary initiative or program to succeed, Harold R. Cook states, the pastor is expected "to have the interest, the vision . . . and the persistence to carry it through."[20]

As a leader in missions, the pastor performs several functions. Paul A. Beals indicates that the pastor is an expositor, an intercessor, an educator, an organizer, a recruiter, a counselor, and a helper. Missions-related messages delivered on Sunday mornings, employing missions-related illustrations and missionary biographies, would have a positive impact. The pastor's private and public prayers for missions and missionaries will set an example for his people. Moreover, the pastor gains helpful information by reading books and missionary prayer letters, listening to messages available on prayer lines, personally corresponding with missionaries, contacting them by fax or e-mail, and keeping in touch with mission boards. A well-informed pastor leads to a better-informed, praying congregation. As an organizer, the pastor learns to delegate while assuming final responsibility for a church's mission program. In his recruiter role the pastor can present to his people options, opportunities, and expectations for missionary service and can also take steps to reinforce commitments made for such ministries. Those who need help with finding God's will for their lives, believers facing mid-life vocational choices, appointees from the home church encountering difficulties, and furloughing missionaries should count on the counseling skills of the pastor. His help should be offered also in other practical areas, such as the preparation of appointees before departure and the readjustment of furloughing missionaries.[21]

Biblical Rationale

Our message is not an improvisation; God revealed it to us (1 Cor. 15:3–8; Gal. 1:11–12). "There is no greater news in this pressured world," writes Henry Lee Allen, "no greater hope for the future regardless of the complexity, inequality, diversity, and apostasy that encroaches anywhere."[22]

The stage is prepared for reconciliation among Christians worldwide. Biblical reconciliation can take place. Jesus broke down the dividing wall between Jew and Gentile (Eph. 2:14–15). The power of the Gospel to reconcile people with God (vertical reconciliation) is clearly demonstrated in the visible reconciliation among believers of diverse ethnic and social background (horizontal reconciliation).

The biblical mandate, however, is often misinterpreted in two main areas: concentration and priority. Acts 1:8 is often misquoted. Some read the text like this: "You will be my witnesses *either* in Jerusalem, or Judea, or Samaria, or to the ends of the earth." Others prefer to read it this way: "You will be my witnesses *first* in Jerusalem, then Judea, then Samaria, then to the ends of the earth." Such interpreters are falling into the "default trap" by assuming that the most important ministry is in their "Jerusalem." They may offer powerful pragmatic arguments in favor of such a reading, yet they are mistaken. The real idea in this verse is not "either/or" or "first/then," but rather "both/and."[23] We need to develop a "bifocal vision" that will enable us to see and care for both the world in our immediate vicinity and the wider world.[24]

The biblical basis for missions has received ample attention among evangelicals in the last fifty years. Literature on the topic is available in most libraries and bookstores. Compelling studies have also been published in recent missiological journals.

Unique "Manifest Destiny"

The belief that African-Americans have a special "manifest destiny" has permeated their spirituals, prayers, and preaching. Scholars have noted that black slaves had a strong attachment to the Old Testament with its emphasis upon God's intervention on behalf of his chosen people.[25]

African-Americans gather in churches "to celebrate what God has done, what He is doing, and in confidence that He will continue to be and do that which has been previously experienced."[26] African-American worship is a participatory event leading to the spiritual assurance that "God is in this place." The "theology of Providence" is prominent.[27] African-American preaching is "a dialogical experience with God, the preacher, and the congregation."[28] It is an art. It employs, among other communication techniques, narrative theology. The preacher keeps the action moving and maintains spontaneity by communicating *with* his people, not *to* them.

The genius of African-American church music is due in part to its free expression, improvisation, adaptation, and ability to nourish the whole being. Spirituals are admired all over the world. Mahalia Jackson, the queen of gospel music, understood her task as one not of entertaining people but of calling them to embrace the Good News. Her performances were often revivals by intent and effect.[29] This writer confirms the inspirational power of spirituals and their reassuring effect during difficult days of Communist persecution in Romania.

Moreover, African-American believers understand better than most other U.S. believers the issues related to injustice, poverty, persecution, and discrimination and can identify with a large number of people around the world who face similar problems. In fact, some closed countries may be more accessible to African-American missionaries than to those of other backgrounds.

African-American believers also display deep emotional energy. When well focused, this energy can demonstrate viability, spearhead reconciliation, help establish new standards, and push for the respect of human rights.

Unique Qualities and Resources

The contemporary African-American church, Rev. Clarence L. James explains, "is a vast repository of underdeveloped resources in the form of people, talents and monies."[30] Accordingly, the African-American Christian community has a number of positive contributions to make in the field of missiology.

Research findings. The subsequent findings come from a report entitled *African-Americans and Their Faith*, written by George Barna. This report, based upon a series of surveys with African-Americans, includes data from interviews with more than eleven hundred adults, approximately four hundred teenagers, and four hundred pastors of black Christian churches across the nation. All of the interviews were based on random sampling techniques and were conducted via telephone.

Survey data paint a positive picture of the African-American population. By their own admission, African-Americans are happy and optimistic and have lower levels of stress.[31] A few other findings: 72 percent consider themselves to be "successful"; 50 percent consider themselves to be "financially comfortable"; 94 percent of black teenagers say they are excited about their future; only 9 percent of black teenagers say they feel "oppressed" in American society; 81 percent of African-Americans describe themselves as "spiritual"; they are more likely than the average American to say that they are "committed born again Christians"; 94 percent say that "having a close, personal relationship with God" is "very desirable" for their future; 91 percent say their faith is a source of emotional strength; 69 percent believe that they will go to heaven because they have confessed their sins and have accepted Jesus Christ as their Savior. African-Americans are more likely than the average American to report that they have prayed to God during the past seven days. They are twice as likely as whites to have read from their Bible in the past seven days.[32] African-American adults spend more time in church (about 120 minutes) than do whites or Hispanic adults (60 to 75 minutes).[33] Barna reports that "[a] majority of African-American adults maintain that the only reason to live is to know, love and serve God. That is a much higher proportion than is found among either Whites or Hispanics. Black adults are also more likely than any other ethnic group to believe that the Bible is totally accurate in all that it teaches. Further, half of all black adults directly attribute their ability to handle prejudice and to endure the injustice that they encounter to their focus on their anticipated life after death, based on their faith in Christ."[34]

Other qualities. African-American believers in general are effective, unembarrassed witnesses. They are action-oriented. In addition, they are event-oriented (concerned with what happens) and person-oriented. Such traits are invaluable for an effective cross-cultural Christian communicator engaged in world evangelism. With its free expression, improvisation, and ability to motivate, the African-American Christian community should introduce the beauty of African-American preaching to the rest of the world, including the "whooping" preaching style.

From the strengths and resources explored above one could conclude that the African-American church has demonstrated its viability and potential for missionary involvement. Yet in spite of such fine qualities, the African-American churches and believers have encountered serious obstacles to missionary participation.

Hindrances to African-American Missionary Involvement

General Hindrances

Regrettably, most African-American leaders and believers are not fully aware of their responsibility to make disciples of all the nations, even though the mandate is inescapable for all who would take seriously the commands of Jesus Christ.

Moreover, most of them are not aware of their rich missions heritage. They should seek to study missions individually and stir up their congregations regarding the Great Commission. This is the best time to catch the vision of God's love for all peoples.

Besides, many African-American believers lack information pertaining to the work of God around the world.[35] Some have adopted an attitude of parochialism (provincialism) and even xenophobia. However, provincialism should be avoided for several reasons. First, each church is part of the universal church. According to Ephesians 2 and 3, this community is God's new humanity in which all barriers have been abolished. As a result, there is no room for racism or for tribalism, whether in its African-American or European-American form. The primary identity of Christians is not in their particular culture but in the culture of the kingdom of God (Eph. 4:3–6), which transcends any culture. A second reason to avoid provincialism is that each church should express gratitude not only for its own cultural heritage, but also for the heritage of others, and should never become so culture-bound as to exclude representatives of other cultures. Third, "no church is, or should try to become, self-sufficient."[36] Churches should enter into partnerships with other churches and share their spiritual gifts, skills, experiences, and resources. They should avoid the two extremes of theological provincialism and theological imperialism. Rather, they must seek to transform and enrich culture for the glory of God.[37]

A major hindrance to missionary involvement is materialism. The Bible warns, "Be on your guard against all kinds of greed; a man's life does not consist in the abundance of his possessions" (Luke 12:15). The African-American churches are tempted to follow other churches' example in falling prey to the temptation of affluence (the Laodicean complex). Yet many African-Americans discover that higher incomes and established careers fail to satisfy the human heart. The success syndrome confounds self-worth and competence. Worldly status and success are ephemeral. They cannot protect an individual from the effects of worldliness and depravity.

Henry Lee Allen, associate professor of sociology at Wheaton College, instructs African-American professionals to "avoid the mythology of the self-made person, the idolatry of materialism, and the ideology of celebrityhood." By using "the spiritual gifts they have, their dominant concern must shift from merely impressing people to impressing God."[38] African-American Christians, like all other Christians, need inoculation from various syndromes that can poison them, their friends, and their families.

Specific Hindrances

African-American Christians as the object of missions. Some African-American Christians see themselves as the object of missions.[39] The deep perception that the needs at home are massive have led to an emphasis on home "missions": benevolent ministries, remedial services of every description, and community life improvement. The most important ministry priorities in African-American churches are helping people in crisis (52 percent), engaging in evangelism (50 percent), providing Christian education (47 percent), offering ministry to children (37 percent), and helping the elderly (27 percent). Additionally, 78 percent of African-American churches are involved in some effort to bring harmony and reconciliation between different racial and ethnic groups.[40] It is true, of course, that the church has the obligation to evangelize its own culture. Caring ministries performed by believers impact a culture in many significant ways. The danger is that an unbalanced church can easily became utilitarian, good mostly for meeting horizontal needs.

The leadership of African-American churches. African-Americans have had high regard for the African-American preacher since the post–Civil War period.[41] The pastor, therefore, is the dominant person in the leadership of African-American churches. In most churches he is the only person in full-time ministry. The greatest frustrations of African-American pastors relate to the need for cooperation and participation in evangelism and missions: 29 percent of pastors feel disappointed by people's lack of commitment to ministry and the church. People's limited participation in evangelism and outreach ranks second (12 percent), followed by the absence of spiritual growth among congregants (9 percent).[42]

In the past, pastors have fulfilled a variety of roles and, in the process, have sgained a wider influence. They counseled, gave legal advice, and supported business ventures.[43] Most African-American pastors today hold to three priorities for themselves and the church in the following order of importance: first, providing the African-American community with a political voice and leadership; second, providing social servsices; and third, providing spiritual leadership.[44] This may surprise many white Christians. However, one must take into consideration the historical development that led to the perception of pastors as defenders of the rights of African-Americans and as social reformers. In most cases it is difficult to separate the spiritual agenda of African-American pastors from the political and social responsibilities they embrace.[45] This is a complex issue that will require additional missiological reflection, solid dialogue with respected African-American leaders, and serious study.

Other hindrances. White Americans could accept blame for the African-American underrepresentation in missions. They need to repent of past mistakes and attitudes, affirms James Sutherland.[46] He quotes one respondent to his survey insisting on the need for whites to reach out to African-Americans. If the whites "can so easily cross cultures outside the U.S. why don't they use the same experience in the U.S. reaching blacks for missions?"[47]

Frequently new missionaries arriving in Africa are asked, "What do you think of the black issue in America?" Africans realize that the missionaries' attitudes toward this problem are a good barometer of what their attitudes will be toward the church in Africa.[48]

Practical Reflections

Most African-Americans (71 percent of adults and 86 percent of pastors) believe that in order to understand the African-American experience, it is necessary to understand the role of religious faith in their lives.[49]

James O. Stallings, a recognized leader in the evangelism office of the Board of National Ministries of the American Baptist Churches in the United States, presumes that "blacks took Euro-American white Christianity, baptized it in African tradition and created a new Afro-American Christianity."[50] Long gone is the view espoused by Joseph R. Washington, who in 1964 wrote in his book entitled *Black Religion* that the black church had "no authentic roots in the Christian tradition" and no "meaningful theological frame of reference." At that time he concluded that the only salvation for black Christians was absorption into the white church structure.[51] Washington's book motivated other blacks to begin research and writing on such issues.

In contrast, most African-American adults perceive their association with an African-American church as comforting, because it is a place where African-Americans have control over their lives. Similarly, African-American pastors are generally viewed as the most significant leaders in the African-American community.[52] In terms of willpower, initiative, motivation, and involvement in missions, they are the real gatekeepers.

While there are some serious gaps between what African-American Christians think and what other ethnic groups think, one needs to understand that achieving unity among the brethren and making disciples of all nations is possible only because the One who commands it also promises to work it out.

Barna notes that some of the stereotypes of blacks will die hard among whites: "For most whites, the perspectives of black people make no sense. Being happy in spite of a very high proportion of single-parent families, feeling financially comfortable in spite of a substantially lower household income, and describing themselves as successful despite being shut out of the highest ranks of government and corporate America makes no sense to the average white person. But what most whites don't comprehend is that African-Americans perceive and approach life on the basis of completely different assumptions. This confusion explains why reconciliation efforts have largely failed in our country. Whites are trying to bring about reconciliation based on a white view of reality and within the context of white lifestyles and goals."[53]

The research findings show also why most of the efforts at developing multiracial congregations or creating multiethnic worship services have failed. "These different population groups have relatively little in common," Barna explains. He elaborates: "They may believe in the same Jesus, but the ways in which they express their faith and experience their Savior are radically different. Frankly, our interviews suggested that most blacks don't have much interest in being part of a multi-racial worship experience. They don't hate whites and they do not dismiss the white spiritual experience—but neither do they feel any need to appropriate it as their own. Their faith culture is unique and is one life element that blacks are neither willing to alter nor abandon."[54]

Some Christians believe that in Christ all our differences should disappear. Such a belief, some explain, is rooted in the myth of the great American melting pot. The early church, on the other hand, was unified but not uniform.[55] Through the power of the Holy Spirit believers dealt with tensions and misunderstandings stemming from cultural differences (see Acts 6:1–6; chap. 10; 11:1–3, 18–20; chaps. 13–14). Consider the following statement made by a veteran missionary: "With my limitations of language and experience, I cannot fully comprehend the meditative nature of Eastern Christianity or the vibrant dynamism of Latin American evangelism or the spiritual freedom of the African mind, but by faith I can accept that Jesus Christ's manifestation of Himself is far greater than I can comprehend on this earth, and I can accept all of these as brothers and sisters because our unity is found in the gospel of Jesus Christ."[56]

How can we best relate to African-American Christians? First, we should avoid the "us versus them" mentality. We should take time to develop relationships. Second, we should relate to African-American missions concerns. Third, as Thom and Marcia Hopler suggest, "We should not attempt to cross the cultural barrier to the non-Christian African-American community. We should first go to the Christian African-American community that is one step closer to our value system though their Christian expression will still be different from what white Christians expect evangelicalism to look like."[57] The white American Christian can ask the Christian African-American community, "How can my particular gifts be of service to you?" Then together, with a bond of trust between them, they should enter into the non-Christian community. The stage of learning about each other should be taken seriously. One should make earnest efforts to listen carefully, eliminate stereotypes, and enhance understanding.

One additional word of caution is needed. African-American churches should not feel pressured to spread their limited resources too thin, to get involved in missions just because other churches are getting involved.

Foreseeable Results

What results of partnership should we expect to see? The most significant outcome from an effective partnership in world missions is obedience to the Great Commission. Also, the serious under-representation of the African-American Christian community in missions could soon be changed.

The African-American Christian community could find its specific niche in the missionary enterprise, intercede for the people of every nation of the world, serve and minister to them, and play its strategic role in the kingdom of God.

The Timing of the Appeal

During the North American Mission Board's second annual Ethnic Presidents Roundtable Conference, held February 1–2, 2000, on the campus of Southeastern Baptist Theological Seminary, in Wake Forest, North Carolina, Paige Patterson, president of the SBC and Southeastern Seminary, declared that "the day is over" when the Southern Baptist Convention is "a White, Anglo Saxon denomination." He expressed his belief that "the future of the Southern Baptist Convention has to be a multi-racial, multi-ethnic future, or quite frankly . . . it has no future."[59]

In 1995 the Southern Baptist Convention overwhelmingly passed a resolution on racial reconciliation seeking forgiveness from African-Americans for any involvement in past injustices of slavery, segregation, and racial prejudice. Similar initiatives have been taken recently by the United Methodist Church and other groups.

A Fervent Appeal

The words of the famous international prophet, Isaiah, reverberate through the ages: "Make known his deeds among the peoples. . . . Let this be known throughout the earth" (Isa. 12:4–5). The magnitude of the task is overwhelming, even for the sophisticated twenty-first-century people of God. No group can do it alone. For this reason and more, African-American brothers and sisters in Christ are entreated to recognize their role in global evangelism, accept their responsibility, and join other groups in the efforts to fulfill the evangelistic mandate. This is the most appropriate time for strategic action, fervent prayer, reconciliation, and unity.

Through effective partnerships the African-American Christian community is invited to explore ways to speed up its integration into the missiological dimension, help clarify the task, participate in workshops, seminars, and strategic consultations, and also initiate pilot projects in key African-American churches. In addition, the African-American community is invited to review relevant findings, strategies, and missiological data accumulated over the last two centuries.

The African-American community could "ask the Lord of the harvest . . . to send out workers into his harvest field" (Matt. 9:38), encourage possible candidates to enter missionary training, consider selective short-term mission projects, expose students in African-American colleges and seminaries to missions, create a new and favorable climate for global evangelism in churches, and even include in its strategy days of prayer for the persecuted church and specific actions on their behalf.

This is not an invitation to join someone else's program. A Christian group can maintain its identity and at the same time work together with other groups of believers. It can develop its own methodology. It can choose strategies appropriate to the values of its members. Nonetheless, due to limitations of resources and high demands on the mission fields, the evangelical community as a whole should make every effort to avoid duplication, competition, and waste of time, personnel, and financial resources.

Emmanuel L. McCall insists that historically, African-American Christians were not attracted to participate in foreign missions by a spirit of adventure, pangs of guilt, or notions of martyrdom.[60] Rather, they were deeply committed to obey the Great Commission, even though resources and conditions were extremely unfavorable. In light of the new, favorable conditions and existing resources, Tom Skinner challenges the African-American Christian community, "Now is the time for Black Christians in this country to rise up and take our rightful place in the body of Christ and to open up ourselves and receive all that God intended for us to have."[61] Likewise, Willie Richardson, the pastor of Christian Stronghold Baptist Church in Philadelphia, invites the believers in the African-American churches to act: "We must accept responsibility to reach the world through foreign and home missions efforts. Our mission for Christ is not complete until the church moves beyond self-interest to getting nothing in return except satisfaction that we are obeying and doing God's will."[62]

The Amsterdam 2000 conference drew 10,732 participants, from 209 countries. In his address, Billy Graham pleaded: "Let us light a fire that will guide men and women into tomorrow—and eternity. Let us light a fire that will roll back the poisons of racism, poverty and injustice. Let us light a fire of renewed faith in the Scriptures as the Word of God, and in worship and evangelism as the priority of the Church. Let us light a fire of commitment to proclaim Jesus Christ in the power of the Holy Spirit to the ends of the earth, using every ounce of our strength. Let us light a fire in this generation that, by God's grace, will never be put out."[63]

The time has come for the Body of Christ to discover the reality of "how good and pleasant it is when brothers live [and work] together in unity" (Ps. 133:1–2).

Notes

1. David L. Larsen, *The Evangelism Mandate: Recovering the Centrality of Gospel Preaching* (Wheaton, Ill.: Crossway Books, 1992), p. 69.
2. W. Edward Glenny and William H. Smallman, eds., *Missions in a New Millennium* (Grand Rapids: Kregel Publications, 2000), p. 23.
3. Luis Bush, "In Pursuit of True Christian Partnership," in *Partners in the Gospel*, ed. James H. Kraakevik and Dotsey Welliver (Wheaton, Ill.: Billy Graham Center, n.d.), p. 7.
4. Kraakevik and Welliver, *Partners in the Gospel*, p. 175.
5. David Garrison, "Integrated Groups Report," in Kraakevik and Welliver, *Partners in the Gospel*, p. 55.
6. Ibid., pp. 56, 118–19, 167.
7. David Cornelius, "The Vision of Lott Carey," *Mission Frontiers* 22, no. 2 (2000): 26.
8. Vaughn Walston, "Ignite the Passion," *Mission Frontiers* 22, no. 2 (2000): 14–20.
9. James O. Stallings, *Telling the Story: Evangelism in Black Churches* (Valley Forge, Pa.: Judson Press, 1988), p. 33.
10. Leroy Fitts, *A History of Black Baptists* (Nashville: Broadman Press, 1985), pp. 109–12; Stallings, *Telling the Story*, p. 41.
11. Stallings, *Telling the Story*, pp. 36–37.
12. L. L. Berry, *A Century of Missions of the African Methodist Episcopal Church* (New York: Gutenberg Printing, 1942), p. 45.
13. Cornelius, "The Vision of Lott Carey," p. 26; Stallings, *Telling the Story*, p. 42.
14. Stallings, *Telling the Story*, p. 42; Marilyn Lewis, "Overcoming Obstacles," *Mission Frontiers* 22, no. 2 (2000): 24–25.
15. Stallings, *Telling the Story*, p. 43.
16. Ibid., pp. 44, 47.
17. Fitts, *A History of Black Baptists*, p. 116; Stallings, *Telling the Story*, p. 70; Lewis, "Overcoming Obstacles," pp. 24–25.
18. Stallings, *Telling the Story*, p. 71; Lewis, "Overcoming Obstacles," pp. 24–25.
19. Reginald L. Matthews, *Missionary Administration in the Local Church* (Schaumburg, Ill.: Regular Baptist Press, 1970), p. 51.
20. Harold R. Cook, *An Introduction to Christian Missions* (Chicago: Moody Press, 1971), p. 222.
21. Paul A. Beals, *A People for His Name* (Pasadena, Calif.: William Carey Library, 1985), pp. 72–77.

22. Henry Lee Allen, "Evangelizing Professionals: Workers in the Field," in *Evangelism and Discipleship in African-American Churches*, ed. Lee N. June (Grand Rapids: Zondervan, 1999), p. 177.

23. Bob Sjogren, Bill Stearns, and Amy Stearns, *Run with Vision* (Minneapolis: Bethany House, 1995), p. 22; James W. Sutherland, "African American Underrepresentation in Intercultural Missions: Perceptions of Black Missionaries and the Theory of Survival/Security" (Ph.D. diss., Trinity Evangelical Divinity School, 1998), p. 164.

24. Paul Borthwick, *A Mind for Missions* (Colorado Springs, Colo.: NavPress, 1987), p. 42.

25. Stallings, *Telling the Story*, pp. 60–61.

26. Emmanuel L. McCall, "Black Christianity in America," in *American Missions in Bicentennial Perspective*, ed. Pierce R. Beaver (South Pasadena, Calif.: William Carey Library, 1977), p. 257.

27. Sutherland, "African American Underrepresentation," p. 68.

28. McCall, "Black Christianity in America," p. 258.

29. Stallings, *Telling the Story*, p. 73.

30. Quoted in Thom and Marcia Hopler, *Reaching the World Next Door* (Downers Grove, Ill.: InterVarsity Press, 1993), p. 178.

31. George Barna, *African-Americans and Their Faith: Research on the Faith, Culture, Values, and Lifestyles of Blacks in America* (Oxnard, Calif.: Barna Institute, 1999), p. 102.

32. Ibid., p. 97.

33. Ibid., p. 54.

34. George Barna, "Existing Stereotypes About African Americans Are Way Off the Mark—and Impede Reconciliation," Current Trends at <http://216.87.../PagePressRelease.asp?PressReleaseID=42&Reference=>, 2000, p. 2.

35. Sutherland, "African American Underrepresentation," p. 165.

36. Lausanne Committee for World Evangelization, *The Willowbank Report* (Lausanne Occasional Papers, No. 2, Report of a Consultation on Gospel and Culture, Charlotte, N.C., 1978), p. 27.

37. Ibid., pp. 28–29.

38. Allen, "Evangelizing Professionals," pp. 175, 176.

39. Sutherland, "African American Underrepresentation," p. 166.

40. Barna, *African-Americans and Their Faith*, pp. 60–62, 63.

41. Stallings, *Telling the Story*, p. 54.

42. Barna, *African-Americans and Their Faith*, p. 76.

43. McCall, "Black Christianity in America," p. 259.

44. Barna, *African-Americans and Their Faith*, p. 64.

45. Ibid., *passim*.

46. Sutherland, "African American Underrepresentation," p. 299.

47. Ibid., p. 291.

48. Hopler, *Reaching the World Next Door*, p. 141.

49. Barna, *African-Americans and Their Faith*, p. 68.

50. Stallings, *Telling the Story*, p. 31.

51. Quoted in McCall, "Black Christianity in America," pp. 250–51.

52. Barna, *African-Americans and Their Faith*, p. 68.

53. Barna, "Stereotypes," p. 3.

54. Ibid.

55. Hopler, *Reaching the World Next Door*, p. 64.

56. Ibid., p. 92.

57. Ibid., pp. 140–41.

58. Sjogren, Stearns, and Stearns, *Run with Vision*, pp. 22–23.

59. Lee Weeks, "SBC to Elect Ethnic President Within Five Years, Envisions Patterson" (press release 2/04/ at http://www.sebts.edu/htm/000204/_ethnic_conference.html, May 15, 2000).

60. McCall, "Black Christianity in America," p. 267.

61. Tom Skinner, "Personal Reflections on Evangelism Among African-Americans," in *Evangelism and Discipleship in African-American Churches*, ed. June, p. 31.

62. Willie Richardson, "The Church's Role," in *Evangelism and Discipleship in African-American Churches*, ed. June, p. 50.

63. Billy Graham, "Let Us Light a Fire," *Decision* 41, no. 10 (October 2000), p. 42.

Chapter Nine

William Carey and the Business Model for Mission

Dwight P. Baker

In 1792 William Carey published his *Enquiry into the Obligations of Christians, to Use Means for the Conversion of the Heathens*. He offered himself for missionary service, arriving in India in November, 1793, and is often spoken of as the father or founder of modern Protestant mission outreach. Here it is argued that his achievement can be seen as a wedding of the contemporary business model and Protestant mission outreach. In the present essay this alliance and its consequences for mission are investigated by examining relationships between mission and business at three "slices of time," the periods surrounding the opening of the nineteenth, twentieth, and twenty-first centuries.

At least since the work of Max Weber a century ago, social scientists and historians have been alert to the roles religions play in undergirding distinctive economic and business patterns. Religion's contribution ranges from undergirding distinctive worldviews at the macrolevel to providing practical certification of particular individuals' trustworthiness at the microlevel. Weber famously found the seeds of Western capitalism in the Protestant ethic: its worldview supplied the foundation upon which an economic system was slowly built up.[1] In the nineteenth-century United States, religion as an institution went further and provided organizational models that nascent business enterprises could copy as their operations spread out across the new country.[2]

In the present instance, however, it is the reverse influence—specifically the impact of the business model upon the conduct of mission—that will be examined. The alliance of mission with the business model will be investigated by looking at the legacy of William Carey and by examining relationships between mission and business at three "slices of time," surrounding the opening of the nineteenth, twentieth, and twenty-first centuries. Carey's lifetime saw the enthusiastic adoption of the business model for mission. By the turn of the twentieth century, "scientific" approaches to business organization and operation provided the model for reorganization of both institutional religion and Protestant mission outreach. The arrival of a truly global economy at the end of the twentieth century raises new questions regarding the direction in which the business model may be taking mission as the twenty-first century opens.[3]

Father of Modern Missions?

Identification of William Carey as "the father of modern missions" is a commonplace of Protestant mission literature. William Carey, the man from England, teacher and translator in India, has been elevated into William Carey, missionary icon. A Carey watchword— "Expect great things from God; attempt great things for God"— epitomizes nineteenth-century North Atlantic Protestantism's robust confidence as it established mission stations across the world. This confidence lasted into the twentieth century. Not as often noted is the fact that Carey stands (1) for a particular style of approach to mission organization (specifically, adapting the joint-stock company for missional purposes) and (2) for a particular era in mission.

The matter of timing was significant for Carey's proposal and for his elevation to Protestant sainthood. The protections of what was to become the modern corporation were just beginning to be extended to ordinary commercial and business ventures.[4] Modern Protestant missions and the modern corporation grew up alongside each other. The business corporation provided the organizational model, and an entrepreneurial spirit permeated both. As exemplar, Carey's lifework gave legitimacy to fusion of the two.

The brilliance of Carey's achievements has, for many, served to obscure the substantial endeavors of his Protestant missionary predecessors. Daniel O'Connor writes of "an evangelical missiography that seems to be obliged to say that nothing of significance happened before William Carey dawned upon the British mission scene at the end of the eighteenth century."[5] If one bears in mind that Carey was consciously building upon Protestant missionary outreach, which by his day had a time depth of a century and a half and more,[6] the question, "Why Carey? Why did *he* become iconic of modern Protestant missions?" becomes pointed. The breadth and diversity of Carey's life interests and missionary engagements supply part of the answer to that question. The cumulative weight of credit accorded to him for work carried out by associates contributes another part. This essay, however, goes beyond Carey and his accomplishments to interrogate the business model of mission itself. What changed in the conduct of mission with the introduction of the business model?

Who Was William Carey?

William Carey's name, observes Timothy George, has become "synonymous with the heroic age of the Protestant missionary movement." In many ways his life and enterprises can be read as exemplifying the very model of a fully modern missionary. George supplies a roll call of nineteenth-century Protestant mission luminaries who "either knew Carey personally or were deeply influenced by his life and example" and states that two centuries after sailing to India, "Carey is universally recognized as the father of modern missions."[7]

That may be. But at the end of a missionary retreat that utilized *Candle in the Dark*,[8] a film dramatization of Carey's life and work, one veteran missionary queried: "Who *was* William Carey? Why is he called the father of modern missions?"

In brief, he was born in 1761. Apprenticed to a shoemaker, Carey was converted through the testimony of a fellow apprentice in 1775 and called as pastor of a Baptist chapel in 1785. In 1792 he published *An Enquiry into the Obligations of Christians, to Use Means for the Conversion of the Heathens* and the following year sailed for India as a missionary with his wife Dorothy and their four children, arriving in mid-November, 1793. Forty years later he died and was buried at Serampore, India, old, full of years, the honored Dr. Carey, orientalist, professor of Sanskrit, Bengali, and Marathi at Fort William College, founder of ongoing missionary enterprises in East India, inspiration and advisor to others beyond India, and the driving force behind translation of the Christian Scriptures in whole or in part into some forty languages and dialects.[9]

Carey was a preacher, teacher, and translator, but further, he was a robust activist, an entrepreneur for God. Ruth and Vishal Mangalwadi offer a litany of firsts: Carey "introduced the idea of Savings Banks to India," "led the campaign for a humane treatment for leprosy patients," "brought the English daisy to India," and "published the first books on science and natural history in India."

He "established the first newspaper ever printed in any oriental language." He was "the first Englishman to introduce the steam engine to India and the first to make indigenous paper for the publishing industry." Carey was "the father of print technology in India," "the founder of the Agri-Horticultural Society in the 1820s, thirty years before the Royal Agricultural Society was established in England," and "the first man to translate and publish great Indian religious classics such as the *Ramayana*, and philosophical treaties [*sic*] such as *Samkhya* into English." He was "a preacher who revived the ancient idea that ethics and morality were inseparable from religion." Further, he struggled against infanticide, campaigned against the burning of widows (*sati*), and as a naturalist continued his study of nature by planting a five-acre arboretum.[10] Malay Dewanji writes along similar lines.[11]

An observation is in order. One may justifiably retain reservations about the notion that all light in India dawned with Carey. Rhetorically, in the rehearsal of his accomplishments, Carey becomes a synecdoche for the larger circle of European expatriates, Indian pundits, and employees working in conjunction with the Serampore mission. As the spotlight is focused more sharply on him, these associates recede from view, and Carey's elevation to symbolic status becomes increasingly pronounced. Still, in Andrew Walls's words, Carey was "by any reckoning a remarkable man."[12] His life, work, writings, social legacy, and mission practice continue to command attention.[13]

Carey and Mission

At one level, facts about Carey as an individual are germane in answering the question, "Why is Carey called the father of modern missions?" If Carey had not had the personal qualities he did (personal focus and drive, and breadth of humane vision) and had not played the roles he did (organizer of a translations factory, publisher, publicist, and social activist), he would not have become emblematic of the Protestant mission enterprise. However, at a deeper level, his work and character "fit" with a Protestant era on the threshold of coming into its own. Carey was the initiator of numerous projects, and his lifework coincided with the inception of an age that was to value entrepreneurialism highly and to reward it magnificently. As a symbol, Carey was carried aloft by the confluence of a number of social and theological currents which he did not originate, but which he had the good fortune, humanly speaking, to exemplify and which were to be foundational to Protestant understanding of the missionary enterprise for the next century and a half. Five of these currents may be mentioned here.

1. He upheld the obligation of Christ's followers to actively engage in *carrying* the Gospel to those who do not yet know Christ with the purpose that they might be converted.
2. He affirmed Christ's missionary mandate to be still in force for the church. He did this in the face of standard—and sterile—Protestant anti–Roman Catholic apologetics, current since Luther, which maintained that the Great Commission had been fulfilled by the apostles and was no longer in force.
3. He proposed to create missionary associations patterned after commercial joint-stock companies to carry out the church's missionary task.
4. Even as a Baptist, and hence a Dissenter, he operated out of a Christendom model of mission.
5. He was the beneficiary of and built on previous missional practice and reflection, including reports coming back from the English colonies in America.

Carey was not the sole adherent of any of these points, nor was he the originator of any of them. A few remarks on each point may help to clarify Carey's contribution.

Christian Obligation to Carry the Gospel

When Carey proposed that the Baptist ministers in Northhampton discuss "the duty of Christians to attempt the spread of the gospel among heathen nations,"[14] he elicited John Ryland, Sr.'s, famous—if apocryphal (according to Walls)[15]—rebuke: "Young man, sit down; when God wants to convert the heathens, He'll do it without your help or mine."

Today it is Ryland's response, not Carey's topic, that needs explanation. Carey was stirring up a theological controversy that had been exercising the Particular Baptists throughout the eighteenth century. In 1781 Robert Hall, a senior minister in the Northhamptonshire Baptist Ministers' Fraternal, had published *Help to Zion's Travellers,* which included the assurance that "the way to Jesus is graciously open for everyone who chooses to come to him." Four years later Carey's friend Andrew Fuller published a treatise seeking to reconcile evangelism and Calvinism.[16] Such rethinking was under way in the wider circles to which Carey and the Particular Baptists related, as well.[17] Carey was not opening a new topic; he was taking sides in an ongoing theological dispute. Not surprisingly, as a newcomer he met initial resistance.

The Great Commission Still in Force

The train of argument against the continuing validity of the Great Commission ran somewhat as follows:

- The apostolic gift was unique.
- Christ's Great Commission was a command given to the apostles as possessors of the unique apostolic gift.
- Being unique, this apostolic gift was limited to the age of the church's founding.
- There is no apostolic succession.

Corollaries:

- In view of the uniqueness of the apostolic gift, the commands and commissions given to the apostles were fulfilled during the apostles' lifetimes.
- Therefore, the Great Commission was fulfilled in the first century and is no longer in force.
- To think otherwise might give the pope a toehold for claiming to be Peter's successor.

As Walls observes, Carey "has no difficulty in reducing this argument to absurdity. Where, he asks his fellow Baptists, is there then any justification for baptizing—is not that equally an apostolic office?"[18]

Carey missed being the first to challenge the standard Protestant apologetic by at least two centuries. Alan Neely traces a "carefully reasoned challenge to the prevailing Protestant view"[19] back to Hadrianus Saravia in 1590. The anti–Roman Catholic animus of the argument came to the fore when the Church Missionary Society was launched. Walls writes that resistance arose in some quarters precisely from the fear that launching a society might be "a distraction from the 'real' work of combating Rome."[20]

Forming a Mission Society

An English Protestant agency under ecclesiastical control intended for the propagation of the Gospel had existed at least since 1701 with the founding in London of the Society for the Propagation of the Gospel in Foreign Parts.[21] Even when it comes to establishing an independent mission society, Carey was not first. Oliver W. Elsbree writes, "In 1787 the American Society for Propagating the Gospel among the Indians and Others in North America was given legal status through an act of the Massachusetts Legislature."[22] This followed through on an effort begun twenty-five years earlier that had been blocked by the Archbishop of Canterbury. Earlier efforts to found mission societies had to await partial disestablishment of the Anglican church.

Yet Carey (1) did advance a rationale for establishing mission societies, (2) was part of the group that carried through and actually established a functioning and long-lived society, (3) gave meaningful reality to his proposal by going in the society's first party of appointees, and (4) attracted an attentive audience of society members and supporters. Diversely engaged over an extended period and possessing linguistic talents far beyond the ordinary, Carey made good missionary press then, and to this day. It is his name, not Ward's, Marshman's, or any of the many others in India during the same period, that has come to symbolize the independent or voluntary mission society patterned as a commercial venture for God.

Operating Out of a Christendom Model

The Christendom model assumes that mission flows from the West to the rest, from the powerful to the powerless, from an established Christian homeland to godless heathendom, and that it does so with all the weight of government, commerce, and public approbation actually or potentially on its side. The presumption that mission could operate out of a Christendom mentality was shared by virtually all Western Europeans in Carey's day and for the next century.[23]

Beneficiary of Previous Missional Practice

In an earlier period reports coming back from the European voyages of discovery played a crucial role in opening new vistas for European Enlightenment thinkers. Traders, travelers, and soldiers of fortune brought tales of other mores, other customs, other languages, and other forms of social organization. These tales extended the conceptual horizons of Europe's intelligentsia. Something similar, Charles Chaney has argued, happened in the history of Protestant missions.[24] Missionary experience from the American colonies spurred British churchmen to rethink entrenched theological positions and to take action. In the colonies, Sir Thomas Browne's sweeping seventeenth-century British inclusivism, "We being all Christians," clearly did not apply. There were daily encounters with exotic peoples outside the bounds of Christian faith. The reconsideration of Particular Baptist theology done by Andrew Fuller, mentioned above, was fueled in part by the writings of Jonathan Edwards from America, and Carey was a reader of David Brainerd's journal. Early American colonial mission experience was foundational for the broadening Protestant missionary movement even as nineteenth-century America's entrepreneurial bent and sense of manifest destiny were to color later development of the Protestant missionary movement.

Carey and Adoption of the Business Model for Mission

These five elements do not exhaust Protestant understanding of mission. However, of these five, it is obvious that the first, second, fourth, and fifth were not exclusive to Protestants. Roman Catholic missionary activity around the world was putting Protestant efforts to shame.[25] The Roman branch of the church was not pretending that the obligation to carry the Gospel into all the world had already been fulfilled, no matter how active the apostles may have been. Roman Catholic missionaries operated, if anything, within an even more encompassing set of Christendom expectations than did Carey and the Protestants. Though they may not have been reading Brainerd's journal and Edwards's theology, Roman Catholic experience in mission among the indigenous peoples of the New World preceded and exceeded that of the Protestants.[26]

That leaves the third point, the business model for mission. Carey cited the example of the way a trading company is formed to carry out business ventures at a distance and then proposed that the Particular Baptists form a mission society along similar lines.[27] It is the widespread adoption of the business model as *the* instrument for mission that is new and that becomes distinctive of Protestant missions. It is to this flexible and endlessly replicable pattern of mission enterprise that Carey has lent his name.

A word of background may bring the distinctiveness of the Carey business model into sharper relief. At the point of the Reformation, the Western church had two predominant structures: (1) a geographical or territorial parish organization for handling congregational life and (2) monastic orders (special-purpose, nongeographically defined entities) as instruments for specialized functions such as teaching, conducting mission outreach, operating hospitals, and maintaining orphanages. When the two dominant streams of the Protestant Reformation, Lutheran and Reformed, jettisoned the monastic orders but retained the geographical parish, they left the Reformation incomplete and foreclosed realization of the missional potential of the congregation.

The third wing of the Reformation, the Anabaptists, was actively missionary. The Anabaptists moved beyond the inclusive geographical parish as well as the monastic orders and looked to the congregation as a mission-focused community. However, persecution came from both sides, Roman Catholic and Protestant. The Anabaptists were hounded from place to place and persecuted nearly to the point of extinction. In return for the concession of being permitted to exist, early Anabaptists allowed initiatives in mission to be cut off virtually at their inception.[28]

When, a century and a half later, Protestant mission outreach again flourished, the Moravians took the lead; William Danker underscores that they did so on a congregational and communal basis.[29] They had a world-encircling vision and sent missionaries widely, to the Americas, the Arctic, Africa, throughout Europe and Russia, and to Southeast Asia. The Moravians have the distinction of having sent out "over half the Protestant missionaries in the eighteenth century," states Paul Pierson.[30] Not every Moravian became a foreign missionary, of course; many worked in the businesses set up to generate profit for the Lord and so to underwrite their mission endeavors. But to join the Moravians was, knowingly, to unite with a mission-focused community. Everyone worked for the cause of missions; everyone aspired to go on a mission. For a time, so as to make a selection among missionary aspirants, the Moravian home base at Herrnhut cast lots to choose who would be released to go as a missionary. In 1759 at the Moravian colony in Bethlehem, Pennsylvania, 36 percent of the male workforce were missionaries on assignment.[31] The Moravian approach may have been inspiring, but it found few emulators. The Moravians' mission-focused model for congregational life was not transferable to the geographically defined, populace-inclusive parish of the Reformed and Lutheran wings of the Protestant church. Becoming fellowships of mission-focused congregations would have required a complete overhaul of those bodies' principle of organization.

It was at this juncture that Carey stepped forward with his proposal of a business-style mission society. The mission society could (1) solicit, receive, and disburse funds; (2) recruit, screen, appoint, second, and dismiss personnel; (3) carry on projects large and small at greater or lesser distances and over shorter or longer periods of time; (4) oversee long-term projects outlasting the lives of both field personnel and members of the board; and (5) undertake large-scale enterprises (the printing establishment at Serampore, educational institutions, and hospitals, for instance). This description will be recognized as falling very close to that of the modern corporation, of which more will be said below. It will also be noted that nothing in the description as given has any necessary connection with either congregations or ecclesial structures either as input or as outcome. Connections, such as they are, come as add-ons. They are not intrinsic.

Carey was cognizant of the need for mission societies to "pay great attention to the views" of those appointed as missionaries.[32] Who is chosen to staff a mission is crucial. Still, focus has shifted to an enterprise administered. Missions become entities that outlast particular gifted persons, and *missionary,* as in "mission agency staff person," becomes a *career* choice to which one can aspire. Most of all, the mission society supplies a model that can be imitated widely without reform or restoration of ecclesiological conceptions. As a supracongregational and supraparish structure, it is adaptable to the needs of both the believers' church/free church tradition and ecclesiastical traditions organized by geographical parish. A particular society *may* become the missionary arm of a particular denomination or, indeed, a particular congregation, but there is no inherently necessary connection. Investors in a joint-stock company come from where they will; in principle, mission administrators, mission candidates, mission backers, and money for mission do the same.

What here is being called the business model of mission differs from both the Moravian model and that of the later Basel Mission, though both engaged in numerous business enterprises. The Moravians engaged in manufacturing and commerce in advance, so to speak, so as to acquire money that could then fund their missionary outreach. The Basel missionaries, Danker reports, saw the day-to-day activities of conducting businesses as themselves missional.[33] They were means through which industrial and commercial missionaries could give living demonstration of Christian character, diligence, thrift, honesty, faith, and compassion in action. Both used business profits to underwrite mission projects. Though Carey also used outside earnings to fund mission expenses, in proposing that mission agencies be formed as joint-stock companies he was pointing in a direction different from that of either the Moravians or the Basel Mission.

Carey symbolizes reconceptualization of mission outreach along the lines of burgeoning capitalistic practice. Along the way, mission is reconstrued. Participation in mission becomes a matter of individual choice, even of personal taste. Some persons have the means and inclination to buy stocks; some give to missions: either or both as individual choice and inclination may dictate. From being the raison d'être of the body of Christ as a whole, mission has retreated conceptually. In Jan Jongeneel's words, mission after Carey pertains only to "some separate members belonging to some congregations."[34] Eventually, Protestantism was to find it necessary to seek to reintegrate congregations and mission. Mission seemingly had become the province of specialists and peripheral to congregational life.

However, the immediate result was a flowering of the business model for Christian mission. Protestantism's pent-up missionary impulse at last had found a mechanism adaptable to the breadth of its ambitions. The significant and long-enduring mission societies founded in the opening decades of the nineteenth century are evidence of the strength and vitality of Protestantism's missionary spirit.[35]

Confluent Streams

The business model for mission did not in itself create the conditions that made mission agencies viable and enabled them to thrive. Powerful social currents already under way made that era especially favorable. Among these were (1) increased social mobility brought about by the ongoing industrial revolution; (2) the rise of the limited liability commercial company, or corporation; (3) enshrinement of individualism, contract-based relationships, and energetic entrepreneurialism as constitutional law in the newly-formed United States; and (4) the blossoming of the "benevolent empire" of which mission agencies formed a part.

Social Mobility

The industrial revolution in England was opening new paths to status and recognition based on personal accomplishment and acquisition of money rather than heredity. Money gained through industry or commerce enabled entrepreneurs to purchase estates for themselves or to "buy" the sons and daughters of landed gentry as spouses for their offspring. Likewise, mission service acted as a mechanism of social elevation. Moving from Britain, rural United States, or the Continent to the foreign mission field raised many to a station in life—with status, control of property, authority, and recognition—that their social origins could have given them no hope of achieving in their homelands, whatever their level of personal capability or accomplishment. The rise in status proved inheritable, passing down to succeeding generations of postmissionary offspring.[36] On the other side of the coin, it has been observed that the number of missionary offspring who played significant roles in their countries' foreign service corps is evidence for the high caliber of the parental missionary stock. Certainly Carey would be a prime example of a rise in status through mission service. He became central to a set of enterprises, including his botanical gardens, beyond anything to which he could have aspired had he remained as a Baptist pastor/cobbler in England.

Rise of the Corporation

Developments in commercial law made the turn of the nineteenth century propitious as well. In God's providence, Carey's proposal of "floating a company"[37] for mission had the good fortune to be issued just as the protections and powers embodied in the limited liability company were being extended to the ordinary commercial sphere. Corporations are so common and so powerful today—and they shape our lives so completely—that it is hard to realize how recently they arrived at anything like their present form.[38] Though today the corporation has "become 'America's representative social institution,'"[39] corporations were uncommon in the United States before 1800.[40] In the nineteenth century the limited liability company blossomed into the corporation of today (though it made slow headway until well into the century). In significant ways, the mission agency and the corporation grew up together.

Legal Setting

United States constitutional law supplied a wholly new impetus. The United States Constitution not only barred establishment of hierarchy, rank, and inherited privilege; it also built rewards for *individual* initiative and achievement into the country's foundational law (see Art. 1, sec. 8). Though the individual had been defined as the basic legal unit, over the course of the nineteenth century the legal status of the chartered company or corporation became ever more sharply defined and refined as an instrument for the expression of American entrepreneurialism—and quite naturally so, for American business interests played a large part in crafting legislation and legal decisions with that very purpose in mind.[41] Two factors determined the unfolding process of simplification of corporate law in the United States, which blazed the trail for British and Continental corporate legal development as well. The first factor was the United States constitutional bar against tariffs on trade between the states. The second factor was the reservation of development of corporation law to the several states. These stipulations set the stage for fierce competition among the states to see which could arrive most quickly at the lowest common denominator in corporate law. In the process, corporate status became ever more widely available, easier to obtain, and accessible for a greater range of purposes. By the latter part of the nineteenth century, equipped with legal protection and stripped of social checks and responsibilities, business (and robber barons) flourished.

Benevolent Empire

An energetic blend of widely dispersed volunteerism, entrepreneurialism, and reformism supplied another significant current, new on the social scene. Especially in the United States, but in Britain and on the Continent as well, voluntary agencies sprang up for many purposes, including Bible societies (American Bible Society, British and Foreign Bible Society, and many others), the Sunday school movement, abolitionist movements, temperance societies, and social reform projects. (According to Martin Marty, more than four thousand temperance societies alone were formed in the United States between 1808 and 1831.)[42] The agencies of the expanding mission movement formed a significant wing of the benevolent empire. They were energized, in part, by the ideas of progress and manifest destiny that buoyed the confidence of the West, particularly the young United States. Throughout the nineteenth century the West was on the ascendant: politically, militarily, industrially, commercially, and culturally; and mission outreach flourished in conjunction with the currents of expansionism emanating from the United States and of empire from Britain and the Continent.[43]

As has been observed, Protestant mission efforts existed prior to Carey. But now, by adopting the capitalistic business model—which itself was being formed into what was to become the modern corporation—Protestant mission had a malleable instrument with limitless potential. Much has been written on the impetus which the American sense of calling as a covenant people gave to American Protestantism and to Protestant foreign mission enterprise.[44] Attention must be given to eighteenth- and nineteenth-century developments in commerce, business, law, and social relations as well.

Consequences for Mission

The movement Carey symbolizes brought a major advance in the quantity of Protestant long-distance and cross-cultural mission engagement. More Protestant mission outreach was undertaken by more people in more places that were more widely separated and more culturally diverse than ever before. There were gains, yes; were there losses as well?

Gains for Mission

What strengths did the new structure of independent mission societies bring to mission?

Flexibility. The mission agency structure is flexible. It can be sized to handle projects large or small. An agency can be started immediately on a shoestring and grow. It can shift with changes in circumstances, starting, stopping, or redirecting energies from one line of activity to another or one mission field to another on short notice. Like a large corporation it can add a new division and undertake multiple projects simultaneously. The mission agency structure has shown itself to be an adaptable instrument.

Durability. Mission agencies, like corporations, answer the concern for durability and continuity, independent of particular individuals. Even if vision and inspiration lag, in a mission agency, managers can succeed one another, carrying on until God grants revival. Institutions have the virtue of sustaining and channeling effort. Long duration also allows for repeated encounters with recurring issues (for example, candidate training, staff deployment, and personnel evaluation) over a number of cycles. Repeated experience, in turn, enables mission agencies to build up a pool of expertise not available elsewhere among the organs of the church and at times rivaling that of large-scale commercial and governmental agencies.

Specialization. Mission agencies facilitate specialization. The number and kinds of mission agencies continue to proliferate. Some agencies focus on one region of the world or one continent, some on a particular religious bloc or people group. Some agencies are the evangelistic or service arm of a particular constituency. Some advertise themselves as specialists in medical work, some in literacy, some in translation, some in education, some in church planting, some in service to other agencies. Some take pride in raising funds in a particular way. The variability and possible specializations are unending.[45]

Cooperation. The agency structure offers a platform for cooperation. It enables congregations to enter together into mission projects that are too large, too distant, or too long-running for any of them individually to undertake. It provides a mechanism for cooperation across denominational lines. It provides a platform from which outreach can be launched that leaves the ecclesiastical divisions and theological quarrels of the West behind. (That has not always happened, but the potential has been there. It can happen, and in some cases it has.) Mission agencies are able to reach out to multiple constituencies at different social levels, with different levels of spiritual or theological understanding, and of differing means—enabling them to become involved to the extent of their understanding and capability.

Losses for Mission

Every strength brings with it corresponding weaknesses. The business model not only allows for specialization but also makes hyperspecialization to the point of fragmentation virtually inevitable, as agencies spot and exploit combinations of "market niches." Commendable readiness to exploit opportunities for the cause of Christ can descend into competition for "brand identity" and "market share." The principle of cooperation, valuable as it is, can function as an "escape valve" that allows complacency in the face of disunity within the body of Christ that begs to be addressed directly. Organizational durability enabling continuation of ministry can degenerate into mere organizational self-perpetuation, staffed by time-servers, obscuring recognition that a ministry has fulfilled its purpose and is due for honorable retirement. Involvement of each person to the extent of his or her capacity too frequently is parsed solely in monetary terms.

In addition to these cautions, four specific concerns may be mentioned here.

Expertism. Through long experience mission agencies have become repositories of expertise. It would be foolish to throw that accumulated knowledge aside and set about to reinvent the wheel. At the same time, excessive deference to Enlightenment-based doctrines of separation of powers or division of labor is hardly warranted. Mission springs from the character of God; it devolves upon the people of God as a whole. Has the business model of mission, which was intended to be an instrument enabling wider mission involvement, instead had the effect of narrowing mission involvement, making it the exclusive preserve of specialists? How many church members see mission as something distant from them emotionally and spatially—something carried out elsewhere by mission agencies staffed by experts—to which from time to time they may give a little money but about which they are not well informed and not inclined to be? How many mission leaders tend to see local churches as spiritual laggards, if not as impediments and competitors for financing that are able to sop up enormous quantities of resources in self-serving and self-indulgent ways?

Corporation as model. Modern Protestant missions and the corporate form of business structure grew up together. Protestant mission enterprise has been heavily molded by the corporate model both in form and in standards used for self-appraisal.[46] This was inevitable, considering (1) the Carey era's enthusiastic embrace of the business model as *the* structure for mission and (2) the dominance of the corporation model for conceiving of and organizing business operations.

Models not only extend but also constrain thought and practice. Instruments, both physical and conceptual, simultaneously enable an objective to be achieved and impose certain ancillary practices. There can be no question that the entities we call corporations constrain modern business practice, often to the detriment of wider human values. Jerry Mander identifies eleven rules of corporate behavior: the profit imperative; the growth imperative; competition and aggression; amorality; hierarchy; quantification, linearity, and segmentation; dehumanization; exploitation; ephemerality and mobility; opposition to nature; and homogenization.[47] How many of these "rules" have analogs in mission practice? If it is wise to choose one's enemies well, it is also sound procedure to be selective about whom or what one calls a friend. At the least, the corporate business model is not neutral.

The stock offerings of a publicly traded corporation, for example, open the door broadly to "ownership" in the sense of money transfers, but actually distance such "owners" from control over vital issues in management of "their" companies. Management is reserved to a relatively small coterie of experts. What safeguards are available to see that the pressure of an overwhelmingly dominant corporate cultural pattern does not similarly alienate and estrange the person in the pew from mission involvement?

Managerialism. The West, it has been observed, has conveyed three "gifts" to the rest of the world. Obvious, of course, is technology (medical technology, industrial technology, communications technology, and so on), techniques of every sort applied to all aspects of the physical world. The second is Western education, both as content and as technique of information dissemination and student formation. The third is management and administration, "technique" applied to human persons and purposes.[48] As is well known, the recipients of those gifts (the colonial world and now the Third World, the peoples subject to "modernization") have valued them variously, at times strongly resisting what is experienced as the onslaught of a Western juggernaut.

It is to this issue that the concerns voiced, for example, by Samuel Escobar and others at the 1999 Iguassu Missiological Consultation[49] and James Engel and William Dyrness[50] are directed. Care must be taken not to caricature the issues they raise, as though they are advocating sloppy administration of mission programs. To point out the limitations of what Escobar has termed "managerial missiology" is not the same as to question the benefits to be realized from good administrative procedures. Mission is carried out, among other ways, through mission agencies with their managers or directors and via the management of resources, financial and otherwise. There is a business aspect to mission; for example, in 1999 Protestant agencies in the United States alone reported income of—and presumably largely disbursed—$2,932,779,966.[51] How to invest the frequently sacrificial gifts of God's children is a weighty responsibility, and wise stewardship is required. Good information and clear plans are essential if one is to discern the leading of the Spirit. Competent administrators and good managers are a gift from God.[52] They are to be received with thanksgiving and nurtured.

Still, heavy-handed emphasis on the language of business (marketing strategy, market niches, managerial approaches, five-year plans, ten-year plans, evangelistic return on investment, and so on) applied to mission becomes problematic and bears close scrutiny. Any displacement of the Gospel of the kingdom by focus on techniques of management, any inflation of personages or programs that threatens to eclipse the centrality and sovereign lordship of Jesus Christ, any reliance on mechanisms that would quench the freedom of the Spirit, or any presumption of a favored place at the table for articulation of Western perspectives and agendas is to be rejected. The Spirit still blows where he wills, and Christ is still sovereign, even within his church! His grace and gifts are not conditioned on either hereditary right or time-sanctioned privilege.

Agenda set by modernity. In a number of ways, Protestant mission effort during the Carey era tied itself to the temper, methods, and objectives of modernity. Modern business enterprise—and the modern corporation—is very much an artifact of the age of modernity. The extreme individualism afflicting the West and especially the United States is an outgrowth of the Enlightenment, "modernity gone to seed."[53] With its shift from the body of Christ to certain saved individuals as the missional base, Protestant conceptions of mission bought into and abetted the rampant growth of Western individualism (see, for example, Bliss's reiterative emphasis on the *individual* acting through voluntary associations).[54] Fixation on means, methods, strategies, goals, deadlines, fulfillment of quotas bespeaks heavy indebtedness to modernity.[55]

To repeat, good information and clear plans are essential, but the collapse of modernity calls mission back, not to more and better techniques alone, but to renewed confidence in the sovereignty of God, proclamation of the good news of the kingdom, and living in step with the Spirit who freely moves and renews where and how he will.

Following the Pattern; Resisting the Pattern

The half century from 1870 or 1880 down to 1920 or 1930 was transformative for the social outlook and practice of the United States.[56] In this period the large modern corporation took something like its present form. Incremental gains had been nurtured throughout the nineteenth century, but the number and scope of corporations rose rapidly in this period, and the ethos of the business corporation permeated all aspects of American life. This was a period of rationalizing all facets of production and consumption of goods. On the side of production, time and motion studies were applied to manufacturing. On the side of management, "scientific" standards of efficiency came into vogue as well as consolidation of business organizations and "scientific" fund-raising. On the side of marketing, concerted effort was exerted to transform the U.S. populace into a nation of consumers.[57] These developments posed an immense challenge for U.S. Protestant mission agencies: would they follow the nation's insistently dominant line of cultural development or would they stand against it?

Denominational leaders and mission agency executives chose to follow the wider cultural pattern and strove to reorganize their handling of mission affairs according to the new ideals of efficient and "scientific" management.[58] "Selling" of mission, for example, fell in step. In 1924, Cornelius Patton could think of no higher or finer value in the name of which to commend mission outreach than that it was a thriving business, "a going concern." "That the missionary is a pioneer of commerce," Patton writes, "is established beyond debate. By his teachings, and even more by his manner of life, he creates a thousand appetites which must then be supplied." However, it is mission itself considered as a business, speaking in "the ordinary business sense," which he wishes to lift up, hoping through the "magnitude and success" of the mission enterprise to enlist "men of vision [who can] appreciate big things and rise to big opportunities."[59]

During this time of transition, not only denominational mission agencies but also women's mission societies "embrac[ed] as their model the corporate structures of their day."[60] In the second half of the nineteenth century, women's mission societies had given their leaders experience in setting up and administering organizations, collecting and disbursing sizable amounts of money, conducting fund-raising campaigns, and deciding upon programs and institutional objectives. Originally an object of scoffing on the part of male mission executives, the leaders of women's missions occupied positions of real and not just apparent power long before women were allowed to exercise comparable levels of administrative and executive responsibility within the business fraternity. The women's mission societies grew from one missionary in 1861 and a $2,000 budget to forty-four societies in 1909 "supporting 4,710 unmarried women in the field" and a budget of $4,000,000.[61] Ironically, as the women's mission auxiliaries bought more and more deeply into the corporate model and perfected their "scientific" fund-raising, their success made them increasingly attractive targets for "corporate takeovers" by parallel male-dominated mission organizations. After all, it would be more efficient and businesslike for denominations to have all mission-related activities under one roof and within one administrative structure. The takeover process was complete before the mid-twentieth century.

As it was a century ago, mission today is being carried out amid massive economic, social, and business upheaval. At the end of the nineteenth century, corporations were "going national." In the latter part of the twentieth they were going international, and today's social and economic dislocations are much more encompassing. Currents and causes of upheaval today include globalization; trends toward economic, political, and religious aggregation into larger blocs coupled with increasing fragmentation within or alongside those blocs; multinational supercorporations; the triumph of free market capitalistic ideology; an unbridled "winner takes all" mentality in corporate rivalries; massive international capital flows; pervasive technological penetration; and emphasis on the short-term bottom line.

Between them, globalization and the aggregation of wealth and power into the hands of fewer and fewer supercorporations are swiftly widening the gulf between the haves and have-nots of the world. In practice, globalization works out to mean enlarged dominance of the West, and particularly of the United States, over all aspects of life in all corners of the world. Values and choices around the globe are being redirected and redefined with a Western twist. In previous years the church sometimes sailed in the wake of conquering armies—but not to her credit. The question today is whether the church will seek to ride the wave of globalization sweeping around the world or whether it will take a stand in solidarity with those being submerged by globalization.

Globalization raises practical issues bearing on the way mission is to be carried out as well. A few examples: How should mission practice relate to the current drive to establish English as the global lingua franca? Are TESOL (Teachers of English to Speakers of Other Languages) programs a God-given means for entry into limited-access countries, or are they one more step solidifying Western hegemony? What of dollarification? Is it a balm for mission accountants or a further diminution of local sovereignty? What of mission coordination by massive and massively expensive global convocations? What of the technologizing of mission? Is translation of Western, predominantly English-language, theological and pastoral training materials an enabling gift or a barrier to indigenous growth? How should their dissemination into the four corners of the earth be viewed? At what point would the life and health of the church worldwide profit more if some of the vast amounts of money so spent were redirected to underwrite cultivation of locally written pastoral and theological materials and development of regional publishing firms?

Organizationally, are there instances of corporate raiding and hostile takeovers of "competing" mission agencies or of their market sectors ("fields") or of their product lines ("field" congregations, national workers, and so on)? Complaints do surface, enough to suggest that this sector of the business model has analogs in mission practice, also. Certainly there are instances of friendly takeovers: absorption of declining smaller agencies' personnel and programs by larger, more robust superagencies. What of indirect takeovers, if one may use that term for efforts to define the program, set the agenda, and specify the goals and objectives by which loosely allied agencies should operate? It is against the pressure of American "activism" in mission and the assumption of "the right to define"[62] that various contributors to *Global Missiology for the Twenty-first Century* have raised their voices.[63]

On the other hand, Protestant fragmentation is rampant. There seems to be no conceivable end in sight, in the United States, to Protestant fissioning or to its generation of new ecclesiastical and mission organizations. Again questions arise. Is the Protestant church in the United States simply moving in step with the dominant business culture, as it did a century ago? In the United States the number of charitable tax-exempt organizations grew explosively from 12,500 in 1940 to over 700,000 in 1992, "over a fifty-fold increase."[64] What does this dissipation and individualization of organizational energy and philanthropic finances portend for mission funding, staffing, and implementation? In view of increasing fragmentation, can Protestantism show that it has an ecclesiology adequate to encompass mission, on the one hand, and the mechanisms through which it seeks to express its faith, on the other?

Multiple Trajectories

When Carey proposed "floating a company" for mission, he helped unleash forces with divergent trajectories beyond his ability to foresee or control. The business model took on a life of its own, with consequences for mission and ecclesiology which continue to reverberate to our day.

On a personal level, many of the difficulties that embroiled Carey's third decade as a missionary sprang from the business model for mission. They either were caused directly or were exacerbated by failure to work out fully from the beginning what the intended scope of the proposal was to be. At the outset the business model for mission launched the Baptist Missionary Society and sent Carey to India. Ironically, within decades maturation of the business model led Carey to sever relations with the society. Viewed in retrospect, it seems that at the Baptist Missionary Society's founding the business model for mission put forward by Carey was not much more than a convenient figure of speech, supplying a paper cover for fund-raising activities by friends. During Carey's third decade in India, the model grew teeth, and it bit hard. Acrimonious questions on finances, lines and levels of authority, and the "corporate" relationships between the entities on the field and the administrators of the home society filled his days, while composing reports and conducting long-distance contests over authorized versus unauthorized publication of his correspondence wearied his soul. The basic issue of who makes decisions and whether directives can be issued by the home administration or whether it may only give advice had not been adequately addressed. Up until 1815, Carey's close friends Sutcliff, Fuller, and Ryland "had almost *been* the [Baptist Missionary Society's] Committee." They had undertaken to raise money and send recruits for the mission and, according to S. Pearce Carey, offered "frank counsel," but had, in Fuller's words, "never pretended to govern" the Serampore trio. As the committee was enlarged and the founders died, newer members of the committee were unknown to Carey and had not known him personally. They heralded fuller implementation of the *business* side of the business model for mission—what Ryland had in mind when he ruefully reflected on the day when all would "fall into the hands of mere counting-house men"[65]—and they were quickly resented by William Carey.

At issue were questions of whether the powers of oversight and administration inherent in the directors of a joint-stock company were to be made effective or not and, preeminently, where the locus of executive power lay. Did it reside in England or at Serampore? Was the Baptist Missionary Society to be essentially an auxiliary for Serampore, or was the work in India a subsidiary over which the home society must exercise strong oversight? By the time the controversies arose, the Serampore trio through their own earnings, subsidies from friends, and direct and indirect appeals to supporters, including ones in the United States, had access to much wider financial support than that supplied by the Baptist Missionary Society, and they eventually withdrew from the society. The support received by Serampore from outside Baptist Missionary Society channels foreshadowed the struggles over "specials," those appeals to congregations for extrabudgetary missionary offerings which were to bedevil denominational efforts to adopt "scientific" fund-raising and to impose businesslike efficiency in missionary support and administration during the latter nineteenth century.

From a wider social perspective, the flowering of the business model for mission was part of a broader movement toward democratization of institutions, including ecclesiastical institutions. Encrusted shackles of ecclesiastical practice were broken, and new avenues, some dramatic, emerged for lay involvement in mission. However, for independent mission agencies to be founded, established ecclesiastical prerogatives had to be relaxed. "Social space" had to be cleared to make room for them to take root. In turn, once mission agencies as voluntary associations were in place, they were instrumental in hastening the process of disestablishment.

The business model brought substantive gains for lay involvement in mission. The wealthy, through endowments and bequests, could set the direction of mission policy and programs. At the same time, penny drives enabled even the humblest to experience giving directly to mission outreach. Mission auxiliaries for raising funds and disseminating mission information were more than just a democratizing of mission: they opened new opportunities for laypersons to gain experience in running an organization. Other persons outside the recognized clergy assumed positions of direct responsibility in mission administration. Laymen such as Rufus Anderson, Henry Venn, and many lesser figures made fundamental decisions affecting missionary placement (including that of ordained missionaries), ecclesiastical forms, ecumenical relations, and mission policy previously reserved to bishops or their superiors. Mission advances created a constituency of readers, not only on the mission fields through mission schools, but in the mission societies' home countries as well. Nineteenth-century mission agencies created a widespread lay appetite for information on missionary progress and then created periodicals and broadsheets to satisfy that appetite. They thereby created an informed body of opinion that even national governments found prudent to take into account.[66]

Over the longer run, other implications of the business model for mission emerge. It is commonly acknowledged that nineteenth-century Protestant mission leaders and personnel were insufficiently self-critical theologically in their identification of God's kingdom with national aspirations. But what specifically of the business model for mission? First, by wedding mission to a particular business model, the Protestant mission movement virtually assured that it would be pulled willy-nilly through the wringer; agency after agency joined the throng in "rationalizing" mission goals and procedures in the latter nineteenth and early twentieth centuries. Following in the wake of bureaucratizing denominations, they too endeavored to become more businesslike. Second, as mission administrators labored to become more "scientific," more efficient, more streamlined, more professional, more goal focused, and, in a word, more businesslike, did mission by the same token become more distant for persons in the Protestant pew? Did the business model, which originally empowered the laity to feel close to and serve in mission, eventually serve to distance them from mission?

Third, how large is the role that mission agencies played, as part of the benevolent empire of voluntary associations, in blazing a trail for the thriving so-called parachurch of today? The church did, indeed, need to break free of the calcified structures comprising the established state churches. But that need does not bestow indiscriminate approval upon the capitalistic-style religious competition that followed as new denominations sought to establish brand identity and gain market share. Today parachurch organizations have trumped denominations, according to Michael Hamilton, as the center of gravity for U.S. evangelical Protestant religious expression.[67] Organizationally, the line of development runs from encompassing ecclesiastical institutions through denominations organized as voluntary associations toward individualistic religious entrepreneurialism. Some credit the "faith missions" of the latter nineteenth century with providing the prototype for today's parachurch.[68] However, the entrepreneurial business model for mission—to the extent that it has been the engine powering this development—was present a century earlier through the example of independent mission agencies.

What Did Carey Accomplish?

William Carey achieved symbolic significance. He stands as emblem for a style in mission (mission as a joint-stock company business venture for God), for a movement (the Protestant wing of the mission movement as contrasted with the Roman Catholic and Orthodox wings), and for an era (roughly from the end of the eighteenth century to the mid-twentieth century). Carey did not "found" Protestant mission outreach in the sense that there was none before him. To say that he was not the founder is not, however, to detract from the honor due him. As Homer Barnett concluded from his extended study of culture change, most innovations are a matter of recombining existing materials and techniques in novel ways or of finding new uses to which old materials can be put.[69] The same holds true in organizing for mission.

A comparison may be made with the "invention" of mail by Rowland Hill in 1836, two years after Carey's death. Hill was truly innovative, yet all the components of the postal service were in use before 1836, including delivery of letters, payment for service, schedules, and even an official postal service. Hill devised no new technology, yet Peter Drucker observes that "Hill did indeed create what we would now call 'mail.' . . . Mail had always been paid for by the addressee, with the fee computed according to distance and weight. . . . Hill proposed that postage should be uniform within Great Britain regardless of distance; that it be prepaid; and that the fee be paid by affixing the kind of stamp that had been used for many years to pay other fees and taxes. Overnight, mail became easy and convenient; . . . 'mail' was born."[70] After Hill the already existing elements of "mail" were put together in a new way and functioned at a new level, generating ease of mail service and quantity of mail handled beyond anything previously imagined.

Carey stands for a similar accomplishment. Carey's was not the first mission society, but his organized itself, established a presence overseas, became widely known, and endured. In Patton's business parlance, it became "a going concern." Further, if the point is to find a larger-than-life person "whose character and career captures the imagination of the Christian world," someone who conveys a "firm image . . . of what a missionary was supposed to be and do,"[71] then Carey fills the bill admirably. The breadth of the activities in which Carey engaged, either directly or through his associates, staggers the imagination. This is true even after judicious discounting to allow for the accumulation of familial and missionary mythmaking.[72]

Was Carey essential? Speaking biographically, he was crucially important to particular Indians who through his ministry came to recognize Jesus Christ as their Lord. For India, Carey was and remains of immense importance. But speaking sociologically regarding the broader Protestant missionary movement, the answer is no. What he did, others had been trying to do. Max Warren credits Carey with giving "the modern missionary movement its geographical perspective."[73] Yet the Moravians had a global perspective before Carey. The business model for mission that Carey epitomizes was caught up in social currents so massive that something like what transpired would have come to pass with him or without him. In this he is comparable to Luther. Both became useful symbols around which forces for change could coalesce and identify themselves.

Beyond the Carey Era in Mission?

Has mission among Protestants moved beyond the Carey era? The answer to that depends on what question is being asked.

Number of Agencies

If it is a question of whether the business model for mission has been laid aside, the answer is that mission agencies independent of governmental sponsorship or ecclesiastical structures continue to exist today. Globally, probably two or three new mission agencies (not all of them Protestant) are being formed every week.[74] Many are agencies intended to fill a gap overlooked by other agencies or to serve as secondary or tertiary agencies providing specialized services to first-order missionary personnel or mission agencies. If the business model for mission by itself defines the Carey era and if numbers count, then surely the Carey era is moving into its most expansive phase yet.

Linking Congregations to Mission

If the question is probing the legitimacy of setting up mission as a parallel track, separate from congregational life and ecclesiastical structures, then protests began early, and today numerous efforts are being made to bridge the gap. On this front, denominational departments of world mission, some established already in the first half of the nineteenth century, were an attempt to bring mission agencies in-house and to regain the initiative from independent mission agencies beholden to no one but themselves. It will be interesting to see how today's increasingly common "church-based" mission projects play out over time. Congregations want to be involved, and the question is the degree to which they will bypass agencies and thereby overlook lessons gained through long travail and hard-won experience. Forward-looking agencies are seeking ways to position themselves as advisory resources to congregations inclined to move out on their own. Though linkages between mission agencies themselves and between agencies and congregations are often couched in a business idiom—for example, partnerships, joint ventures, and consortia—to the degree that they are an effort to overcome a parallel-track mentality which distances mission from congregations, these efforts can be seen as an attempt to move beyond the legacy of the Carey era.

Missionary Role

Does the question address itself to the qualities expected of a prototypical missionary: sterling personal character, lengthy term of service, energetic enterprise, and level of commitment? Carey's forty years in India and breadth of engagement stand as a challenging, even daunting, model of service, blazing a trail for the heroic era in Protestant mission. However, if the "traditional career missionary"— with a lifetime commitment, pith helmet, and furlough every fifth year, working as adjunct to colonial administrations and as ecclesiastical supervisor of an overseas parish or diocese—is identified as *the* defining feature of the Carey era, then the game is surely up. Already a century ago missionary writers such as Bliss were marking the difference between Carey's day and their own in regard to patterns of missionary service (granting furloughs every five to ten years had replaced earlier lifelong terms of service as being more "economical of ability and strength").[75] Today the character and service pattern for long-term missionaries continues to evolve in the direction of increasing fluidity. God calls into being instruments for his purpose to meet the exigencies of the age and situation. Will career missionaries be "short-termed" into extinction? There would be losses if they were; but might there be gains as well?

End of Christendom

But the question of whether mission among Protestants has moved beyond Carey might be looking in a completely different direction. Might it be addressing the constellation of assumptions that comprised the Christendom model for doing mission? In the Christendom model, mission proceeds from the West; mission comes from above, from a position of power; and the missionary occupies the role of tutor and guide. These assumptions (along with a fourth bedrock conviction of the compelling need of people to hear and respond to the Gospel) provided the ideological framework within which Carey operated, as did succeeding generations of Protestant missionaries. That constellation as a seemingly coherent whole is gone. It no longer is tenable, though vestigial remains may be encountered in one setting or another.

Mission from the West. In Carey's day, mission traveled from west to east, from north to south. The West supplied missionaries; the rest of the world received them. In many ways it could hardly have been otherwise. The Christian population resided primarily in the West. Today the very success of the missionary project has planted the church around the world, and missionaries travel from every continent to every continent.

Mission from above. In Carey's day the geographical reference to the West was ideologically and culturally significant. As well as being messengers of Christ, Western missionaries were representatives of the social group that was striving to make itself the master of humankind, and they carried that sense of entitlement with them. Today the rise in numbers of non-Western missionaries is shifting practical realities in the field.

Missionary as tutor. In Carey's day and long after, the Western church assumed the role of tutor, providing instruction but also checking and correcting the copybooks of the "younger" churches. Today with gifted teachers, scholars, and writers residing in every corner of the globe, the Western church no longer has exclusive claim to the role of teacher. It needs to listen to what the Spirit is saying to and through other branches of the church rooted in other cultures as well. By calling upon insights from East and West, North and South, the global church can sharpen its understanding of God, his Word, and his mission through mutual correction and instruction.[76]

Collapse of Christendom. Wilbert Shenk writes that what Kenneth Scott Latourette called the Great Century of missionary advance (1792–1914) was a powerful last thrust of Christendom that led to its dismantling.[77] Christendom had a geopolitical locus. It consisted of a symbiotic relationship among religious, political, and cultural powers that had been Constantine's long-lasting legacy to Europe. As nineteenth-century missionaries moved out into every corner of the globe, they carried the church far beyond the bounds of Europe's "Christendom." The church moved outward, but the boundaries of Christendom did not. In its new countries of residence the church was buttressed neither by political regime nor by traditional culture. In some places it was actively persecuted. Yet over the course of the twentieth century the church outside of Europe and the West grew. The church in the south and the east has become numerically preponderant, shifting the church's demographic center of gravity away from Christendom's heartland. Further, Shenk writes, the experience of the church in mission lands had a reflexive effect "by driving Christian leaders back to first principles of Christian discipleship"[78] in ways that undercut Christendom assumptions and forced reevaluations "back home" of formerly accepted church and state linkages.

Insofar as the Carey era in mission stands for a Christendom outlook, with its uncritical blending of missionary and national purposes, the Carey era is—and on biblical grounds ought to be—over. It is to William Carey's credit that his labors, along with those of untold numbers of other missionaries, contributed to bringing about that momentous change.

In Sum

The interplay between the currently dominant Western capitalistic business model as means and Christian mission outreach as purpose presents a dual reminder. We are humbled to be reminded that we must always be open to the Spirit's freedom to work through obviously flawed instruments. Humanly and societally, there is no other kind. At the same time, we must always be vigilant lest we find ourselves working at cross-purposes to Christ's mission through thoughtless adoption of unworthy means. The church's proper stance is not to be antibusiness per se: not all conduct of business is stamped from the same mold. However, the church does well to be wary of a business- and success-intoxicated outlook lest its witness be sullied through association with the idols of the marketplace. The case is similar to that of politics. The church would not do well to be politically apathetic or stridently antipolitical. This is so even though political machinations and political powers have done much over the past two millennia to distort, suppress, and co-opt Gospel witness. The potency and pervasiveness of both business and politics in human life require both vigilance and, whether we wish it or not, participation.

The church does well to engage in serious reflection on the character of mission and the means appropriate for carrying out mission. But to become fixated on a search for the *one* right model for the conduct of mission is to chase after an illusion, a mere will-o'-the-wisp. Shenk well observes that "various mission models have been employed over the past two millennia. All reflect the socioeconomic and political contexts in which they arose."[79] All models for mission have strengths and all have weaknesses. None are wholly good, none are without drawbacks, none are neutral, and none are wholly adapted to the purposes at hand. Christ's followers must work to cultivate and enhance points of congruence with the values inherent in Christ's kingdom, and to guard against instrumental values that mock or thwart the worldwide reign of God. The missionary church today, also flawed, can be bold, remembering the condescension of God who heretofore has been pleased to work through imperfect vessels, trusting that he will do so again.

Notes

1. Max Weber, *The Protestant Ethic and the Spirit of Capitalism* (London: Allen & Unwin, 1930). At the level of lived experience, Weber found religious approval to have an immediate, almost cash, value. He writes that "admission to the congregation is recognized as an absolute guarantee of the moral qualities of a gentleman, especially of those qualities required in business matters. Baptism secures to the individual the deposits of the whole region and unlimited credit without any competition. He is a 'made man.'" Max Weber, "The Protestant Sects and the Spirit of Capitalism," in *From Max Weber: Essays in Sociology*, ed. H. H. Gerth and E. Wright Mills (New York: Oxford Univ. Press, 1958), p. 305.

2. Peter Dobkin Hall, "Moving Targets: Evangelicalism and the Transformation of American Economic Life, 1870–1920," in *More Money, More Ministry: Money and Evangelicals in Recent North American History*, ed. Larry Eskridge and Mark A. Noll (Grand Rapids: Eerdmans, 2000), pp. 159–67. See also Peter Dobkin Hall, *The Organization of American Culture, 1700–1900: Private Institutions, Elites, and the Origins of American Nationality* (New York: New York Univ. Press, 1982); and Gregory H. Singleton, "Protestant Voluntary Organizations and the Shaping of Victorian America," in *Victorian America*, ed. Daniel Walker Howe ([Philadelphia]: Univ. of Pennsylvania Press, 1976), pp. 47–58.

In nineteenth-century United States, contributions of religion to business included providing replicable patterns of organization for large-scale and widely dispersed enterprises, bolstering development of the nonprofit sector, and stimulating technological innovation and intensive capital investment in certain sectors of the economy. These aspects of religion's contribution to business lie outside the scope of this chapter, but see the work of Peter Dobkin Hall, e.g., "Religion and the Organizational Revolution in the United States," in *Sacred Companies: Organizational Aspects of Religion and Religious Aspects of Organizations*, ed. N. J. Demerath III, Peter Dobkin Hall, Terry Schmitt, and Rhys H. Williams (New York: Oxford Univ. Press, 1998), pp. 99–115; "Religion and the Origin of Voluntary Associations in the United States," Yale University, Program on Non-Profit Organizations, Paper No. 213, 1994; "Inventing the Nonprofit Sector," in *Inventing the Nonprofit Sector and Other Essays on Philanthropy, Voluntarism, and Nonprofit Organizations*, Peter Dobkin Hall (Baltimore: Johns Hopkins Univ. Press, 1992); David Paul Nord, "The Evangelical Origins of Mass Media in America,

1815–1835," *Journalism Monographs* 84 (May 1984): 1–30; and Peter J. Wosh, *Spreading the Word: The Bible Business in Nineteenth-Century America* (Ithaca, N.Y.: Cornell Univ. Press, 1994).

3. Earlier drafts of this material were presented at the U.S. Center for World Mission's forum on missiology, Pasadena, California, March 27, 2001; the Southwest Regional Meeting of the Evangelical Missiological Society, Biola University, La Mirada, California, May 4, 2001; and the Midwest Fellowship of Professors of Missions, North Park Theological Seminary, Chicago, Illinois, November 3, 2001.

I wish to express appreciation to Dr. Paul Stuehrenberg, librarian, and the faculty of Yale Divinity School for appointment as a Research Fellow. The research upon which this paper is based was greatly strengthened through access to Yale University's library holdings and especially the Divinity School's Day Missions Library.

Note that "mission" without the "s" refers to God's overarching and ongoing purpose to spread abroad knowledge of himself and his loving redemptive activity to all humankind. By extension, mission also refers to the church's mandate to participate in God's redemptive purposes. "Missions" as a collective refers to specific entities and agencies set up by Christ's followers as instruments for achieving God's redemptive purposes.

4. Lawrence M. Friedman, *A History of American Law* (New York: Simon & Schuster, 1985).

5. Daniel O'Connor, "United Society for the Propagation of the Gospel, 1701–2000: Chronicling Three Centuries of Mission," *International Bulletin of Missionary Research* 25, no. 2 (April 2001): 75.

6. Charles L. Chaney, *The Birth of Missions in America* (Pasadena, Calif.: William Carey Library, 1976).

7. Timothy George, *Faithful Witness: The Life and Mission of William Carey* (Birmingham, Ala.: New Hope, 1991), p. xvii.

8. *Candle in the Dark: The Story of William Carey* (Worcester, Pa.: Christian History Institute, 1998; distributed by Vision Video, Worcester, Pa.), 97-min. videotape.

9. George, *Faithful Witness*, pp. 140–41.

10. Ruth and Vishal Mangalwadi, *Carey, Christ, and Cultural Transformation: The Life and Influence of William Carey* (Carlisle, Cumbria, U.K.: OM Publsishing, 1993), pp. 1–8.

11. Malay Dewanji, *William Carey and the Indian Renaissance* (Delhi: ISPCK, 1996).

12. Andrew F. Walls, *The Missionary Movement in Christian History: Studies in the Transmission of Faith* (Maryknoll, N.Y.: Orbis, 1996), p. 161.

13. Among many others, see E. Daniel Potts, *Baptist Missionaries in India, 1793–1837: The History of Serampore and Its Missions* (Cambridge: Cambridge Univ. Press, 1967), pp. 79–113; William A. Smalley, *Translation as Mission: Bible Translation in the Modern Missionary Movement* (Macon, Ga.: Mercer Univ. Press, 1991), pp. 40–52; A. Christopher Smith, "A Tale of Many Models: The Missiological Significance of the Serampore Trio," *Missiology: An International Review* 20, no. 4

(October 1992): 481–500; Ralph D. Winter, "William Carey's Major Novelty," *Missiology: An International Review* 22, no. 2 (April 1994): 203–22.

14. George, *Faithful Witness*, p. 53.

15. Walls, *Missionary Movement in Christian History*, p. 246.

16. George, *Faithful Witness*, pp. 54–57.

17. D. Bruce Hindmarsh, *John Newton and the English Evangelical Tradition: Between the Conversions of Wesley and Wilberforce* (Grand Rapids: Eerdmans, 1996), pp. 119–68.

18. Walls, *The Missionary Movement in Christian History*, p. 246. Carey's 1792 argument is reprinted in George, *Faithful Witness*, p. E.5.

19. Alan Neely, "Missiology," in *Evangelical Dictionary of World Missions*, ed. A. Scott Moreau (Grand Rapids: Baker Books, 2000), p. 633. See also John Howard Yoder, "Reformation and Missions: A Literature Survey," in *Anabaptism and Mission*, ed. Wilbert Shenk (Scottdale, Pa.: Herald Press, 1984).

20. Walls, *Missionary Movement in Christian History*, p. 247.

21. Paul H. Friesen, "Society for the Propagation of the Gospel in Foreign Parts (SPG)," in *Evangelical Dictionary of World Missions*, ed. A. Scott Moreau, pp. 887–88; O'Connor, "United Society for the Propagation of the Gospel, 1701–2000," pp. 75–76, 78–79.

22. Oliver Wendell Elsbree, *The Rise of the Missionary Spirit in America: 1790–1815* (Williamsport, Pa.: Williamsport Printing, 1928), p. 49.

23. See O'Connor, "United Society for the Propagation of the Gospel, 1701–2000," pp. 78–79; J. N. Ogilvie, *Our Empire's Debt to Missions: The Duff Missionary Lecture, 1923* (London: Hodder & Stoughton, [1924]); Andrew F. Walls, "British Missions," in *Missionary Ideologies in the Imperialist Era: 1880–1920*, ed. Torben Christensen and William R. Hutchison (Struer, Denmark: Aros, 1982), pp. 159–66.

24. Chaney, *Birth of Missions in America*.

25. Kenneth B. Mulholland, "From Luther to Carey: Pietism and the Modern Missionary Movement," *Bibliotheca Sacra* 156, no. 1 (January–March 1999): 85.

26. Angelyn Dries, *The Missionary Movement in American Catholic History* (Maryknoll, N.Y.: Orbis Books, 1998).

27. William Carey, in George, *Faithful Witness*, pp. E.54–57.

28. See the essays in Shenk, ed., *Anabaptism and Mission*.

29. William J. Danker, *Profit for the Lord: Economic Activities in Moravian Missions and the Basel Mission Trading Company* (Grand Rapids: Eerdmans, 1971), pp. 13–75.

30. Paul E. Pierson, "Moravian Missions," in *Evangelical Dictionary of World Missions*, ed. A. Scott Moreau, p. 660.

31. Danker, *Profit for the Lord*, pp. 23, 27–29.

32. William Carey, in George, *Faithful Witness*, p. E.55.

33. Cf. Danker, *Profit for the Lord*, pp. 126–27.

34. Jan A. B. Jongeneel, "European-Continental Perceptions and Critiques of British and American Protestant Missions," *Exchange* 30, no. 2 (April 2001): 107.

35. Edwin Munsell Bliss, *The Missionary Enterprise: A Concise History of Its Objects, Methods, and Extension* (New York: Fleming H. Revell, 1908), pp. 66–92.

36. Jon Miller, "Class Collaboration for the Sake of Religion: Elite Control and Social Mobility in a Nineteenth-Century Colonial Mission," *Journal for Scientific Study of Religion* 29 (March 1990): 35–53.

37. Walls, *Missionary Movement in Christian History*, p. 247.

38. Harold J. Laski, *The Foundations of Sovereignty: And Other Essays* (New York: Harcourt, Brace, 1921), pp. 171–208; Friedman, *A History of American Law*, pp. 188–201, 511–31; Richard S. Tedlow, *The Rise of the American Business Corporation* (Philadelphia: Harwood Academic Publishers, 1991).

39. Richard L. Grossman and Frank T. Adams, "Exercising Power over Corporations Through State Charters," in *The Case Against the Global Economy: And for a Turn Toward the Local*, ed. Jerry Mander and Edward Goldsmith (San Francisco: Sierra Club Books, 1996), p. 385.

40. Friedman, *History of American Law*, p. 198.

41. Grossman and Adams, "Exercising Power over Corporations," pp. 374–89; Jerry Mander, "The Rules of Corporate Behavior," pp. 309–22; Tony Clarke, "Mechanisms of Corporate Rule," pp. 297–308, all in *The Case Against the Global Economy*, ed. Mander and Goldsmith.

42. Martin Marty, *Righteous Empire: The Protestant Experience in America* (New York: Dial Press, 1970), p. 96.

43. See Stephen C. Neill, *A History of Christian Missions*, revised by Owen Chadwick (London: Penguin, 1986), p. 414; Ogilvie, *Our Empire's Debt*; Max Warren, *The Missionary Movement from Britain in Modern History* (London: SCM Press, 1965).

44. E.g., Marty, *Righteous Empire*; William R. Hutchison, *Errand to the World: American Protestant Thought and Foreign Missions* (Chicago: Univ. of Chicago Press, 1987); Robert T. Handy, *A Christian America: Protestant Hopes and Historical Realities*, 2d ed. (New York: Oxford Univ. Press, 1984); Sidney E. Mead, *The Lively Experiment: The Shaping of Christianity in America* (New York: Harper & Row, 1963).

45. For a helpful typology of mission organizations, see Ralph D. Winter, "The Six Spheres of Mission Overseas," *Mission Frontiers* 20 (March–April 1998): 16–24, 40–45.

46. See Ben Primer, *Protestants and American Business Methods* (Ann Arbor, Mich.: UMI Research Press, 1979).

47. Jerry Mander, "Rules of Corporate Behavior," in *The Case Against the Global Economy*, ed. Mander and Goldsmith, pp. 315–21.

48. For sustained analysis and critique of the twentieth century's bent toward "technicizing" all aspects of human life, see the work of Jacque Ellul, especially his *Technological Society* (New York: Knopf, 1970), *Technological System* (New York: Continuum, 1980), and *Technological Bluff* (Grand Rapids: Eerdmans, 1990).

49. In William D. Taylor, ed., *Global Missiology for the Twenty-first Century: The Iguassu Dialogue* (Grand Rapids: Baker Academic Publishers, 2000).

50. James F. Engel and William A. Dyrness, *Changing the Mind of Missions: Where Have We Gone Wrong?* (Downers Grove, Ill.: InterVarsity Press, 2000).

51. A. Scott Moreau, "Putting the Survey in Perspective," in *Mission Handbook: U.S. and Canadian Ministries Overseas, 2001–2003*, ed. John A. Siewert and Dotsey Welliver, 18th ed. (Wheaton, Ill.: Evangelism and Missions Information Service, 2000), p. 45.

52. Levi T. DeCarvalho, "What's Wrong with the Label 'Managerial Missiology'?" *International Journal of Frontier Missions* 18, no. 3 (Fall 2001): 141-46.

53. Charles R. Taber, *To Understand the World, to Save the World: The Interface Between Missiology and the Social Sciences* (Harrisburg, Pa.: Trinity Press International, 2000).

54. Bliss, *Missionary Enterprise*, pp. 52–53, 66–67, 378, and elsewhere.

55. See Edward R. Dayton and David A. Fraser, *Planning Strategies for World Evangelization*, rev. ed. (Grand Rapids: Eerdmans; Monrovia, Calif.: MARC, 1990); and David B. Barrett and James W. Reapsome, *Seven Hundred Plans to Evangelize the World: The Rise of a Global Evangelization Movement* (Birmingham, Ala.: New Hope, 1988).

56. For numerous references, see Eskridge and Noll, eds., *More Money, More Ministry*.

57. For overviews, see Robin Klay and John Lunn, with Michael S. Hamilton, "American Evangelicalism and the National Economy, 1870–1997," pp. 15–38; Gary Scott Smith, "Evangelicals Confront Corporate Capitalism: Advertising, Consumerism, Stewardship, and Spirituality, 1880–1930," pp. 39–80; Peter Dobkin Hall, "Moving Targets: Evangelicalism and the Transformation of American Economic Life, 1870–1920," pp. 159–67; all in *More Money, More Ministry*, ed. Eskridge and Noll.

58. See Primer, *Protestants and American Business Methods*.

59. Cornelius H. Patton, *The Business of Missions* (New York: Macmillan, 1924), pp. vii, ix, 5.

60. Susan M. Yohn, "'Let Christian Women Set the Example in Their Own Gifts': The 'Business' of Protestant Women's Organizations," in *More Money, More Ministry*, ed. Eskridge and Noll, p. 205.

61. Yohn, "Let Christian Women Set the Example in Their Own Gifts," in *More Money, More Ministry*, ed. Eskridge and Noll, p. 181.

62. William R. Hutchison, "American Missionary Ideologies: 'Activism' as Theory, Practice, and Stereotype," in *Continuity and Discontinuity in Church History*, ed. F. Forrester Church and Timothy George (Leiden: Brill, 1979); "A Moral Equivalent for Imperialism: Americans and the Promotion of 'Christian Civilization,' 1880–1910," in *Missionary Ideologies in the Imperialist Era*, ed. Christensen and Hutchison.

63. Taylor, ed., *Global Missiology for the Twenty-first Century: The Iguassu Dialogue*.

64. Klay and Lunn, with Hamilton, "American Evangelicalism and the National Economy," in *More Money, More Ministry*, ed. Eskridge and Noll, p. 31. They continue, "By contrast, the number of for-profit corporations rose during the same period from 473,000 to three million—a sevenfold increase." Cf. Hall, *Inventing the Nonprofit Sector*, p. 13.

65. Samuel Pearce Carey, *William Carey, D.D., Fellow of the Linnean Society*, 8th ed. (London: Carey Press, 1934), pp. 337, 338.

66. Walls, *Missionary Movement in Christian History*, pp. 250–51.

67. Michael S. Hamilton, "More Money, More Ministry: The Financing of American Evangelicalism Since 1945," in *More Money, More Ministry*, ed. Eskridge and Noll, pp. 110–12; see also Klay and Lunn, with Hamilton, "American Evangelicalism and the National Economy," pp. 33–37, in the same volume; and Wesley K. Willmer and J. David Schmidt, with Martyn Smith, *The Prospering Parachurch: Enlarging the Boundaries of God's Kingdom* (San Francisco: Jossey-Bass, 1998).

68. Klay and Lunn, with Hamilton, "American Evangelicalism and the National Economy," in *More Money, More Ministry*, ed. Eskridge and Noll, p. 35.

69. Homer G. Barnett, *Innovation: The Basis of Cultural Change* (New York: McGraw-Hill, 1953).

70. Peter F. Drucker, *Innovation and Entrepreneurship: Practice and Principles* (New York: Harper & Row, 1985), pp. 243–44.

71. Chaney, *Birth of Missions in America*, p. 71.

72. For example, the report that Carey introduced the first steam engine to India in 1820 is "doubtful," according to Daniel Potts. He writes that "a steam-engine was used by the Military Department of the Government no later than March 1809." See his *Baptist Missionaries in India*, p. 112. For an assessment of Carey's approach to Bible translation, see Smalley, *Translation as Mission*, pp. 40–52, and Potts, *Baptist Missionaries in India*, pp. 79–90. For a description by Carey of the Serampore translation process, see Terry G. Carter, ed., *The Journal and Selected Letters of William Carey* (Macon, Ga.: Smith & Helwyn, 2000), p. 226.

73. Warren, *Missionary Movement from Britain*, p. 22.

74. David B. Barrett and Todd M. Johnson, "Annual Statistical Table on Global Mission: 2000," *International Bulletin of Missionary Research* 24, no. 1 (January 2000): 24–25.

75. Cf. Bliss, *Missionary Enterprise*, pp. 133–34.

76. Cf. Charles R. Taber, "Contextualization and Mutual Correction in the World Church" (paper read at the conference on Christianity as a World Religion, Calvin College, Grand Rapids, Michigan, April 28–29, 2001).

77. Wilbert R. Shenk, *Changing Frontiers of Mission* (Maryknoll, N.Y.: Orbis, 1999), pp. 142–52.

78. Ibid., p. 147.

79. Wilbert R. Shenk, ed., *The Transformation of Mission: Biblical, Theological, and Historical Foundations* (Scottdale, Pa.: Herald Press, 1993), p. 12.

Chapter Ten

A Survey of the Local Church's Involvement in Global/Local Outreach

Bruce K. Camp

This essay presents an overview of the past, present, and future practices of the local church in global/local outreach. The focus will be upon the Western evangelical church. In addition to analyzing historical and current practices of the church in outreach, the author offers possible trends and future activities of the church in missions.

Sizable and significant shifts have occurred and are occurring regarding Western evangelical local church participation in global and local outreach. Many churches seek to play a role that is different from what the local congregation historically has practiced. This new role will have profound ramifications in global/local outreach.

This essay will begin with a summary of local church practices in world evangelization during five periods of history.[1] These periods are as follows:

1. Spontaneous expansion (A.D. 33–311)
2. Expansion by the state (311–1700)
3. Influence of Pietism (1700–1800)
4. Expansion by mission structures (1789–1914)
5. The reawakening of the local church to its involvement in missions (1910–present)

After a review of the historical periods the author will explain three paradigms of current missions involvement by congregations and then offer several trends and forecasts for future involvement by churches.

Spontaneous Expansion (A.D. 33–311)

The expansion in the early church immediately following Christ's ascension can be categorized best as spontaneous. Church growth was accomplished by the witness of ordinary men and women, missionaries and local assemblies who followed the promptings of the Holy Spirit. Roland Allen writes: "In the beginning the Church was a missionary society: it added to its numbers mainly by the life and speech of its members attracting to it those who were outside."[2] James Scherer explains how this spontaneous expansion most likely occurred: "In part, it seems to have resulted from an awareness that mission was the task of ordinary Christians and of congregations acting together. Professional agents and special boards did not yet exist. Unconsciously these early Christians grasped that mission was a total activity involving preaching, teaching, baptism, personal witness and service to humanity."[3] Harry Boer believes that the early church was propelled into action based upon the work of the Holy Spirit. He argues that it was not the Great Commission that motivated people to witness; rather, it was the Pentecost event. In fact, Boer maintains that the early church leaders were reluctant to share the Gospel with non-Jewish people. He states that, as a result of the Spirit's work, the church became, by nature, a witnessing community. "Witnessing is not one among many functions or activities of the Church; it is of her essence to witness," Boer says, "and it is out of this witness that all her other activities take their rise."[4]

Whether evangelism and missions took place as a result of obedience to the Great Commission or as a by-product of the work of the Holy Spirit, the early church up until the time of Constantine spontaneously spread the Good News throughout much of the world. This spontaneous expansion is corroborated by the Scriptures and church history.

Verification by Scriptures

Sections of the Scriptures that highlight the extent of a gospel witness in the early church include the following: "Those who had been scattered [believers from the Jerusalem church] went about preaching the word" (Acts 8:4). "First, I thank my God through Jesus Christ for you all, because your faith is being proclaimed throughout the whole world" (Rom. 1:8). "For the word of the Lord has sounded forth from you [the church in Thessalonica], not only in Macedonia and Achaia, but also in every place your faith toward God has gone forth, so that we have no need to say anything" (1 Thess. 1:8). The Bible tells that the church grew both in times of peace and in times of persecution (Acts 2:41; 8:1–12). It expanded as a result of individuals declaring the Gospel wherever they happened to be *and* as a consequence of intentional witness (Acts 3:1–4:4; 16:6–10). Sometimes local assemblies were commended for their part in sounding forth the Good News; on other occasions an individual's missionary endeavors were highlighted for his ministry in furthering the gospel message (1 Thess. 1:8–10; Phil. 2:25–29). The extent of the declaration of the Gospel is described in the Scriptures as being worldwide, at least to the world as known to the early church.

J. Herbert Kane summarizes the geographic expansion of the early church in this way: "The Book of Acts opens with 120 timid disciples meeting secretly in an upper room in Jerusalem for fear of their enemies. A generation later, when the Book of Acts closes, the gospel had been preached as far west as Rome; and there was a thriving Christian church in almost every city of significance in the Eastern part of the empire. What began as a Jewish sect in A.D. 30 had grown into a world religion by A.D. 60."[5] The Scriptures give substantial indication of this rapid expansion of the church in the first century. But what the Scriptures do not tell us, historical evidence does.

Verification by Historical Documents

One of the earliest historical evidences of the rapid growth of the Christian faith is found in correspondence between Pliny the Younger, who was an imperial legate in Bithynia in Asia Minor, to Trajan Pliny, the Roman emperor who reigned from A.D. 98 to 117. Pliny the Younger mentions that Christianity had made great progress and that it had spread not only in the cities but also in the villages and the countryside.[6]

Another indication of success in the spreading of the Gospel is found in Justin's work, *The First Apology* (*ca.* 153), chapter 39, where he mentions that twelve men went out from Jerusalem and announced the Gospel to men of every nation: "For twelve illiterate men, unskilled in the art of speaking, went out from Jerusalem into the world, and by the power of God they announced to the men of every nation that they were sent by Christ to teach everyone the word of God."[7] From the evidence contained in these two documents, one could conclude that by the middle of the second century the Gospel was making such inroads throughout the world that it attracted attention from politicians and social historians alike. Who were the people that God was using to declare his message?

Missionaries

During the first two centuries of the early church, apostles (not the original twelve) ministered as itinerant missionaries. The Scriptures (in Acts 14:14, 2 Cor. 11:13, and Rev. 2:2, among others) highlight the activity of both true and false apostles.

This apostolic missionary activity is also documented in the *Didache*, written about A.D. 130–160, also known as *The Teaching of the Twelve Apostles*. This Christian writing contains moral exhortations for believers, instructions on baptism and fasts, the Lord's Prayer, and rules concerning hospitality towards apostles and prophets.[8] In addition, the document indicates that the apostles, as itinerant missionaries, were not permanently elected officials of an individual church. Rather, they were dedicated to poverty, and they could not settle down in any one place. Adolf Harnack believes that apostles, prophets, and teachers were all called to have a ministry to the church as a whole but not to have a permanent ministry like that of bishops, elders, and deacons. In addition, according to Harnack, the apostles received much honor for their ministry, a fact which, in turn, apparently resulted in abuses by others posing as apostles.[9] To correct this abuse, the *Didache* says, "But let him not stay more than one day, or if need be a second as well; if he stays three days, he is a false prophet."[10]

While the first-century work of the apostles is well documented, the missionary ministry of the apostles during the second century is largely unknown. With the exception of Pantaenus, who ministered in India, very few details of the ministry of the apostles were recorded during this period.[11] Apostle missionaries were an important element in the spread of the church in the first century. However, they were not the primary cause of the spread of the Christian faith, for laymen and women provided an even greater witnessing force.

Laymen and Laywomen

Besides the professionals (apostles, prophets, and teachers), there were others whom God used to declare his message. Harnack says: "We cannot hesitate to believe that the great mission of Christianity was in reality accomplished by means of informal missionaries."[12] Latourette concurs: "The chief agents in the expansion of Christianity appear not to have been those who made it a profession or a major part of their occupation, but men and women who earned their livelihood in some purely secular manner and spoke of their faith to those whom they met in this natural fashion."[13]

So powerful was the witness of these informal missionaries, according to Stephen Neill, that by the end of the third century 10 percent of the population of the Roman empire, estimated at 50 million, was Christian. Neill reminds the reader, however, that distribution of the Christian faith was very uneven. Some parts of Asia Minor were 50 percent Christian, while other sections of the world, such as the inland parts of Greece, were hardly penetrated with the Gospel.[14]

Overall, however, the believers apparently were able to expand the faith quite rapidly. Michael Green identifies several reasons why people may have been so attracted to the Gospel during this period: the evidence of transformed lives, the opportunity for fellowship that a church offered for all people, the joy and endurance of believers even under persecution, and spiritual power that included healings and exorcisms.[15] Henry Chadwick adds that the most potent single cause of Christian success during this time was the practical application of charity. He mentions that believers would care for the poor, widows, and orphans, would visit the brethren in prisons and mines, and would help others in times of calamity.[16] The early Christians also used several evangelistic methods to draw people into the church: public evangelism (in synagogues or open air, and through prophetic preaching as well as personal testimony), household evangelism, personal evangelism, and literary evangelism.[17]

To provide an overview of this epoch, Bavinck summarizes this period of spontaneous expansion as follows: (1) Outreach was spontaneous, and there was little reflection on the motive for missions. (2) Missionary work was primarily monocultural. (3) Political aims were not attached to missions. (4) Missionary work was not comprehensive, but rather, ministries developed out of a sense of Christian compassion in specific situations.[18]

James Bergquist postulates a reason why local congregations have not been acknowledged more for their involvement in missions: "Many if not most of the standard histories of the early church have dealt with the fact of Christian expansion, but have seldom looked in detail at how the growth was achieved."[19] He suggests that individuals look to specialized studies such as John Gager's[20] and E. Glenn Hinson's[21] in order to gain a more accurate picture of ways the local church has contributed to the expansion of Christianity. Gager maintains that while many external and internal factors contributed to the growth of Christianity, the single overriding internal factor was "the radical sense of Christian community," which was open to all but required absolute and exclusive loyalty and involved every aspect of a believer's life.[22] Hinson documents that the corporate church played a major role in evangelizing the ancient world during the first three or four centuries. He believes that churches served as missionary communities and would evangelize and incorporate persons in their areas.[23] By the mid–second century, Hinson observes, the clergy began to take a more active role in the dissemination of the gospel message. He offers four patterns of starting churches: (1) sometimes a bishop or group of bishops would send another bishop to evangelize and start a church; (2) at other times a bishop would send presbyters or deacons to start a church; (3) now and then the closest bishop to a group of Christians would instruct the group until they were ready to elect a bishop or presbyter who would complete the constitution of the church; and (4) sometimes a bishop would evangelize an area until he had prepared a suitable candidate to replace himself.[24]

In conclusion, the first era of the expansion of the church can be characterized by spontaneous witnessing by laymen and laywomen as well as intentional missionary efforts by local churches to send representatives to declare the Gospel. Global evangelism was prompted by the Holy Spirit and was not the result of a developed theology of missions. Mission agency structures had not yet come on the scene. Missions was the duty of every Christian. But what was accomplished so well by individual missionaries in the first few centuries was carried on by the state during the next fourteen centuries.

Expansion by the State (A.D. 311–1700)

During the 1,350-year-plus period of A.D. 311–1700, the vehicle of expansion changed from ordinary believers to governments. No longer were individuals primarily responsible for declaring the gospel message; rather, it became the duty of the political hierarchy. The statement has been made that the monastic movement was the primary means by which Christianity expanded during these years.[25] However, while there were many monks talking about Jesus Christ, their impact in converting non-Christians was relatively small compared to that of the political rulers. Latourette says, "The age [A.D. 500–1500] was one in which Christianity owed its spread largely to the patronage of rulers."[26] In fact, he describes this growth as "almost monotonous uniformity."[27] His synopsis of the way Christianity spread during this time was that a few individual converts were won by either merchants, captives, or monks. These new believers had little or no effect on the country as a whole. Later there was a mass movement into the church, usually led by rulers and not infrequently hastened by the use of force. Then, slowly, the masses learned about the Christian faith, usually through the ministry of the monks.[28]

Christianity as State Religion

This new mode of expansion dates back to approximately A.D. 311, the year when the Edict of Milan was decreed by Emperor Constantine. The edict granted tolerance to Christians, allowed for conversion to Christianity, and stipulated that church property that had been taken during the persecutions must be restored to the Christian communities. Before this time Christians frequently had been persecuted for their faith, the extent of persecution depending upon which emperor was in power. Now they were recognized by the state as being an official religion. Thus began the movement of Christianity toward becoming a state religion. Will Durant comments: "By his [Constantine's] aid Christianity became a state as well as a church, and the mold, for fourteen centuries, of European life and thought."[29] Williston Walker adds: "To Constantine's essentially political mind Christianity was the completion of the process of unification which had been long in progress in the empire. It had one Emperor, one law, and one citizenship for all free men. It should have one religion."[30]

When Christianity became a state religion, the churches were flooded with people who wanted, or were forced, to adopt the emperor's religion. With these new "converts" came pre-Christian belief systems that were incompatible with the Gospel. Latourette writes: "The Church, in alliance with a state of pre-Christian origin and flooded by those who had come over lightheartedly from paganism, was found acquiescing to much in its membership and in the society which it now embraced within its fold which was quite antagonistic to its professed principles."[31]

Monasticism

From within, the church faced nominalism and syncretism; from without, it now was intertwined with a political system. Moral decay inside the church led many to separate from it and form monastic movements, which originally were not intended to carry out a missionary function but to allow individuals to practice Christianity uninhibited by the evils of society around them. However, the quiet zeal of the monks attracted others, and monasteries rapidly proliferated.

Ralph Winter provides an example of the use of the monastic movement even by the state church to plant a new diocese. Gregory the Great, bishop of the diocese of Rome in A.D. 596, wanted to plant a diocesan structure in England, but he had no ministry vehicle to accomplish this goal. He requested help from Augustine, a member of the Benedictine monastery, to plant a diocesan structure in England. Winter's point is that, as strong as Gregory was in his own diocese, he had no structure to utilize to reach out in this intended mission other than a sodality.[32]

Bruce Shelly notes that the monastic calling seemed, for many, the truest form of Christian life. While abuses and evils were indeed present in the monastic movement, the immense service which the monks rendered in the spread of Christianity and development of civilization should not be underrated.[33] Philip Schaff says: "By drawing to themselves the best spirits of the time, the convents became in their good days, from the tenth well into the thirteenth century, hearthstones of piety, and the chief centers of missionary and civilizing agencies."[34]

In any discussion of monasticism such notable missionaries as Ulfilas (*ca.* 311–383), Patrick (*ca.* 389–461), Columba (521–596), Alopen (seventh century), and Boniface (680–754) warrant mention. These individuals, along with others, were instrumental in the spread of Christianity. However, as noted earlier, while the monastic movement played a major role in the expansion of the Christian faith that Protestant histories tend to ignore, governments and political forces probably played an even more significant role in world evangelism.

Government Involvement

In their quest for expansion, governments in this era also became involved in the missionary enterprise. Ruth Tucker writes: "From the beginning, Roman Catholic missions were closely tied to political and military exploits, and mass conversions were the major factor in church growth. Political leaders were sought out and through promises of military aid became nominal Christians, their subjects generally following suit."[35]

Schaff[36] provides specific examples of governments assisting the masses to become Christians. His illustrations include Charlemagne (771–814) conquering and Christianizing the Saxons; Alfred the Great in 878 forcing some thirty Vikings to accept Christianity; Ratislav, a prince in Moravia, requesting missionaries for his homeland (*ca.* 862); and Vladimir of Russia (988) forcing his countrymen to be baptized.

The Crusades and the activities of the kings of Portugal and Spain further assisted the spread of Christianity. In 1493 Pope Alexander VI issued a Demarcation Bull that divided the world into two spheres of influence: Portugal was given Africa and the East Indies, and Spain was given the New World. In return for these areas, the kings of Portugal and Spain were responsible for the conversion of the heathen in their overseas dominions. This system became known as the *Patronato*.

The civil authorities of Portugal and Spain took their Christian responsibility seriously. Joseph Schmidlin writes: "Beginning with Columbus and Vasco da Gama, all the Spanish and Portuguese explorers regarded their expeditions as likewise crusades and missionary voyages, for the purpose of seeking Christians (as well as spices) and of opposing the unbelievers with fire and sword if they rejected the Christian law which the missionaries first preached with the spiritual sword."[37]

Redefinition of Missions

While the Roman Catholic Church utilized the *Patronato* system to expand its domain, it also had at its disposal many religious orders that were willing to take the Catholic Church's message to any part of the world. Four orders, in particular, are noteworthy for their missionary endeavors. They are the Franciscans (established 1210), the Augustinians (1215), the Dominicans (1216), and the Jesuits (1540). Some consider these orders as the first missionary societies and thus date the beginning of societies around 1210. However, missionary societies of today have as their primary emphasis the spreading of the Gospel; and to argue that the Catholic orders were concerned primarily with the expansion of the church would be debatable, although it was one of their objectives.[38] The Jesuits, for example, had a great missionary tradition, but their primary goal was to render unlimited obedience to the Pope.[39] The first Catholic mission society, established by a pope for the purpose of disseminating the Christian message and under his authority, began when Pope Gregory XV in 1622 founded the Sacred Congregation for the Propagation of the Faith.[40]

Addison Soltau suggests that since Christianity was at this time a religion of the state, the church redefined the way it understood its mission. "Mission now came to be understood in a geographic sense. The unbeliever who needed to be evangelized was no longer one's neighbor, but the barbarian who lived on the borders of the empire. In a comparatively short time missions changed from being an activity of the local congregation and became a task carried on by special agents in remote areas. Unbelievers were no longer within the reach of the daily witness of the ordinary believer. This new understanding of mission dominated the thinking of the church from then on. From the fourth century missions was thought of as something distinct from the mainstream of the church's life."[41] Soltau offers an important insight to the discussion of the local church's role in missions. He maintains that missions was seen as the obligation of local churches and all believers prior to the Edict of Milan. But from the time of Constantine, missions became separate from the normal life of a church and was seen only in geographic dimensions of reaching the barbarian tribes outside of the empire. David Bosch concurs: "No local church in Europe could still undertake any mission work in its own neighborhood since the only remaining pagans now lived far across the ocean. Mission thus became the task of travellers to distant lands."[42]

Bavinck provides the following overview of the missionary activity of the church during the Middle Ages: (1) In the broadest sense, the transmission of culture was now connected with missions. (2) A political background was acquired by missions, as it was the state that initiated the work of expansion. (3) The church as a whole viewed missionary work as drawing wild and uncivilized people into the light of Christian culture and assimilating them into the Christian empire.[43]

The practice of missions changed radically during the Middle Ages. No longer was it the ministry of individuals and congregations; now it was the responsibility of governments. The imparting of Christian culture was now more important than saving souls. No longer was the goal evangelizing a neighbor, but "Christianizing" the barbarians outside of the empire. With the government and monastic involvement in missions during this period, it is easy to understand how local congregations could have lost their missions vision. Interestingly enough, local assemblies did not regain their zeal for missions even during the Reformation. In fact, it took several hundred years—well into the 1700s—before any significant change came in terms of the local church and its influence in missions.

Influence of Pietism (1700–1800)

Reformation Context

To understand properly the Pietistic era, one must go back to the Reformation, to the context within which Pietism began. Walker provides a description of the religious and economic situation and events in Germany at the beginning of the sixteenth century: papal taxation and interference with churchly appointments, unworthy clergy, monasteries in need of reform, economic unrest, rising German humanism, and the stirrings of popular religious awakenings that resulted in a deepening sense of terror about death and concern for salvation.[44]

While the Reformers were successful in bringing many people back to the early church's (biblical) view of salvation by faith alone, they did not bring individuals and congregations back to the earlier missions paradigm for evangelism either locally or globally. Latourette offers six reasons why missions was not actively considered by the Reformers:

1. In the initial stages of the movement, Protestantism was so engrossed in making a place for itself against Roman Catholicism—in working out its own theological positions, adjudicating controversies among its various leaders, and effecting the organization—that its members had little time for non-Christians outside of western Europe.

2. Several of the early leaders of Protestantism disavowed any obligation to carry the Christian message to non-Christians. Luther and Melanchthon both believed that the end of the world was so imminent that no time remained to spread the Gospel throughout the world. In addition, Luther and others believed that the command to "preach the gospel to every creature" was binding only on the original apostles and that the Gospel already had been proclaimed through out the earth. (According to Gustav Warneck, Melanchthon believed it was the duty of the civil authorities, and not the individual believers, to extend the gospel message. Zwingli's position was to allow messengers "called of God" to go at their own risk to declare the Gospel, but he was silent regarding the duty of the church to send out missionaries. Calvin also did not emphasize the missionary duty of the church. He believed that the kingdom of God was not to be advanced or maintained by the industry of men, but that it was to remain the work of God alone through "election." While a few churchmen believed and taught that the Great Commission still applied to the church, most of the better-known church fathers either did not write about the subject or were silent about it.)

3. Protestantism was preoccupied with the wars which arose out of the separation of the Protestants from the Roman Catholic Church.

4. Protestant governments were relatively indifferent to spreading the Christian message among non-Christians.

5. Protestants lacked the monastic system that, for over a thousand years, had been the chief agent for propagating the faith. Luther had rejected the monastic orders (sodalities) because of their lack of spiritual vitality.
6. Protestants were not active in missions because they had relatively little contact with non-Christians. It was not until British and Dutch sea power arose that Protestants had direct commercial contact with non-Christians.[45]

In summary, according to Latourette, theology, internal and external struggles, lack of a missionary structure, and inadequate means of expansion all resulted in the failure of the Reformers to recapture the missionary vision of the early church.

It should be noted that there were several missionary endeavors during this era, such as Calvin's sending of evangelists back to his homeland in France and commissioning four missionaries and a number of Huguenots to travel to Brazil and establish a colony to evangelize the Indians. George Fox sent three missionaries to China, and Justinian von Weltz called for the church to recognize its missionary obligation, organize a missionary society to accomplish the task, and set up a school for missionary training. Although none of these activities succeeded,[46] the Anabaptists stand out as an exception to these failures. They maintained that the Great Commission was mandatory for all believers.[47] Yet, generally speaking, it took a renewal within the Protestant churches before Protestants recaptured a vision for a lost world.

Pietism was born in this environment and in turn gave birth to the modern Protestant missions movement. Gustav Warneck writes: "It was in the age of Pietism that missions struck their first deep roots, and it is the spirit of Pietism which, after Rationalism had laid its hoar-frost on the first blossoming, again revived them, and has brought them to their present bloom."[48] Neill agrees: "The history of missions supported by Churches on the European continent begins only with the emergence of the movement called pietism."[49]

Renewal Through Pietism

The Pietist movement was a reaction against the dead orthodoxy found in the Protestant state churches at the time. Some of the major tenets of Pietism were (1) that individuals need a personal and growing relationship with God, (2) that every Christian should have an understanding of the Bible, and (3) that believers have a responsibility to live holy lives, proclaim the Gospel, and help the needy. Kane's analysis of the movement is that "[t]here can be no missionary vision without evangelistic zeal; there can be no evangelistic zeal without personal piety; there can be no personal piety without a genuine conversion experience."[50]

Pietism began with an individual's personal relationship with God and moved forward from there. As a consequence, the universal priesthood of the believer received a new emphasis, and personal Bible study, prayer, and meditation became the hallmarks of Pietists. Unfortunately, Pietists were ridiculed and labeled as heretics by religious leaders because the Pietists saw Christianity as beginning with the individual and not merely belonging to the state church.

The "Father of Pietism," Philip Spener (1635–1705), was a Lutheran pastor who in 1670 began to have a small group meet in his home for Bible reading, prayer, and a discussion of the Sunday sermons. His purpose for the group was to deepen the spiritual life of those who attended. Spener proposed the gathering of circles (small face-to-face groups) within the various congregations—*ecclesiolae in ecclesia* (circles within a church)—for Bible reading. He also suggested better training for the clergy and believed that ministers should be held responsible for their lifestyles. In addition, he recommended that since Christianity is more than intellectual knowledge, a new type of preaching was in order.[51] As a result of his many new ideas, Spener was labeled a heretic. From the beginning Spener's goal was never to separate from the church but rather to gather those from within the church who were concerned for their own salvation and the salvation of others. Pietism began to blossom, and when the universities of Saxony did not allow Pietists to enter their schools, Pietists founded their own University of Halle in 1691, formally opening it in 1694. Spener taught at the university for ten years and had August Francke join the faculty at the school.

As a result of Francke's efforts the University of Halle became the fountainhead of Pietism. Mark Noll says, "Under his leadership Halle became the center of Protestantism's most ambitious missionary endeavors to that time."[52] Walker says, "At a time when Protestants generally still failed to recognize the missionary obligation, Francke and his associates awoke to it."[53] Protestant missions began from this institution, first with the Danish-Halle Mission and then, more notably, with the Moravians.

Missionary Efforts

The Danish-Halle Mission originated as a result of King Frederick IV of Denmark's 1705 commissioning of Franz Lutkins, court chaplain of Copenhagen, to find missionaries for Danish colonies. Not finding any willing and suitable men in Denmark, Lutkins contacted Spener and Francke for assistance. They suggested two Germans: Bartholomew Ziegenbalag and Heinrich Plütschau, both of whom had studied at Halle under Francke. The German church hierarchy and the orthodox Danish church authorities opposed the missionary endeavor, primarily because of its connection with the Pietistic movement. Nevertheless, the two missionaries did make it to India in 1706, and ultimately the Danish-Halle Mission recruited sixty missionaries from Halle.

It was Francke's desire that missions would again be associated with local churches. While that dream never came to fulfillment, he was successful in helping some Christians understand that world evangelism was the duty not of the government, but of believers. Warneck writes: "True, he did not succeed in making missions the actual business of congregations or of the church, for the 'official' church declined the service. It was (and it remains still) only 'ecclesiolae in ecclesia,' which formed the missionary church at home. But there was this great advance, that from Francke's time onward missions were no longer regarded merely as a duty of the colonial governments, but as a concern of believing Christendom, that individual voluntarism (freewillinghood) was involved in them, and that this voluntarism was made active in furnishing means for their support. Without Francke the Danish mission would soon have gone to sleep again."[54]

In addition to assisting the Danish-Halle Mission, Francke and Spener were influential in the spiritual life of Count Nicolaus Ludwig von Zinzendorf (1700–1760), who became the bishop of the Moravian Church. Zinzendorf was sent to Halle at the age of ten and studied under Francke. During this time he and some other school friends formed the "Order of the Grain of Mustard Seed," a Christian fraternity dedicated to "loving the whole human family" and to spreading the Gospel.

In 1722 German-speaking Moravian refugees settled on Zinzendorf's Berthelsdorf estate and founded a community named Herrnhut (meaning "the Lord's watch"). Soon other religious refugees from various backgrounds arrived. In 1727 a revival swept the community which resulted in a passion for missions. After a trip to Copenhagen, where the count met two native Greenlanders and a Negro slave from the West Indies—each of whom pleaded for him to send missionaries to their lands—von Zinzendorf returned to his home convinced of the urgency to send out missionaries. "Within a year the first two Moravian missionaries had been commissioned to the Virgin Islands, and in the two decades that followed, the Moravians sent out more missionaries than all the Protestants (and Anglicans) had sent out in the previous two decades."[55]

Bavinck notes the following characteristics of this era:

1. Missions no longer operated in close connection with the government agencies of colonial powers.
2. The message of missions was individual repentance and faith in Christ. Other emphases were deep personal piety and anticipation of Christ's immediate return.
3. In general, the churches were not able to exert much effort in the task of missions. The state church was not inclined to risk missionary activities. Thus, missions was separated from the official church leadership and was conducted by small groups.
4. The motive for missions was the believers' need to tell others about Christ's love as experienced in their own spiritual life.
5. The Pietistic concepts of missions that excluded the questions of national community and culture were not accepted by others.[56]

Soltau offers a provocative insight on the Pietistic movement. He maintains that the movement had a nontheological missions basis and that it did not challenge the theology of its day: "Those involved in the spread of the gospel were content to do the work of missions rather than seek a broad theological base for what they believed to be God's clear and unmistakable purpose. On the one hand the church utilized theology to serve its own ends, to excuse its unwillingness to participate in missions. But on the other hand, while the Pietists remained steadfast in their pursuit, they did so without much recourse to theology. In short, the modern missionary movement was primarily a non-theological one."[57]

Scherer offers an additional insight on Pietism, pointing out that the Pietistic movement contributed to the divorce of the church and missions: "In making mission work the special concern of spiritually regenerated groups and individuals, rather than the task of the entire church, pietists contributed to a divorce between church and mission which still formally exists in many European regional churches. Even in those churches where mission has been 'integrated' into the life of the church, mission work is generally seen as the cause of special-interest groups. Pietism activated many persons in mission, but it did not establish a genuine universal priesthood based on Baptism."[58]

Expansion by Mission Structures (1789–1914)

While the expansion of the Protestant Christian faith during the first three hundred years after the Reformation was noteworthy, it was not a triumphant success. Neill writes, "In 1800 it was still by no means certain that Christianity would be successful in turning itself into a universal religion."[59] However, by the end of the century Protestant Christianity had spread like wildfire. Latourette writes: "Never before in a period of equal length had Christianity or any other religion penetrated for the first time as large an area as it had in the nineteenth century in the regions covered by this volume [the Americas, Australasia, and Africa]."[60]

A number of factors fueled the rapid expansion of the Protestant Christian faith during this era. Tucker[61] mentions that it was a time of reform movements, as the Age of Enlightenment and eighteenth-century rationalism had given way to the Age of Romanticism—a time to put theory into practice. Other religions such as Hinduism, Buddhism, and Islam were relatively quiescent, and Catholicism was actually declining in many parts of the world as the French Revolution cut the economic purse strings of Roman Catholic missions. It was a time of relative world peace. People no longer saw religion as something that the state organized and administered, but as the responsibility of each individual—to take care of his own spiritual condition and to reach out to others. Harold Cook adds, "Increasingly missions were held to be the responsibility of the organized church. The church, rather than the state, had to take up the task and carry it through, even at times in opposition to the state's desires."[62]

While there was a shift of emphasis from governments to believers, in the matter of whose duty it was to take the Christian message to the unevangelized, there was no corresponding change in attitude for many local congregations to facilitate this process. Because there was a reluctance to take up the challenge of global evangelism, mission societies arose to tackle the task. Neill comments: "[T]his was the great age of societies. In many cases the Protestant Churches as such were unable or unwilling themselves to take up the cause of missions. This was left to the voluntary societies, dependent on the initiative of consecrated individuals, and relying for financial support on the voluntary gifts of interested Christians."[63]

William Carey

During this time William Carey, the "father of modern missions," began his work. Kane says of Carey, "What Luther was to the Protestant Reformation, Carey was to the Christian missionary movement."[64] Carey was converted to Christ at the age of eighteen and left the Church of England to join the Particular Baptists. His view of missions began to evolve while reading *Captain Cook's Voyages.* As he pinpointed regions of the world on a map, he saw places where people were still living in ignorance of God. As he studied the Bible, he became convinced that the Great Commission still applied to the church in his day. He posed the following arguments for this view: first, if the command to teach all nations was restricted to the apostles, then so should be the command to baptize; second, if the command applied only to the apostles, then those who had gone out after that time had done so without warrant; third, if the command applied only to the apostles, then the promise of God's divine presence in this work would also be limited.[65]

In the spring of 1792 Carey published a small book entitled *An Enquiry into the Obligations of Christians, to Use Means for the Conversion of the Heathens,* which presented the biblical rationale and the need for world missions. One of the "means" to which he referred was mission societies. Prior to 1792, only three mission societies were in existence, all designed to operate within the colonial framework of North America. These were the Society for the Propagation of the Gospel in New England (founded in 1649), the Society for Promoting Christian Knowledge (founded in 1698 as an independent mission within the Anglican Church), and the Society for the Propagation of the Gospel in Foreign Parts (founded in 1701 as a mission agency of the Church of England).[66]

Development of Mission Societies

Ralph Winter describes Carey's *Enquiry* as the "Magna Carta of the Protestant missions movement."[67] As a result of that publication, as well as encouragement from Carey, several mission societies formed within the next thirty years: the London Missionary Society (1795), the Scottish and Glasgow Missionary Societies (1796), the Netherlands Missionary Society (1797), the Church Missionary Society (1799), the British and Foreign Bible Society (1804), the American Board of Commissioners for Foreign Missions (1810), the American Baptist Missionary Union (1814), and the American Bible Society (1826).[68]

During this time mission agencies were not governed by denominations. Even Carey's mission, the Baptist Missionary Society, while it had arisen within the denominational framework, was not sponsored or directed by the denominational hierarchy. However, as the nineteenth century progressed, denominations themselves began to initiate mission societies.[69] Some of the denominational mission societies of this era were the Wesleyan Methodists, American Congregationalists, Baptists, Presbyterians, and United Presbyterian Church of Scotland.

What began as a handful of mission societies in the 1790s had, by 1999, increased to at least 693 agencies in the United States and 121 in Canada, according to the 2001–2003 edition of the *Mission Handbook*.[70]

Why was there not more involvement by local congregations in global evangelism during Carey's era? Neill suggests that it was because the majority of Protestant missionaries in the nineteenth century were not churchmen and because the doctrine of the church played a far lesser role in theology in those days than it does today. "The emphasis was on the Church as an administrative organization, as a corporation, rather than on the Church as the divine creation, the body of Christ," says Neill.[71]

Latourette has noted some of the main features of Protestant Christianity in the nineteenth century:

1. The mission societies were influenced by individualism, the Pietistic tradition, the Wesleyan movement, and the revivals of the eighteenth and nineteenth centuries.[72]
2. Students, women, and laypeople played a significant role in mobilizing individuals to help spread the Gospel.[73]

3. The financial base of support for missions changed from governments and a few wealthy individuals, or the missionaries themselves, to hundreds of thousands of givers. For the first time, a substantial minority of laymen and clergy became interested in and contributors to world missions.[74] Latourette expounds further on this subject: "While in any one congregation those actively interested in 'missions' were generally in the minority, and although much opposition was voiced by the church members and indifference characterized the majority, in the aggregate, by the latter part of the century, the contributors to these societies numbered several hundred thousands."[75]

4. The latter part of the nineteenth century saw a rapid increase of the nondenominational societies for the spread of Christianity.[76]

While it is true that Christianity was expanding geographically during this era, this expansion was not a direct result of a strong local church emphasis. Denominations supported missionary endeavors, but the major efforts in expansion came from individuals and independent societies. The chasm between the local church and missions that began during the reign of Constantine continued through what might be called the age of mission societies. A theology of missions that included the local church had yet to be developed.

The Reawakening of the Local Church to Its Involvement in Missions (1910–Present)

While early Christian churches played a significant role in world evangelism during the first few centuries A.D., the role of the church was minimal during the following sixteen hundred years. It was not until 1910 and the first World Missionary Conference that the local church began to reawaken to its role in world missions. Most ecumenical churches trace their missions histories back to this 1910 conference. This, together with several subsequent missions conferences, in fact, facilitated the church's movement in world evangelism from virtual noninterest to active involvement in the missionary enterprise. This section will briefly review the role of the church in missions from an evangelical conference perspective and then articulate the activities of churches in missions from a practical perspective.

World Missionary Conference (1910)

In June of 1910 over twelve hundred individuals from 159 missionary societies gathered in Edinburgh, Scotland, for what proved to be an extremely significant missionary conference. It was a conference devoted to strategizing a final campaign to present the offer of salvation to everyone on the face of the earth.[77] But the Edinburgh conference began an emphasis on missionary cooperation without a prior doctrinal consensus between the many denominations in attendance. Indeed, there was very little discussion of theology.

One of the conference's greatest accomplishments was the establishment of a Continuation Committee that eventually became the International Missionary Council (IMC). It was set up to promote international missionary cooperation. The IMC had no doctrinal guidelines of its own; its aim was "to further the proclamation to the whole world of the Gospel of Jesus Christ, to the end that all men may believe in him and be saved."[78] However, because of a lack of doctrinal agreement, important differences would emerge between the many denominations desiring to cooperate.

By the conclusion of the World Missionary Conference, delegates agreed that the responsibility for the task of world missions fell upon the church as a whole. While local assemblies were charged to take part in this commission, they were *not viewed as the only catalyst* in world evangelization. In the final message of the conference the emphasis was made that the responsibility for evangelism "is committed to all and each within the Christian family; and it is incumbent on every member of the Church. . . . The missionary task demands from every Christian, and from every congregation, a change in the existing scale of missionary zeal and service."[79]

Wheaton Congress (1966)

Building upon the foundation laid at the 1910 Edinburgh conference, the Wheaton Congress has been regarded by evangelicals as a key event that has resulted in current-day evangelical cooperation in missions. The Wheaton Congress marked the beginning of evangelicals coming together to discuss global evangelism on a large scale. It was here that the importance of the local assembly in world missions was widely recognized. Two American inter-mission organizations, the Interdenominational Foreign Mission Association (IFMA) and the Evangelical Foreign Missions Association (EFMA), representing thirteen thousand overseas missionaries, jointly sponsored a conference at Wheaton College in Illinois and entitled it "The Congress on the Church's World-Wide Mission." Nine hundred thirty-eight delegates from seventy-one countries attended the conference. Harold Lindsell wrote the following five points as rationale for the necessity of such a conference:

1. In the events of the past decade which culminated in the demise of the International Missionary Council in 1961,
2. In the subsequent need for evangelicals to define their own position in light of this change,
3. In the desire for a closer fellowship of evangelicals committed to fulfill the terms of the Great Commission,
4. In the realization that changing modes of thought require a reaffirmation of Biblical missionary principles and a re-examination of missionary attitudes,
5. In the conviction of the continually pressing spiritual needs of a world that is shrinking in size but increasing in complexity,
   Therefore it becomes the duty of evangelical leadership to make plain to the world their theory, strategy and practice of the Church's universal mission.[80]

The Wheaton Declaration, which was unanimously adopted by the delegates, stated that the local church has primary responsibility for world evangelism. One of its more pointed statements in this regard is: "In the Acts of the Apostles local congregations were God's primary agents for the widespread dissemination of the gospel. The total mobilization of the people and resources of the churches in effective, continuous evangelistic outreach is indispensable to the evangelization of the world (Acts 17:1–4 and I Thessalonians 1:8–9; Ephesians 4:16)."[81]

Berlin Congress (1966)

From October 24 to November 4, 1966, evangelicals held another significant missions convention in Berlin, Germany. *Christianity Today* magazine sponsored the convention, entitled "The Berlin World Congress on Evangelism," which drew over eleven hundred evangelical leaders from over a hundred countries. The theme of the congress was "One Race, One Gospel, One Task." In his opening address Billy Graham, the honorary chairman of the conference, spelled out the necessity for convening the congress at that time. He stated that there was confusion in the church worldwide as to the very meaning, message, and method of evangelism as well as the strategy of the enemy of evangelism.[82]

At Berlin many messages exhorted the delegates to practice evangelism, but little was said about the role of the local church in missions and evangelism. Bassham comments on this lack of emphasis on the local church: "Berlin's participants assumed the place of the church in the total process of evangelism. The church received little attention in the theological addresses. Yet probably most would have agreed with the theological presuppositions made by Künneth about the church when he stated: '"Gospel" and "Church" . . . stand in an indissoluble relationship. The Gospel points to the Church, and the Church derives from the Gospel.'"[83]

Green Lake (1971)

For evangelicals the issue of the local church's role in missions, from a theological viewpoint, surfaced for the first time in the 1960s at both the Wheaton and Berlin conferences. Still, a theological rationale for local church involvement in global evangelism needed further clarification. This clarification began in the 1970s and 1980s. Green Lake '71 (GL '71) was a significant conference because it brought this issue to the forefront.

An important convention occurred for U.S. mission agency executives in Green Lake, Wisconsin, from September 27 through October 1, 1971, as delegates tried to address many significant issues related to both the "home church" and the "receiving church." Sponsored by the IFMA and EFMA, GL '71 was designed to address, on the one hand, tensions in the relationship between the local church in the United States and the mission agency (church/mission) and, on the other hand, tensions between the mission agency and the national church (agency/church).

The IFMA prepared a list of subjects with primary and subsidiary questions for each topic and sent the list to its constituency for study before the convention. The topics and primary questions which related to the church/mission tension were:

1. Recruitment: Has consideration been given to the wide variety of churches, pastors and officers with which the IFMA deals? What problem is presented by the mobility of students and consequent limited contacts with any one church? How should the largely impersonal relationship between mission and churches regarding recruits be improved? How can the mission help the many candidates who apparently fail to demonstrate in their home churches qualifying gifts for missionary service?

2. Mission Structure: How can the mission increase the voice of a local church in mission affairs? How can communications between the church and mission on official matters be improved? How can meaningful involvement of churches or pastors in mission affairs be secured considering the diversity of structures in churches and missions?

3. Finances and Publication: Has the mission defined the responsibility of the church and the mission in the securing of support for missionaries, candidates and administrative expenses? How can communication be improved between home churches and mission boards? How can help be given to meet the support needs of nationals who replace missionaries in overseas service functions? How can IFMA missions adequately project a favorable contemporary image to supporting churches?

4. Mission Personnel: How can local churches receive from mission agencies an accounting of the stewardship of missionary manpower? How can the missionary on furlough best serve within the program of a local church? How can the church exercise a spiritual ministry to the children of missionaries in North America in post–high school training? How can the mission and the local sending church cooperate to minister to the specific pastoral care needs of the missionary family during furlough?[84]

It is apparent that these questions were asked from a practical perspective. But the primary thesis question—Biblically, how should a church be involved in global evangelism?—was not addressed.

Perhaps this is why Harvie Conn writes: "The only radical theological perspectives were provided by Edmund P. Clowney's morning messages on 'The Biblical Doctrine of the Ministry of the Church (Biblical Ecclesiology and the Crisis in Missions).' And, judging from the essays published after Green Lake, they played little normative part in the structuring of solutions. The activism of evangelical missions thinking continued to present the picture of a 'church without theology' and a 'mission without theology.' Biblical theology functioned on a devotional, not a canonical level." Conn concludes: "We are convinced that, as long as evangelical missions theory continues to develop on a purely functional level, without the operative judgment of biblical theology, the tension areas cannot be isolated and solutions cannot be found. We are also convinced that the tension areas of a basic sort are theological in nature."[85]

Lausanne I (1974)

The Lausanne International Congress on World Evangelism, held in Lausanne, Switzerland, in July of 1974, featured Billy Graham as the honorary chairman and the primary catalyst for the gathering. He had four hopes for this congress: (1) to see the congress frame a biblical declaration on evangelism, (2) to see the church challenged to complete the task of world evangelization, (3) to state the relationship between evangelism and social responsibility, and (4) to develop a new koinonia or fellowship among evangelicals of all persuasions throughout the world.[86]

While Berlin 1966 was predominantly Western in representation, Lausanne 1974 was not. The 2,700 delegates and 1,000 observers, guests, and staff came from 150 countries. Close to 50 percent of the participants were from the Two-Thirds World.

Three of the most significant outcomes of the Lausanne conference were (1) the emphasis on the unreached peoples and the priority of cross-cultural evangelism, (2) the formation of the Lausanne Committee for World Evangelization (LCWE), and (3) the adoption of the Lausanne Covenant (a statement of evangelical mission theology). Saphir Athyal, a leader in the Lausanne movement and the principal of Union Biblical Seminary in India, writes about the covenant: "This historical statement served as a theological basis for the evangelicals for their fuller understanding of the nature of the gospel and the task of evangelization. Thus, the covenant has since become a basis for fellowship and cooperation in world evangelization."[87] The covenant is divided into fifteen sections. Of these, two deal directly with the issue of the local church's involvement in global evangelism: section 6, "The Church and Evangelism," and section 8, "Churches in Evangelistic Partnership." Because of the significance of the Lausanne Covenant and its recognition of the local congregation's role in evangelism, both sections are quoted below.

The Church and Evangelism (Clause 6)

We affirm that Christ sends his redeemed people into the world as the Father sent him, and that this calls for a similar and deep and costly penetration of the world. We need to break out of our ecclesiastical ghettos and permeate non-Christian society. In the church's mission of sacrificial service evangelism is primary. World evangelization requires the whole church to take the whole Gospel to the whole world. The church is at the very center of God's cosmic purpose and is his appointed means of spreading the Gospel. But a church which preaches the Cross must itself be marked by the Cross. It becomes a stumbling block to evangelism when it betrays the Gospel or lacks a living faith in God, a genuine love for people, or scrupulous honesty in all things including promotion and finance. The church is the community of God's people rather than an institution, and must not be identified with any particular culture, social or political system, or human ideology.[88]

Howard Snyder's address, entitled "The Church as God's Agent in Evangelism," dealt specifically with the question of parachurch structures in evangelism.[89] Several of the major thoughts in section 6 were adopted from his address. Snyder believes that the church is the community of God's people, not institutional structures. The institutional structures are the parachurch.[90] He argues from the biblical perspective that evangelism can best be understood as the outgrowth of the normal body life of the church.[91] Furthermore, neither denominational structures nor paradenominational structures such as Christian schools, evangelistic associations, and missionary societies existed in New Testament days. Therefore, it should be self-evident, according to Snyder, that such structures have no explicit biblical basis.[92] Finally, the church is God's agent of evangelism as it truly becomes the community of God's people.[93]

Peter Savage, coordinator of the Latin American Theological Fraternity, was asked to expand on the topic "The Church and

Evangelism." In writing about whether the church is adequate for the evangelistic task or if the task should be given to the para-ecclesiastical structures, Savage suggests that giving the task to parachurch agencies would not take into account the biblical view of the local church and would also fail to acknowledge that "[t]he greatest outreach in evangelism has often sprung from community churches." He concludes by saying: "The church today finds itself faced with two great inter-related challenges: the challenge of the massive task of world evangelisation and the challenge of being the truly biblical community described in Scripture that is capable of carrying out that task."[94]

While the issue of the church and evangelism is discussed in clause 6 of the Lausanne Covenant, clause 8 explains the nature of evangelistic partnership, especially considering the role of the younger churches.

Churches in Evangelistic Partnership (Clause 8)

We rejoice that a new missionary era has dawned. The dominant role of western missions is fast disappearing. God is raising up from the younger churches a great new resource for world evangelisation, and is thus demonstrating that the responsibility to evangelise belongs to the whole body of Christ. All churches should therefore be asking God and themselves what they should be doing to reach their own area and to send missionaries to other parts of the world. A re-evaluation of our missionary responsibility and role should be continuous. Thus a growing partnership of churches will develop and the universal character of Christ's church will be more clearly exhibited. We also thank God for agencies that labour in Bible translation, theological education, the mass media, Christian literature, evangelism, missions, church renewal and other specialist fields. They too should engage in a constant self-examination to evaluate their effectiveness as part of the Church's mission.[95]

Costas elaborates on this clause: "The centrality of God's redemptive mission in the message of the Bible also underscores the importance of the church as a missionary agent."[96]

As seen, the Lausanne Covenant stresses the church's duty in evangelism. This emphasis differs from the emphasis at Berlin 1966, where personal evangelism was stressed. Johnston wrote, about Lausanne, that a strong ecclesiology permeated the congress, covenant, and Continuation Committee deliberations; the Planning Committee declared their intention to convene the congress "as members of Christ's body."[97]

The Lausanne '74 congress was, indeed, significant to the evolving discussion of the local church in missions theology. Snyder reminded those in attendance of the biblical view of the church regarding missions; the Lausanne Covenant stated that the church is God's appointed means to spread the Gospel. Stott even questioned the indefinite survival of parachurch agencies in his commentary on the covenant.[98] All these items and others indicate a renewed perspective on the involvement of local congregations in world evangelism.

Pattaya (1980)

The LCWE sponsored its second Consultation on World Evangelism at Pattaya, Thailand, in June of 1980, with over eight hundred delegates and observers meeting to discuss the development of new strategies for cross-cultural evangelism and to evaluate the progress of world evangelization since Lausanne 1974.

Two items pertinent to this discussion came out of the Pattaya consultation. First, the Thailand Statement recognized the local church as "the principal agency for evangelism, whose total membership must therefore be mobilized and trained."[99] Second, *Co-operating in World Evangelization: A Handbook on Church/Para-church Relationships* was published. This Lausanne occasional paper, number 24, published in 1983, was the first book that highlighted the tensions between local churches and mission agencies. These tensions included dogmatism about nonessentials and differing scriptural interpretations, the threat of conflicting authorities, the harmfulness of strained relationships, rivalry between ministries, and suspicion over finances.

Overall, the book is written from a practical rather than a theological perspective. Stott, in the "Theological Preamble," notes that the legitimacy of parachurch agencies is still under debate. From his point of view, the key question is regarding who should initiate and operate the specialist organizations. Stott believes that the argument in favor of parachurch organizations is largely historical, while the contrary argument begins with the Scriptures. His solution is to place agencies on a graded axis: "*independence of the church is bad, co-operation with the church is better, service as an arm of the church is best."* Stott concludes: "Here then are the two extremes to be avoided. The tendency of the 'establishment' to control individual initiatives runs the risk of *quenching the Spirit* [italics in original]. The tendency of voluntary organisations to insist on their independence runs the risk of *ignoring the Body.* It is the age-old tension between authority and freedom. To quench the Spirit and to ignore the Body are both serious sins; they grieve the Christ whose Body and Spirit they are."[100]

A pertinent observation about the role of the local church in world evangelism in connection with Lausanne II is offered by Scherer: "In my opinion the wholistic emphasis picked up by Lausanne at Manila 1989 (whole gospel—whole church—whole world, etc.) and emphasized by the IMC after Willingen 1952 is of limited help because while it makes the "whole church" responsible for mission, it stops short of demonstrating how local congregations can effectively carry out the missionary obligation."[101] Scherer's analysis of the Lausanne movement from 1966 to 1986, with regard to the local church's role in missions, is encouraging. He writes: "Evangelicals now moved increasingly toward a church-centered mission stance in which the local church was viewed as the principal agent in evangelism, and elements from the older IMC formulas were taken over. Parachurch groups were held accountable for maintaining a spirit of Christian unity, and urged to move toward something like de facto integration with local churches."[102] If his observation was correct, then the next several years should have shown signs of local church activity outside of the Lausanne umbrella; unfortunately, controversy continued instead.

Wheaton (1983)

In June of 1983 the World Evangelical Fellowship sponsored a conference in Wheaton, Illinois: "The Nature and Mission of the Church." Over half of the 320 participants came from non-Western churches. Delegates were divided into three working groups or "consultations" to deliberate over (1) the church in its local setting, (2) the church in new frontiers for missions, and (3) the church in response to human need. John Gration believes that Wheaton '83 is very significant to the discussion of church and parachurch relationships: "The growing crescendo of interest and attention given to this subject [church and parachurch relationships] across the decade and a half of this brief survey reaches its climax in the

Wheaton '83 Congress on the Nature and Mission of the Church."[103] A news release about the conference, dated July 19, 1983, reads, "'The local church is God's primary agent in his mission for the world': this was the consensus of the participants in the Wheaton '83 conference."[104]

While many speakers, such as Wilson Chow, Valdir Steuernagel, Theodore Williams, Peter Kuzmic, Luis Bush, and Tokunboh Adeyemo, spoke about various facets of the local church's ministry, it was Pablo Pérez's presentation, "The Relationship Between Church and Para-Church: A Theological Reflection," that was most germane to the subject of the local church having primary responsibility in world evangelism. He offered an important insight about the nature of parachurch agencies, based on pragmatic reasoning, when he exclaimed: "Sad to say, the very pragmatic consideration that the para-church agencies are doing efficiently what the church as a whole has not been able to do, seems to be more important than trying to determine their nature. If there cannot be found a Biblical basis for this nature, are these agencies to disappear from the picture or should we learn to live with these 'abnormalities'?"[105]

A brief summary of the conference discussions about the local church was released in a Wheaton '83 newsletter entitled "Letter to the Churches" where the mission of the universal church, expressed in local assemblies, was stated to be that of the Great Commission. With regard to cooperation between local churches and mission agencies, the conference declared about agencies (both denominational and parachurch): "We view them as servant agencies supplementing the mission of the church to the world. Let us bear in mind that para-church agencies have a responsibility to relate their ministries to the full fellowship of the church."[106]

Indeed, Gration was correct in his observation that the topic of the local church and parachurch relationship reached its climax in 1983 at Wheaton. The conference was the first attempt to apply a biblical understanding of the local church and its duty to minister in the world. While the subject may have reached its climax at this conference, it has not diminished in importance, and the issue continues to be debated and discussed to this day.

Lausanne II (1989)

The International Congress on World Evangelization held in Manila, Philippines, in July of 1989 was the second international congress sponsored by the Lausanne Committee for World Evangelization. More than 4,300 Christians from 173 nations participated. The large number of women (22 percent) and younger leaders under age forty-five (50 percent) gave special significance to this gathering.[107]

While Lausanne I gave a summons to the local church to involve itself in world evangelism, Lausanne II provided an even more pronounced emphasis. Not only were plenary sessions devoted to the subject, but the "Manila Manifesto" and a special track on the local church highlighted the congregational structure's obligation in world missions.

Jong-Yun Lee, a Korean pastor and conference speaker, stated: "Each local church visibly represents the whole church. When we call for 'The Whole Church to Take the Whole Gospel to the Whole World,' we are calling for each and every church to take the whole gospel to the whole world. . . . The local church is primary both in terms of the call and the task of workers in the harvest field. The call is issued from within the local church and the task is to plant more local churches."[108]

Eduardo Maling, a pastor in the Philippines and plenary conference speaker, told the audience that the local church is the key to world evangelization: "The church is God's instrument, chosen to demonstrate and declare to the whole world Jesus Christ, the Saviour and Lord."[109]

In a video presentation on the primacy of the local church in mission, Luis Bush discussed what God was doing in the world, especially in Latin America, Asia, and Africa. Bush concluded, "It is the local church that is having a key role in the effort of missions launching out from these different continents."[110]

The Manila Manifesto, similarly to the Lausanne Covenant, outlines what the delegates at the conference signed as a public declaration of their convictions. Two declarations in particular relate to the subject of the local church having primary responsibility in world evangelization. They are numbers 16 and 17:

16. We affirm that every Christian congregation must turn itself outward to its local community in evangelistic witness and compassionate service.

17. We affirm the urgent need for churches, mission agencies, and other Christian organizations to cooperate in

evangelism and social action, repudiating competition and avoiding duplication.[111]

The manifesto gives emphasis to the local church reaching its own community but broadens the responsibility of spreading the Gospel in the world to both congregations and agencies.

The summary of the track on the local church, coordinated by James Wong, Canon in the Anglican Church of Singapore, draws the following conclusions about the local church:

- We believe that the local church is the God-ordained channel to fulfill the Great Commission.
- We believe that the local church bears primary responsibility for the spread of the gospel.
- We believe the local church is God's primary instrument for world evangelization.
- Church and parachurch organizations should also work together, for the parachurch agency is a servant of the church, while the church can benefit from its specialist expertise.[112]

Lausanne II, like Lausanne I fifteen years prior, saw the local church as the primary vehicle God intends to use to reach the world with his Gospel. Both congresses stressed the importance of local assemblies being involved in the Great Commission. Participants at the two events stated that it is the duty of churches to reach the lost with the Good News, and at Lausanne II, that agencies are servants of the church.

While the growing recognition of the role of the local church in missions is encouraging, it should be noted that at both events, as well as at the other major evangelical meetings discussed above, there was no in-depth study of the biblical role of the local church in missions. Scriptural texts were given at all the gatherings to support the local church's involvement in missions, but these were used as proof texts rather than providing a theological rationale or analysis. Many evangelicals have returned to the early church perspective that the local church has primary responsibility in world evangelism. Yet throughout the many writings suggesting such a position, one looks in vain for a detailed scriptural analysis to support it.

Since 1910 many evangelicals have felt a growing desire that local churches be more significantly involved in missions. This concern was first *expressed* in the 1960s at the Wheaton Congress (1966) and the Berlin Congress (1966), *grew* in the 1970s at the Green Lake Conference (1971) and Lausanne I (1974), and *blossomed* in the 1980s at Pattaya (1980), Wheaton (1983), and Lausanne II (1989).

This summary of the historical practices of the local church yields several important conclusions. First, the expansion of the Christian faith was accomplished primarily via three movements: the spontaneous witness of individual believers, the conquering and colonizing activities of state governments, and the work of mission societies. Local churches have been involved in the growth of Christianity sporadically, but they have not played a significant role throughout history. Only during the nineteenth century did God begin to use mission agencies as his primary means to spread the Gospel.

Second, it is important to keep in mind the distinction between evangelism and missions. Just as the apostle Paul planted a congregation in Thessalonica and then from that church the gospel message spread out to new communities, so a similar pattern of Christian expression can be observed throughout church history. Often it was missionaries who would pioneer the spread of the Gospel to a new area and plant a church, and then the church would be the major catalyst to evangelize the surrounding region.

Third, a major transition occurred in the life of the Christian church in A.D. 311 when Christianity was recognized as a state religion by Constantine's decree, the Edict of Milan. Previous to his decree the spread of the Christian faith was the obligation of individual believers and local assemblies. After 311 the duty to Christianize people was inherited by the state. No longer were nonbelievers acknowledged as neighbors; now, they were perceived as outside of the Christian empire and therefore to be conquered and "Christianized." Missions thus became distinct from the normal life of the church.

Fourth, when individual believers *did* rediscover the command to "make disciples in every nation" during the age of Pietism, it was understood as the obligation of a few enthusiasts, not the work of every Christian. This understanding continues in many congregations today. The modern missionary movement has its origin in the Pietistic movement, when nonchurch structures composed of a few enthusiasts began to plant churches in various parts of the world.

Fifth, a well-developed theology of missions that includes the local church has yet to be formulated. When Christianity first spread, it was by spontaneous expansion, with little reflection on a missionary theology. Outreach simply happened. With the advent of governments that assumed the responsibility for Christianizing their citizens, a theological study of the subject was not warranted. As Protestants rediscovered the Great Commission during the age of Pietism (ca.1694) and the era of William Carey (1761–1834), Matthew 28:18–20 became a primary text to support global missions. However, the challenge of world evangelism, again, belonged to a few, not to the whole church. At present, while discussions have taken place about the missionary nature and duty of the universal church, a comprehensive theology of missions from a local church perspective has not been written from either an ecumenical or an evangelical point of view.

Sixth, though the structures for carrying out missions have evolved over the last two millennia, the purpose of God was not thwarted. If his people were not going to be faithful in fulfilling the Great Commission, he found other ways to declare his message. Sometimes his declaration was made through volunteers; at other times it was through slaves who were taken by force by opposing armies. Occasionally God would use local bodies of believers, such as the Moravians or Anabaptists; at other times he would use monks, governments, or mission societies. God's desire to see men and women come into a personal relationship with his Son would not be circumvented by the inactivity of the local body of Christ.

History proves useful when explaining what has already occurred. Yet how are churches currently involved in world evangelization? What paradigms of global/local ministry do congregations utilize?

Paradigm Shifts

In the last twenty-five years local evangelical churches have begun to make major paradigm shifts with regard to their role in obeying the Great Commission. More specifically, numerous congregations have conducted their global missions activities based upon two paradigms: supporting and sending. Currently a third, the synergistic or focused paradigm, continues to emerge. Presented in this section is a descriptive analysis of these paradigms.[113]

A major shift occurring within churches is that they increasingly seek a more active responsibility in world missions. Granted, many are willing to take a less active role. But many are not. The paradigms presented here represent a continuum of

Summary of Paradigm Shifts

PARADIGMS	SUPPORTING	SENDING	SYNERGISTIC
Key word	"They"	"My"	"We"
Description	Dependent	Independent	Interdependent
Key Question	What is *their* game plan?	What is *my church's* plan?	What is *our* role in obeying the Great Commission?
Mission Agency	High loyalty to a given agency	Awareness that an agency is one of many	Recognition of a global Christian community
Decision Making	Agency making decisions	Partnership with an agency	Forming a strategic ministry
Geographical Support	Support outside the region	Support within the region	Support of non-Western missionaries
Philosophical Support	Support missionaries	Recruit/train/ support our own	Partnership with others (Americans/nationals)
Congregational Outreach	Nondirective philosophy	Directive philosophy	"Empower church constituency" philosophy
Relationships	Superficial contact with missionaries	Quality/quantity time with our missionaries	Make a significant impact on the non-Christian world
Missions Education	By outsiders	By insiders and quality teachers	High-tech and high-touch
Church Participation	Emphasis on goers	Emphasis on goers and senders	Emphasis on everyone participating in outreach
Focus on	Money	People	Opportunity
Strategy	No church strategy	A single church strategy	Multipronged strategy
Signs of Success	Bigger budgets for missions and better missions conferences	Bigger budgets and more missionaries sent	Souls saved and churches planted

missions activities. No congregation fits one paradigm entirely and perfectly. A particular church may utilize selected ideas within each of the three paradigms. For the sake of illustration, however, the paradigms will be presented as if each one is an all-inclusive pattern of a particular church's activities. Thus, while these paradigms overlap and oversimplify reality, they enable us to make certain observations.

Paradigm 1: The Supporting Church

The supporting paradigm is still the predominant model for evangelical churches. From this perspective, the role of the local church in world missions is understood largely as supporting. The involvement is passive. The prevailing question is "What is *their* game plan?" In other words, churches look to mission agencies to set the missions agenda. Basically, whatever agencies want to do is accepted as correct, because they are perceived to be the experts. A descriptive summary word for this model is "dependence" in regard to the way the local church conducts its global/local activities through the agencies. The way that churches perceive success in this model is that they have bigger budgets and better missions conferences each year.

The age group that responds best to this model is believers over sixty years of age. The Boomer generation does not enthusiastically support it as it is currently practiced. James Engle comments: "[I]t is time for churches still functioning in the mode of Paradigm 1 (the vast majority) to recognize that they are seriously out of phase with today's missions realities."[114]

Paradigm 2: The Sending Church

Instead of maintaining a supporting role, many churches in the 1980s increasingly began to assume a sending role in world missions. The key word became "my," and the key question became "What is *my church's* plan?" In this model, churches have shifted from a more dependent mode to an independent one in their relationship to mission agencies. Congregations utilize the services of mission agencies when they want to, but churches are no longer dependent on any one agency. Some churches send their own missionaries, bypassing the agencies altogether.

Several factors characterize this second paradigm. The agency to which a church was loyal in the previous decade now becomes one of many. Denominational and/or organizational loyalty is predominantly a notion of the past for churches that have accepted the sending paradigm. Financial support is regionalized. Congregations insist upon both quantity and quality time with their missionaries.

Missions education and partnerships also changed significantly. Church members began to speak about involvement in missions based upon their missions training in a Perspectives class or on a short-term missions trip. Congregations still may work with agencies, but only as equal partners. If an agency does not accept this new role of the church as a partner, then a church may opt to find an agency that cooperates with the church's sending task. The signs of success for this model are bigger budgets and more missionaries sent.

Paradigm 3: The Synergistic (Focused) Church

The definition of the synergistic paradigm contains the idea of joint action by agents that, when taken together, increases the effectiveness of both. This model starts with a recognition of the end goal of souls saved and churches planted. It focuses on the end result (world evangelization), not on the means to the end (such as sending missionaries). Synergistic churches want to use all the resources at their disposal to accomplish the task.

The key word of this paradigm is "we." The question the church asks is "What is *our* role in obeying the Great Commission?" Instead of trying to accomplish numerous missions activities by themselves, synergistic churches focus on a few items they can do well. They have emotional ownership of these activities. They partner with others and combine their efforts to produce greater effectiveness than either party can accomplish independently. The partnership model assumes an interdependent perspective. The churches realize that they do not have to respond to every need—and that they are not able to—and so instead, concentrate their energies and finances on a few needs. Frequently such concentration of energies and finances is channeled to evangelize an unreached people.

Synergistic churches desire to make a significant impact on the non-Christian world. They adopt various approaches to missions, including an entrepreneurial one. Congregations utilizing the synergistic paradigm likely will reflect many of the Boomers' values, such as a desire for multiple options in ministry, appreciation for diversity among individuals (men and women, lay and professional, ethnic and Anglo), desire for change, and a hope for significance in their lives.[115]

Engel grasps the implications of this model. He writes: "This paradigm presents major challenges to mission agencies which are still functioning in the resource-funneling mode of Paradigm 1. Proactive churches have little interest in passive involvement and hence will be increasingly nonreceptive unless there are distinct opportunities for mutually beneficial relationships. In other words, the onus is placed on the agency to let the church become a part of the action and demonstrate that real partnership can be established."[116]

Reasons for the shift in attitudes toward this new model include technological advances that allow for ease of communication and travel, a different set of values of Boomers and Generation Xers, and a wealth effect that allows many people the option of travel (such as for short-term missions).

It is readily acknowledged that no one paradigm is best for every church to follow. As churches consider their role in global/local outreach, they will need to ponder the pros and cons of each of these models. Probably many churches will want to use elements from all three.

Now that the church's practice in missions has been surveyed from both a historical and a present-day perspective, the question needs to be addressed: How will Western evangelical churches participate in global/local outreach in the future?

Trends and Forecasts

Below are macropredictions that many proactive churches may choose in the coming years regarding issues relating to the local church and world evangelization. Some individuals may interpret these as positive changes; others will view them as negative. They are listed to suggest what the future increasingly might bring and to help people plan for such changes. After each trend or forecast is stated, an explanation is provided. Implications are mentioned to highlight possible ramifications of each trend or forecast.[117]

A shift from being means oriented to being goal oriented. Historically, congregations focused their efforts on sending missionaries, which presupposes that the role of the church is to send. In the future, churches will change models based upon the question: What needs to happen in order to see this people reached with the Gospel?

Assemblies will not limit themselves to sending long-term missionaries. They will want to include any possible resource to see a group evangelized and discipled. Thus, they may not send long-term missionaries from the church. Instead, they might support nationals, radio broadcasts, short-term professional teams, and literature distribution.

Implications: (1) Churches will increasingly question the role of the long-term church planter where the church is already in existence. (2) Churches will not support ministries of which they do not readily see the value. (3) Agencies will need to prove *why* a missionary with a particular set of abilities is needed in a certain ministry and area.

A shift from being missions focused to being mission focused. The shift from a focus on missions to a focus on mission acknowledges that the entire church is to participate actively in the Great Commission. Overseas missions is not viewed as the ultimate ministry. Outreach is the calling of the church. It is the nature of the church, as opposed to the task of a minority within the assembly. Acts 1:8 is seen as the model for the entire congregation. The hierarchy of lostness of those overseas is not assumed as it was in previous generations.

Implications: (1) Support for ministries outside the homeland will decrease as demand for funds for overseas efforts will compete more intensely with needs in the homeland. (2) Agencies will want to assist churches in meeting their entire Acts 1:8 concerns. A sole focus on overseas ministries will not satisfy churches. However, as agencies assist churches in their ministries, greater trust will be built between the two entities.

A shift in the church's perspective of mission agencies from dependency to expediency. Agencies will not play the same role as they have in the past. Historically they served as intermediaries. They were needed to interpret the world to churches. Their expertise was required to send people to the field, keep them there, and ensure their effectiveness. As we look to the future, these roles diminish in importance given technological advances. Often churches have a more accurate picture of what is occurring in the life of one of their own missionaries than does the leadership of an agency. Churches increasingly will realize that agencies, while helpful, are not the only ones with expertise.

Implications: (1) Agencies will need to fulfill different roles with different churches. For some, they will create and control ministry opportunities as they have in the past. In other cases, they will serve churches and let them set the agenda. (2) Churches will look to networks and peers for ideas and inspiration. (3) Agencies will want to approach entrepreneurial churches as learners.

A shift from the missionary being over the national church to serving under the national church. As church leaders travel and see the quality of national leaders that God has raised up, they will question the need for the missionary to be in control. They will assume that where there is a national church, missionaries will work under its leadership. Short-term ministries will further this vision.

Implications: (1) Agencies that do not work under national churches will be viewed as paternalistic. (2) More and more finances will go directly to support national workers. (3) The role of the missionary will change from church planter to expert in areas that the national church lacks. (4) In many situations, churches will experience frustration as they begin to feel stifled by national churches that do not share their entrepreneurial bent or vision for closure. As this happens, churches will shift their focus from working under a national church to working alongside a national church.

A shift in emphasis from professional missionaries to lay involvement. While long-term missionaries will still be needed and crucial to world evangelization, churches will focus their efforts on mobilizing as many of their laity as possible in outreach. Short-term missions is just the beginning of this trend. As people seek to make a difference in the world, churches will offer opportunities as well as encourage laity to pray and dream about meaningful participation in the Great Commission based upon who they are and the resources God has given them.

Implications: (1) Church missions conferences will not focus predominantly on the unevangelized; they will focus on empowering laity for both local and global involvement. (2) Agencies with quality short-term ministries that are family-oriented will thrive. (3) The establishment of nonprofit corporations by churches and individuals will increase in order to simplify and expedite giving and outreach. Often, these nonprofit corporations will facilitate broader participation among a variety of churches.

A shift in the donor's attitude about outcomes. Boomers and Generation Xers will take a harder look at results and consult with multiple experts on how finances can best be utilized for the kingdom. Their desire to leverage money will be a significant dynamic in the missions equation. They want "bang for their buck," so to speak. Therefore, major donors who want to give to missions will in essence become active partners, sitting at the table with agencies, churches, and training institutions.

Implications: (1) Money will be available, but people will have to be persuaded that what they are giving to matters. (2) Agencies will be forced to consider donors' intent and offer projects within their parameters. (3) Agencies will experience increasing challenge in tapping into networks of people who have money and a concern for global outreach. Simply having representatives in various parts of the country will not suffice. (4) Agencies will be forced to trim operating expenses in order to reduce missionary support requirements. (5) The perception that supporting Western missionaries costs too much will motivate individuals to look for alternative ways to participate in missions. (6) Many churches will abandon their commitments to persons, projects, and ministries if they do not see the expected results from their investments.

These trends and forecasts are based upon materials read, discussions with church and agency leaders, and present realities extrapolated into the future. They are my best informed conjectures as to what the future holds. I readily acknowledge that in the future additional trends will occur and events will take place that we never imagined.

We all orient our lives and ministries based upon an expected future. My questions to my readers are: What are your forecasts in regards to the local church and world evangelization? What are the implications of these shifts? How are you and your organization preparing for the implications?

Notes

1. Bruce K. Camp, "Scripturally Considered, the Local Church Has Primary Responsibility for World Evangelization" (D.Miss. diss., School of Intercultural Studies, Biola University, 1992).

2. Roland Allen, *The Spontaneous Expansion of the Church and the Causes Which Hinder It* (Grand Rapids: Eerdmans, 1962), p. 117.

3. James A. Scherer, *Missionary, Go Home!* (Englewood Cliffs, N.J.: Prentice-Hall, 1964), p. 43.

4. Harry R. Boer, *Pentecost and Missions* (Grand Rapids: Eerdmans, 1964), p. 100.

5. J. Herbert Kane, *A Concise History of the Christian World Mission* (Grand Rapids: Baker Book House, 1982), p. 7.

6. Kenneth Scott Latourette, *A History of the Expansion of Christianity*, 7 vols. (Grand Rapids: Zondervan, 1974), 1:141.

7. Justin Martyr, *Writings of Saint Justin Martyr*, trans. Thomas B. Falls (New York: Christian Heritage, 1948).

8. Henry Chadwick, *The Early Church* (New York: Penguin, 1976).

9. Adolf Harnack, *The Expansion of Christianity in the First Three Centuries*, trans. and ed. James Moffatt, 2 vols. (New York: G. P. Putnam's Sons, 1904), 1:419–38.

10. Michael Green, *Evangelism in the Early Church* (Grand Rapids: Eerdmans, 1970), p. 168.

11. Latourette, *A History of the Expansion*, 1:116.

12. Harnack, *The Expansion of Christianity*, 1:460.

13. Latourette, *A History of the Expansion*, 1:116.

14. Stephen Neill, *A History of Christian Missions* (Middlesex, England: Penguin, 1975), p. 44.

15. Green, *Evangelism in the Early Church*.

16. Chadwick, *The Early Church*, p. 56.

17. Green, *Evangelism in the Early Church*.

18 J. H. Bavinck, *An Introduction to the Science of Missions* (Phillipsburg, N.J.: Presbyterian & Reformed, 1960), pp. 288–89.

19. James A. Bergquist, "The Congregation in Mission—Worth a Second Look," *International Review of Mission* 81, no. 321 (April 1992): 15.

20. John H. Gager, *Kingdom and Community* (Englewood Cliffs, N.J.: Prentice-Hall, 1975).

21. E. Glenn Hinson, *The Evangelization of the Roman Empire* (Macon, Ga.: Mercer Univ. Press, 1981).

22. Gager, *Kingdom and Community*, p. 140.

23. Hinson, *The Evangelization of the Roman Empire*.

24. Ibid., pp. 40–42.

25. C. Peter Wagner, *Leading Your Church to Growth* (Ventura, Calif.: Regal Books, 1984), p. 153.

26. Latourette, *A History of the Expansion*, 2:19.

27. Ibid., 2:15.

28. Ibid., 2:15–18.

29. Will Durant, *Caesar and Christ* (New York: Simon & Schuster, 1944), p. 664.

30. Williston Walker, *A History of the Christian Church*, 3d ed. (New York: Charles Scribner's Sons, 1970), p. 105.

31. Latourette, *A History of the Expansion*, 1:368.

32. Ralph D. Winter, "The Two Structures of God's Redemptive Mission," *Missiology: An International Review* 2, no. 1 (January 1974): 121–39.

33. Bruce Shelly, *Church History in Plain Language* (Waco, Tex.: Word, 1982), pp. 138–39.

34. Philip Schaff, *History of the Christian Church*, 8 vols. (Grand Rapids: Eerdmans, 1910), 2:136.

35. Ruth A. Tucker, *From Jerusalem to Irian Jaya* (Grand Rapids: Zondervan, 1983), p. 43.

36. Schaff, *History of the Christian Church*, 2:47–66.

37. Joseph Schmidlin, *Catholic Mission History*, 1933, cited in Kane, *A Concise History*, p. 58.

38. Newman C. Eberhardt, *A Summary of Catholic History* (St. Louis, Mo.: B. Herder, 1961); Marian McKenna, *Concise History of Catholicism* (Patterson, N.J.: Littlefield, Adams & Co., 1962); John Dowling, *The History of Romanism* (New York: Edward Walker, 1870).

39. Dowling, *The History of Romanism*, p. 473.

40. Neill, *A History of Christian Missions*, p. 178.

41. Addison P. Soltau, "Mobilizing the Seminaries," in *Reaching the Unreached*, ed. Harvie M. Conn (Phillipsburg, N.J.: Presbyterian & Reformed, 1984), pp. 150-51.

42. David Bosch, *Witness to the World* (London: Marshall, Morgan & Scott, 1980), p. 116.

43. Bavinck, *An Introduction to the Science of Missions*, pp. 290–91.

44. Walker, *A History of the Christian Church*, p. 301.

45. Latourette, *A History of the Expansion*, 3:24–26.

46. Kane, *A Concise History*, p. 76.

47. Wilbert R. Shenk, ed., *Anabaptism and Mission* (Scottdale, Pa.: Herald Press, 1984), p. 216.

48. Gustav Warneck, *Outline of a History of Protestant Missions from the Reformation to the Present Time* (New York: Fleming H. Revell, 1901), p. 53.

49. Neill, *A History of Christian Missions*, p. 227.

50. Kane, *A Concise History*, p. 77.

51. Walker, *A History of the Christian Church*, p. 446.

52. Mark A. Noll, "Pietism," in *Evangelical Dictionary of Theology*, ed. Walter A. Elwell (Grand Rapids: Baker Book House, 1984), p. 856.

53. Walker, *A History of the Christian Church*, p. 448.

54. Warneck, *Outline of a History of Protestant Missions*, pp. 55–56.

55. Tucker, *From Jerusalem to Irian Jaya*, p. 71.

56. Bavinck, *An Introduction to the Science of Missions*, pp. 295–97.

57. Soltau, "Mobilizing the Seminaries," p. 151.

58. Scherer, *Missionary, Go Home!* p. 73.

59. Neill, *A History of Christian Missions*, p. 243.

60. Latourette, *A History of the Expansion*, 5:469.

61. Tucker, *From Jerusalem to Irian Jaya*, pp. 109–12.

62. Harold R. Cook, *Highlights of Christian Missions* (Chicago: Moody Press, 1972), p. 54.

63. Neill, *A History of Christian Missions*, p. 252.

64. Kane, *A Concise History*, p. 83.

65. William Carey, *An Enquiry into the Obligation of Christians, to Use Means for the Conversion of the Heathens*, ed. John L. Pretlove (Dallas: Criswell, 1988), p. 5.

66. Kane, *A Concise History*, pp. 81–82.

67. Ralph D. Winter, "The Long Look: Eras of Missions History," in *Perspectives on the World Christian Movement: A Reader*, ed. Ralph D. Winter and Steven C. Hawthorne (Pasadena, Calif.: William Carey Library, 1981), p. 167.

68. Kane, *A Concise History*, p. 86.

69. Cook, *Highlights of Christian Missions*, p. 65.

70. A. Scott Moreau, "Putting the Survey in Perspective," in *Mission Handbook: U.S. and Canadian Christian Ministries Overseas, 2001–2003*, 18th ed., ed. John A. Siewert and Dotsey Welliver (Wheaton, Ill.: Evangelism and Missions Information Service, 2000), p. 33.

71. Neill, *A History of Christian Missions*, pp. 510–11.

72. Latourette, *A History of the Expansion*, 4:18, 43.

73. Ibid., 4:95–99.

74. Ibid., 4:48–49.

75. Ibid., 4:86–87.

76. Ibid., 4:100.

77. James A. Scherer, *Gospel, Church, and Kingdom* (Minneapolis: Augsburg, 1987).

78. Ibid., p. 17.

79. World Missionary Conference, *World Missionary Conference, 1910* (New York: Fleming H. Revell, 1910), p. 109.

80. Harold Lindsell, *Church's Worldwide Mission* (Waco, Tex.: Word, 1966), p. 3.

81. Ibid., p. 228.

82. Quoted in Carl F. H. Henry and W. Stanley Mooneyham, eds., *One Race, One Gospel, One Task: World Congress on Evangelism, Berlin 1966, Official Reference Volumes*, 2 vols. (Minneapolis: World Wide Publications, 1967), 1:24–30.

83. Rodger C. Bassham, *Mission Theology, 1948–1975: Years of Worldwide Creative Tension—Ecumenical, Evangelical, and Roman Catholic* (Pasadena, Calif.: William Carey Library, 1979), p. 224.

84. Vergil Gerber, *Missions in Creative Tension* (Pasadena, Calif.: William Carey Library, 1971), pp. 16–19.

85. Harvie M. Conn, *Theological Perspectives on Church Growth* (Phillipsburg, N.J.: Presbyterian & Reformed, 1976), pp. 107, 108.

86. Quoted in J. D. Douglas, ed., *Let the Earth Hear His Voice* (Minneapolis: World Wide Publications, 1976), p. 34.

87. Saphir Athyal, "Lausanne 1974," *World Evangelization* 16, no. 62 (1989): 22.

88. Quoted in Douglas, ed., *Let the Earth Hear His Voice*, p. 5.

89. Howard Snyder, "The Church as God's Agent in Evangelism," in *Let the Earth Hear His Voice*, ed. Douglas, p. 356.

90. Ibid., p. 356.

91. Ibid., p. 352.

92. Ibid., p. 353.

93. Ibid., p. 353.

94. Peter Savage, "The Church and Evangelism," in *The New Face of Evangelicalism*, ed. C. René Padilla (London: Hodder & Stoughton, 1976), pp. 121, 125.

95. Quoted in Douglas, ed., *Let the Earth Hear His Voice*, p. 6.

96. Orlando Costas, "Churches in Evangelistic Partnership," in *The New Face of Evangelicalism*, ed. Padilla, p. 148.

97. Arthur P. Johnston, *The Battle for World Evangelism* (Wheaton, Ill.: Tyndale House, 1978), pp. 294–95.

98. John Stott, *The Lausanne Covenant: An Exposition and Commentary* (Wheaton, Ill.: Lausanne Committee for World Evangelization, 1975), pp. 22–23.

99. Edward R. Dayton and Samuel Wilson, eds., *The Future of World Evangelization* (Monrovia, Calif.: MARC, 1984), p. 151.

100. John Stott, "Theological Preamble," in Lausanne Committee for World Evangelization, *Co-operating in World Evangelization: A Handbook on Church/Parachurch Relationships* (Wheaton, Ill.: Lausanne Committee for World Evangelization, 1983), pp. 13, 15.

101. James A. Scherer, personal communication, August 25, 1992.

102. Scherer, *Gospel, Church, and Kingdom*, p. 191.

103. John Gration, "Church and Parachurch: Partner or Competitor?" (paper presented at the meeting of the Association of Evangelical Professors of Missions, Pasadena, Calif., September 24–28, 1984), p. 5.

104. Wheaton '83, news release, July 19, 1983, p. 1 (available from Wheaton '83, P.O. Box 1983, Wheaton, Ill.).

105. Pablo Pérez, "The Relationship Between Church and Para-Church: A Theological Reflection," in *The Church: God's Agent for Change*, ed. Bruce J. Nicholls (Devon, U.K.: Paternoster, 1986), p. 206.

106. Wheaton '83, "Letter to the Churches," June 1983, p. 2.

107. J. D. Douglas, ed., *Proclaim Christ Until He Comes* (Minneapolis: World Wide Publications, 1990), pp. 11–14.

108. Jong-Yun Lee, "Primacy of the Local Church in World Evangelization," in *Proclaim Christ Until He Comes*, ed. Douglas, pp. 69–71.

109. Eduardo M. Maling, "The Importance of the Local Church to World Evangelization," in *Proclaim Christ Until He Comes*, ed. Douglas, p. 75.

110. Cited in Douglas, ed., *Proclaim Christ Until He Comes*, p. 79.

111. Cited in Douglas, ed., *Proclaim Christ Until He Comes*, p. 27.

112. Cited in Douglas, ed., *Proclaim Christ Until He Comes*, p. 409.

113. Bruce K. Camp, "Paradigm Shifts in World Evangelization," *Mobilizer* 5, no. 1 (Winter 1994): 1–16.

114. James F. Engel, *A Clouded Future* (Milwaukee, Wis.: Christian Stewardship Association, 1996), p. 16.

115. Gary R. Collins and Timothy E. Clinton, *Baby Boomer Blues* (Dallas: Word Publishing, 1992).

116. Engel, *A Clouded Future*, p. 17.

117. Bruce K. Camp, "Forecast," *Mobilizer* 8, no. 2 (1998): 23–27.

Chapter Eleven

The Demographics of World Religions Entering the Twenty-first Century

Michael Jaffarian

The many facts and figures of this essay, as well as the category titles, are largely drawn from the second edition of the *World Christian Encyclopedia*. After a brief look at eight smaller religions, a countdown of the world's top ten religions in the year 2000 presents significant, instructive, and sometimes surprising statistics for each. Islam is indeed the world's fastest-growing major religion, but its growth is driven much more by high birth rates than by high conversion rates. The world's largest religion, Christianity, is examined in more detail—by continent, by ecclesiastical megabloc, and by renewal movements, including Evangelicalism. Special attention is given to the Independent, or postdenominational, churches, which represent Christianity's most dynamic sector. Concluding exhortations advocate serious thought about affecting the global demographics of religion in the twenty-first century, and religion-specific missionary ventures and structures.

Religions have members and adherents who can be counted. Counting them is not an easy task, but not impossible. Numbers speak. They tell stories of success or failure, of growth or decline, of significance or unimportance. The statistics of religions raise, and help to answer, such questions as, Which religions are strong, and which are weak, and why? Where are religions growing, and where declining, and why? What kinds of religious movements attract people, and which lose people, and why?[1]

The twentieth century closed upon a world of many religions. Evangelicals believe "indeed there are many 'gods' and many 'lords,' yet for us there is but one God, the Father, from whom all things came and for whom we live; and there is but one Lord, Jesus Christ, through whom all things came and through whom we live" (1 Cor. 8:4–6). Evangelicals believe "salvation is found in no one else, for there is no other name under heaven given to men by which we must be saved"

(Acts 4:12). Most Evangelicals believe that of all the religions on earth, salvation can be found in only one. So we listen with great interest to the Christian numbers and with great sorrow to all the others.

For us, these statistics tell a story of life, death, heaven, hell, destiny, and eternity. They point to realities that could not be less trivial or more serious. They compel our hearts to urgency and our minds to strategy. We care deeply about these numbers, because we care deeply about people. Behind each number are real names, faces, bodies, and souls, soon to "take their places at the feast with Abraham, Isaac and Jacob in the kingdom of heaven," or to "be thrown outside, into the darkness, where there will be weeping and gnashing of teeth" (Matt. 8:11–12).

This report is largely drawn from the *World Christian Encyclopedia*, second edition, and the book that was originally intended to stand as the third volume of that set, *World Christian Trends*. I worked on this project for seven years. David Barrett and Todd Johnson began a few years before me, and George Kurian helped early in the process. Actually, hundreds of scholars, missionaries, sociologists, pastors, demographers, missiologists, journalists, professors, bishops, church growth specialists, and researchers, secular and religious, from many religions, from all Christian traditions, and from nearly every country in the world, contributed to this research project.

This account of our findings begins with this fact: at the close of the twentieth century a few major players dominated the world religious scene. The world's largest religion single-handedly accounted for nearly one-third of the world's population in 2000. The top five together covered 85.1 percent of the world's population; Buddhism was number six. The top ten religious categories together accounted for 99.4 percent of the world's population. So beyond these ten, the other hundreds or thousands of smaller religions together counted only 0.6 percent of humanity among their followers. If these followers all lived in one country, it would be about the size of Argentina, Poland, or Tanzania. It would also, no doubt, be a fascinating place to live and witness.

At this point, a simple demographic note: change in the number of adherents to any religion comes by way of four factors, two related to natural increase and two related to change in faith or religious adherence. In Islam, for example, every day children are born into Muslim families. These children are counted as Muslims until they grow up and choose a different religious path, if they do; in fact, most remain Muslims all their lives. Every day Muslims die. The difference between the number of births and the number of deaths produces the figure of natural increase (or decrease). Every day people convert to Islam from other religions or no religion. Every day people defect from Islam to other religions or to no religion. The difference between the number of conversions and the number of defections produces the figure of conversion increase (or decrease).

The heart of this essay is a countdown of the world's ten largest religions. But first, some comments on those with fewer adherents.

Smaller Religions

The world's largest population of Zoroastrians in 2000 was found in Iran (1.9 million). There were more Zoroastrians in Afghanistan (304,000) than in India (213,000). The fourth country on the list was the United States (53,000). The global total was 2.5 million.[2]

There were 2.6 million Taoists in 2000, with 86 percent of them living in Taiwan and only 360,000 in China.[3]

The figure for Shintoists would be much higher if all who visit Shinto shrines were counted. Most shrine visitors, however, are really Buddhists, and only 2.8 million in the year 2000 considered Shintoism their first or major religion. Japan is home to 98 percent of the world's Shintoists (no surprise there), and this is a religion whose adherents are all Japanese, all from this single ethnic stock.[4] Shintoism is the world's largest religion that is in absolute decline. There are several larger religions that lose more by defection than they gain by conversion year by year, but in each of those their gains through natural increase of births over deaths keeps them growing overall, at least slowly. Not so with Shintoism.

There were 4.2 million Jains in 2000, 98 percent of them in India.[5] Only recently, for the first time in my life, did I hear of a Christian missionary commissioned to witness specifically to the Jains. Were they an ethnic group instead of a religious one, they would easily be listed as one of the most significant, and neglected, least-evangelized peoples.

Confucianism is a religion whose influence is far wider than its actual membership. Most books on the world's religions devote a chapter to it even though it held only 0.1 percent of the world's population in 2000, a figure that, interestingly, reflects definite growth in the twentieth century. Of the world's 6 million Confucianists in 2000, 87 percent lived in South Korea. Fewer than a hundred have remained in China itself, and there are none in Taiwan. The others are mainly in Thailand, Myanmar, Japan, and Australia.[6]

The Baha'i religion shows a remarkable missionary achievement: for a religion founded in 1863, which is very recent in global religious history, the Baha'is have established their presence in 218 of the world's 238 countries—more than any other religions but Christianity and Islam. Of the world's 7 million Baha'is in 2000, 3.5 million lived in Asia and 1.7 million in Africa, including large numbers in D.R. Congo, Kenya, South Africa, and Zambia. The largest number of Baha'is in 2000 lived in India (1.7 million), then the United States (753,000), both with many more Baha'is than Iran, the third on the list (with 463,000), where this religion was born.[7]

Consider the rapid growth of the religion Spiritism. At the start of the twentieth century there were only 269,000 Spiritists in the world; at the close of it there were 12.3 million. Even in the thirty years between 1970 and 2000, Spiritism nearly tripled.[8] More than 8 million Spiritists lived in Brazil in 2000, with 4 million in Cuba and large numbers in Colombia, Haiti, Jamaica, and Venezuela. The United States in 2000 had 138,000 Spiritists, and Britain had 69,000.[9] Spiritist religions, which call on the spirits of the dead for mediumistic activity, are mainly Afro-Brazilian, Afro-Caribbean, and Afro-Cuban.[10] The global figure of 12.3 million does not include those who are baptized Roman Catholics but who also participate in Spiritist rituals and activities. With those added in, the global total would swell to 94 million and Spiritism would jump onto the top ten list of the world's largest religions. Spiritist religions include Umbanda, with 31 million followers, Voodoo, with 6 million, and Xango and Candomble, each with a million.[11] Evangelicals recognize the fingerprints of the devil on every non-Christian religion, but here he shows his face most brazenly, in a religion centered on what we easily recognize as demon possession.

Many are surprised to learn that Judaism is no longer among the world's ten largest religions. At 14.4 million globally in 2000, Jews accounted for only 0.2 percent of the world's population. The United States had more Jews than did Israel by a wide margin, with 5.6 million in the United States and 3.9 million in Israel. The only other countries with more than a half million Jews were Russia (951,000) and France (591,000). At the start of the twentieth century, Judaism was number seven on the global list, and even in 1970 it ranked tenth.

Though it is not in absolute decline, its growth rate is well below the global growth rate, and it continues to slide down the list.[12] By natural increase, the number of Jews in the world is growing, though slowly. But many more people leave the Jewish faith each year than are converted to it.[13] The Evangelical missions movement has devoted much energy and attention to the Jews. This is partly explained by our natural interest in the olive tree root to which we Gentile Christians are but wild, engrafted shoots (Rom. 11:17–18). It is also because of various prophetic speculations, because of our obvious interest in the lands and people of the Bible, and because of Romans 1:16.

Beyond these eight smaller religions remain hundreds and thousands of others, new and old, syncretistic and original, from East and West, from North and South. When a journalist recently asked David Barrett about the world religious scene, he replied, "The main thing we've discovered is that there is *enormous* religious change going on across the world, all the time. It's massive, it's complex, and it's continual. We have identified nine thousand and nine hundred distinct and separate religions in the world, increasing by two or three new religions every day. What this means is that new religious movements are not just a curiosity, which is what people in the older denominations usually think they are. They are a very serious subject."[14]

The Ten Largest Religions

10. Sikhism

There were 23 million Sikhs in the world at the close of the twentieth century, 95 percent of them in the religion's home country of India and 83 percent of them in one ethnolinguistic people group: the Eastern Punjabis of India. Three other countries each had populations of more than 200,000 Sikhs: Britain, Canada, and the United States. Sikhism is not a monolithic religion. There are at least twenty submovements or religions among the Sikhs, including holiness movements calling for greater purity, reform movements calling for accommodation to modern realities, militant movements opposing the Indian government (notably the Akali Dal), and factions dating back to the early history of Sikhism.[15] I remember once hearing Donald McGavran encourage evangelization of the Sikhs. He commented on their martial values and suggested that missionaries who were former military men might particularly be granted a hearing.

9. New Religions

'New Religions' is not a generic, descriptive phrase, but a specific term for a group of religions, most of which are syncretistic, indigenous to Asia, and founded since 1945.[16] Some of the religions in this group include:

- From China, San-Chio (Three Ways), with 106 million adherents, a combination of Confucianism, Taoism, and Buddhism.
- From Japan, Soka Gakkai, with 18 million adherents.
- Also from Japan, Tenrikyo (Religion of Heavenly Wisdom), with 3 million adherents, 17,000 churches, 20,000 mission stations worldwide, and a deliberate global missionary effort.
- From Indonesia, the Abangan and Kebatinan mystical Javanese movements with 24 million and 62 million adherents respectively.
- From Vietnam, the Cao Dai Missionary Church with 3.2 million adherents, with elements from Roman Catholicism.
- From Taiwan, I-kuan Tao, with 3 million adherents, a syncretistic mix of Buddhist, Taoist, and Christian elements.
- From Syria, the Nusairis, with 1.1 million adherents, with a mix of quasi-Muslim, Gnostic, Ismaili, and Christian teachings.
- From South Korea, the Religion of the Heavenly Way, with 1.2 million adherents, drawing on Confucianism, Taoism, and Shamanism.

Also in this category are such religious groups as the world's 10 million Astrologists, 12 million New-Agers, and 1.5 million Occultists.[17]

Globally, at the close of the twentieth century there were 102 million New-Religionists, with 99 percent of them in Asia. The countries most affected: (1) Japan, where 26 percent of the population were New-Religionists; (2) Indonesia, where 22 percent of the population were; (3) South Korea, where 13 percent were; and, interestingly, (4) North Korea, where 13 percent were.[18] For North Korea this was the third largest category of religious affiliation in the country, after only Nonreligion and Atheism.[19]

8. Atheism

The religious category of 'Atheist' is different from the category of 'Nonreligious', just as the person who insists there is no God and who opposes religion is different from the person who is unsure or indifferent about God and who simply follows no religion. There are five times more Nonreligious in the world than Atheists. Most Atheists are Communists, and more than three-fourths of the world's Atheists live in China. Mainly because of Communism's enormous influence in the world through the twentieth century, the relatively tiny group of 226,000 Atheists at the start of the twentieth century ballooned to 150 million by the year 2000.[20]

7. Ethnoreligion

For the second edition of the *World Christian Encyclopedia* Barrett decided to use the term 'Ethnoreligionists' instead of the term 'Tribal Religionists' used in the first edition. In the first edition 'Shamanists' were listed as a separate religion; in the second edition, Shamanists and Animists are listed as two subcategories under Ethnoreligionists.[21] It is surprising that there are still so many Ethnoreligionists in the world: 277 million at the close of the twentieth century. In the 1800s and early 1900s it was widely and confidently predicted that this religion would disappear from the earth, and soon. Instead, Africa began the twentieth century with 63 million Ethnoreligionists and ended it with more—97 million in 2000, or 12 percent of the continent's population. There were also 51 million Ethnoreligionists in Asia in 1900, which through the century grew to 128 million.[22] In 2000 there were four countries in Asia that each had more than 7 million Ethnoreligionists (China, India, South Korea, and Vietnam) and four in Africa (Ethiopia, Madagascar, Mozambique, and Nigeria). Madagascar's population was 48 percent Ethnoreligionist, and Mozambique's was more than 50 percent.

6. Buddhism

Many are surprised to discover that the extremely well-known and influential religion of Buddhism is not higher on the global list for population. In 2000 the world's 360 million Buddhists lived in 126 different countries. Though 98 percent of the world's Buddhists lived in Asia, even for that continent it was only the fifth largest religion, and less than 10 percent of all Asians were Buddhist. In a few countries, some of them quite large, Buddhism was the dominant religion. Thailand in 2000 was 85 percent Buddhist, Myanmar 73 percent, and Sri Lanka 69 percent.[23]

5. Chinese Folk-Religion

In the first edition of the *World Christian Encyclopedia* (1982) Barrett listed 23.1 percent of China's population and 5.2 percent of the global population in mid-1975 under the title of 'Chinese Folk-Religionists'. That introduced an important and, I believe, more accurate way to understand the categories of religious adherence in the Chinese world.[24] The person who studies only Buddhism, Taoism, and Confucianism will fail to learn about the religions that most Chinese follow. Actually, for those Chinese who have a religion, traditional Chinese folk-religious beliefs and practices are by far the most popular forms of religious life. At the close of the twentieth century 93 percent of the world's 385 million Chinese Folk-Religionists lived in China. We should not let the size of that number escape our notice. Only two countries in the world, China and India, have a larger total population than this religion. The entire population of the United States is smaller than the global population of Chinese Folk-Religionists by a margin of 107 million.

4. Nonreligion

Next on the list is Nonreligion. This is the second-largest religious category in Europe, North America, Latin America, and Oceania.[25] Of those four continents, Europe has the most Nonreligious, 107 million in 2000. But there are far more Nonreligious people in Asia than there are in Europe; in fact, more than five and one-half times as many. And that fact is not just driven by the reality of Asia's enormous population. The percentage of Asians that are Nonreligious (16.5 percent) is greater than the percentage of Europeans that are Nonreligious (14.7 percent). Do not think of Nonreligion as primarily a Western reality. In today's world it is more Asian than European or Northern American; it is especially Chinese. Nonreligion was China's largest religious category at the close of the twentieth century, with 42.2 percent of the national population; Chinese Folk-Religion was second at 28.5 percent. In 2000 there were 533 million Nonreligious in China; that is 13 times more than the number in Russia and 21 times more than the number in the United States, the second and third countries on the global list for most Nonreligious. In fact, if every person in the United States was Nonreligious (which is very far from the reality), the number of Nonreligious in China would still be almost twice as large.[26]

Actually, the great surprise should be that the category of Nonreligious is as small as it is today. Through much of the twentieth century and before, in the Western world, most futurists and social observers predicted and expected religion to shrink to a tiny remnant, or even disappear from the global human experience.[27] Voltaire, Marx, Freud, H. G. Wells, Bertrand Russell, B. F. Skinner, and many, many other great thinkers now dead, including many Christian theologians, would be shocked to read the second edition of the *World Christian Encyclopedia* and discover that at the end of the twentieth century nearly 85 percent of the people of the world belonged to a religion. Religion has persisted, stubbornly, on the face of the earth. Today no global analysis is possible without taking into account the huge reality of religion, and many of today's serious thinkers have found this factor to be central to their view of the world.[28] And now a more astute and informed demography of religion can project with confidence that this persistence will continue into the future. In 2050 the world will likely be 88 percent religious and only 12 percent Nonreligious and Atheist (combined).[29]

3. Hinduism

The world total of 811 million Hindus at the close of the twentieth century is projected to pass the one billion mark by 2025. In 2000, 93 percent of the world's Hindus lived in India. There are well more than twice as many Hindus in the world as Buddhists. Hinduism is growing globally, but not at all as a result of conversion. Hinduism is growing because the population of India is growing. This religion is presently losing in the battle of defections versus conversions. In the average year of the 1990s many people converted to Hinduism, but many more defected from this faith—about 660,000 more defected than converted each year of the decade.[30]

2. Islam

The second largest religion in the world is Islam, with 1.2 billion adherents in 2000, or 19.6 percent of the world's population. At the close of the twentieth century, 40.5 percent of Africa was Muslim, and Islam was the largest religion in Asia by a plurality of 22.5 percent. These two continents together accounted for 96 percent of the world's Muslims. On the list of the ten countries with the most Muslims in 2000, the top six were in Asia (Pakistan, India, Indonesia, Bangladesh, Turkey, and Iran, in that order), and the next four in Africa (Egypt, Nigeria, Algeria, and Morocco, again in order). Europe was 4.3 percent Muslim in 2000 with 31.6 million adherents.[31]

Islam is growing. In the decade of the 1990s it was the fastest growing major religion in the world. So what we have repeatedly heard in news broadcasts since September 11, 2001, is true, though there is more to the statistical story than that. Islam grew at an average annual rate of 2.13 percent in the 1990s, which compares to the global population growth rate of 1.41 percent. Islam is growing at a rate faster than that of the global population, and Christianity is not. But Islam's growth is largely driven by the high birth rate in many predominantly Muslim nations. Of Islam's global growth in the 1990s, 96 percent was by natural increase (births over deaths) and only 4 percent by conversion increase (conversions over defections); the corresponding figures for Christianity were 90 percent and 10 percent. Each year far more non-Christians convert to Christianity than non-Muslims convert to Islam—probably more than three times as many.[32]

1. Christianity

We take no pride in the fact that our Christian faith is the world's largest religion. For one thing, that there is even one Christian on earth is a miracle of God's grace and goodness. For another, we grieve over the vast numbers who are not Christians. As evangelicals, we also grieve over the many who are Christians in name but who, we fear, will not be in heaven.

Most of the people in the world are not Christians of any kind. In 1987 Father Tom Forrest, leader of the Roman Catholic billion-dollar plan for world evangelization called Evangelization 2000, announced, "The project is to give Jesus Christ a 2,000th birthday gift of a world more Christian than not."[33] This goal was missed by a margin of about one billion. At the close of the twentieth century the world had more than 4 billion non-Christians, or 67 percent of the global population.[34]

How many Christians are there in the world? This is a simple question to ask, but difficult to answer, for two reasons.

First, what is a Christian? People often try to ask us missionary researchers how many people are truly saved. They do not use these words, but what they want to know is, "If the world were to end today, how many people would be in heaven tomorrow?" That is a question only God can answer. We mission researchers can make informed estimates on many complex questions, but we cannot touch that one. It is hard enough for pastors who know their flock well to assess the true spiritual state of those under their care. It is impossible to assess statistically the true spiritual state of any population segment—city, people, language, or country. But we can count external, observable phenomena, such as church membership and affiliation, which, we believe, tell important stories in themselves and which, we also believe, point to related spiritual realities.

In the glossary of the *World Christian Encyclopedia*, 'Christians' are defined as "followers of Jesus Christ as Lord, of all kinds, all traditions and confessions, and all degrees of commitment."[35] So those who are strong in Christian obedience and those who are weak, even very weak, in their Christian obedience are both counted as Christians—if they hold Christianity as their religious adherence or if a church, any church, counts them as among its community. In the WCE2 dictionary a 'Christian' is defined as "one who believes in, or professes, or confesses Jesus Christ as Lord and Savior, or is assumed to believe in Jesus Christ; an adherent of Christianity."[36] This definition allows us researchers to compare the number of Christians in the world to the number of Muslims, or Buddhists—since those religions also include faithful Muslims and unfaithful Muslims, strong Buddhists and weak Buddhists, and so on. It also frees us from the contentious, disputable, and in fact impossible task of sorting out the better or truer Christians from the rest and only letting the term 'Christian' be attached to the former.

Second, this is a difficult question also because of the huge amount of tedious work needed to produce a credible answer to this basic question, considering the vastness and complexity of the world's peoples and the world's churches. Our global total comes from a set of 238 country totals (each of which required serious work), which come from the statistics of nearly 34,000 distinct Christian denominations (which required an enormous effort to gather).[37] Many other cross-checking tests were applied at many points in the process.

But—we have done the work, and this is what we found.

At the close of the twentieth century there were almost exactly 2 billion Christians in the world.[38] The majority of these, 58 percent, lived in the Four-Fifths World (Asia, Africa, and Latin America), with 42 percent in the Western world. The continent with the most Christians was Europe, with 560 million, followed by the 481 million Christians of Latin America, the 360 million of Africa, and the 313 million of Asia.[39]

As a percentage of the global population, Christianity declined in the twentieth century, from 34.5 percent of the world in 1900 to 33.0 percent in 2000. Even in the last decade, on this measurement Christianity declined slightly, from 33.2 percent of the world in 1990 to 33.0 percent in 2000. This is despite the large growth of Christianity in China and the fact that during the decade of the 1990s large numbers of people in former Communist countries converted from Nonreligion or Atheism to the Christian faiths of their ancestors or to new Christian movements. That certainly does not mean that Christianity declined in number during either the century or the decade. There were about 558 million Christians on earth in 1900, so the number of Christians grew in the century by more than 1.4 billion, or 258 percent. There were about 1.7 billion Christians on earth in 1990, so the number of Christians grew in the following decade by about 253 million, or 14 percent. Yet while Christianity grew in the twentieth century by 258 percent, world population overall grew by 274 percent; and while Christianity grew in the decade of the 1990s by 14 percent, world population overall grew by 15 percent.[40]

In the final decade of the twentieth century the global growth of Christianity was due much more to natural increase than to conversion, which is the normal situation for most religions in most sizable population segments. In the average year of the 1990s, the number of Christians in the world increased by 25.2 million; 22.7 million came by natural increase and 2.5 million by conversion. So 90 percent of Christian growth came by natural factors and 10 percent by changes in religious adherence.[41] Remember that the 2.5 million figure is a *net* increase. If the question is, "How many people convert to Christianity every year from other religions or no religion?" the answer (for the year 2000) is about 19.0 million. There were also 16.5 million defections from Christianity that year.[42]

By continent, relative to population growth, in the twentieth century Christianity saw amazing growth in Africa, strong growth in Asia, slight decline in Northern America, even slighter decline in Latin America, but more serious decline in Europe.[43]

At the start of the twentieth century there were only 10 million Christians in all of Africa; at its close that had grown to 360 million. Africa's population grew by 626 percent in the century, but its church grew by 3,500 percent. In 1900 only 9.2 percent of Africans were Christian; in 2000, 45.9 percent were. But the nature of this growth has changed in recent years. In the last decade of the twentieth century, only 4.8 percent of the growth of Christianity in Africa came by way of conversion, which is much lower than the global average of 10 percent. So the growth of Christianity in Africa now is much more driven by the natural increase of births over deaths than by the gains of conversion over defection, to an extent greater than the global average.[44]

Asia grew from 2.3 percent Christian in 1900 to 8.5 percent Christian in 2000—not nearly as dramatic a change as in Africa, but the sheer population size of Asia is also a factor. Africa had 350 million more Christians at the end of the century than at the start, and Asia had 291 million more. Asia's population grew by 287 percent during the century, and its church grew by 1,322 percent.[45]

Christianity is not only the largest religion in the world, it is also the largest religion in five of the world's six continents. The only exception is Asia, where Christians are only the sixth largest religious group, after Muslims, Hindus, Nonreligious, Chinese Folk-Religionists, and Buddhists. Christians dominate four of the continents; they account for 77 percent of the population of Europe, 82 percent of Oceania, 84 percent of North America, and 93 percent of Latin America.[46]

Europe began the twentieth century 94.5 percent Christian and ended it 76.8 percent Christian. So where did all those Christians go? Most of this decrease came from those who left the faith of their parents for no faith. The categories of Nonreligious and Atheist together accounted for only 0.5 percent of Europe's population in 1900, but for 17.8 percent of the continent's population in 2000. But an interesting thing happened in Europe in the final decade of the century. Christianity grew again, even as a percentage of the population. This is a significant reversal of the trend of the 1900s overall. Christians formed 76.2 percent of Europe's population in 1990 and 76.6 percent in 2000, and that growth was not due to a high birth rate; it was more due to conversion back from Atheism or Nonreligion to Christianity following the fall of Communism. Thirty-four percent of the growth of Christianity in Europe in the 1990s was due to conversion; that compares to the global average of 10 percent. There were still many hundreds of thousands in Europe who defected from Christianity to Nonreligion in the last decade, but the number of conversions each year surpassed the number of defections by an average of about 315,000 per year. This contrasts with North America, Latin America, and Oceania, each of which had more defections than conversions in that same decade. In North America, for example, in the last decade of the twentieth century, the number of people leaving Christianity each year was 338,000 greater than the number of people converting to Christianity.[47]

What about the cities? In the year 2000, though Christians accounted for 33.0 percent of the world's population, they accounted for 44 percent of the world's urban population. There are more Christians living in cities than in rural areas; 62.7 percent of the world's Christians lived in cities in 2000 and 37.3 percent in rural areas. In messages on the imperative of urban ministry, I have heard it declared that "the world is largely urban but Christianity is largely rural"—or something along those lines. There are many important reasons to pursue and support Christian urban ministry, but the above slogan, though it preaches well, is incorrect on both counts. In fact, the world population in 2000 had a rural majority (52 percent, not a large margin), and Christianity had an urban majority (almost 63 percent).[48]

No other religion on earth is spread as widely as Christianity among the diversity of the human family. Only Christianity has adherents among every one of the world's 238 countries. There are at least some Christians in about 11,500 of the world's 12,600 ethnolinguistic peoples, and Christians speak about 12,500 of the world's 13,500 distinct languages.

Groups Within Christianity

No major world religion is a monolith, with all of its adherents holding the same beliefs on every point, following the same practices in every religious activity, or belonging to a single organizational structure. Christianity, as we know well, is hardly an exception. So what kinds of Christians are there?

There are crypto-Christians and professing Christians; affiliated, unaffiliated, doubly-affiliated, and disaffiliated Christians. The WCE2 sorts organized Christianity into six ecclesiastical megablocs, 300 major traditions, and nearly 34,000 distinct denominations (by country), with 3.4 million local churches or worship centers. Cutting across these are megatypologies of renewal that quantify Evangelicals, Great Commission Christians, and Pentecostals/charismatics.[49]

With the first edition of the *World Christian Encyclopedia*, Barrett found it necessary to coin a neologism to describe the 70 million people (in 1980), most of them in Communist countries, who quietly and secretly confessed Jesus as Lord, treasured the Bible as their holy book, and worshiped in the way of Christ—but did not openly or publicly profess their Christian faith. His choice of a term was 'crypto-Christians', defined in the glossary of the second edition as "secret believers, hidden Christians, usually known to churches but not to state or secular or non-Christian religious society."[50] So the total number of Christians in the world is larger than the number of those professing to be Christians. 'Total Christians' is the sum of 'professing Christians' plus 'crypto-Christians'. In 2000 there were 124 million crypto-Christians in the world, or 6.6 percent of the global Christian population. Seventy-five million of those were in China alone; virtually all in the house-church movement were counted here.[51]

This term also includes a group called 'non-baptized believers in Christ', which are defined in the glossary of the second edition as "members of non-Christian religions who become converted to faith in Christ as Lord but choose not to join denominations but to remain in their religions as witnesses there to Christ."[52] In the course of our research we became convinced of this reality, so therefore recognized and enumerated groups that can be called 'hidden Hindu believers in Christ', 'hidden Muslim believers in Christ', and so on. We believe this is a significant reality. Ralph Winter called it "potentially the most explosive revelation in the entire work."[53] The WCE2 estimates that India in 2000 had 21.5 million such crypto-Christians and Indonesia had 6.8 million.[54]

Also, the total number of Christians in the world is larger than the number of those counted by the churches as belonging to them. 'Total Christians' is the sum of 'affiliated Christians' plus 'unaffiliated Christians'—the latter being those who are indeed Christian in their religious faith but who hold no official membership in an organized church or denomination. Interestingly, this is a smaller number than crypto-Christians—111 million globally in 2000 as against 124 million.[55]

The seven ecclesiastical megablocs in the *WCE1* evolved into a six-part typology in the second edition. Roman Catholics, Protestants, Orthodox, and Anglicans remained unchanged as categories. So also did Marginal Christians, the category that includes the Church of Jesus Christ of Latter-day Saints (commonly called Mormons), Jehovah's Witnesses, and other groups like them "holding mainstream Christian doctrines except on the nature of Christ, and existence of the Trinity; also professing a second source of revelation in addition to the Bible" (from the *WCE2* glossary).[56] The earlier categories of 'Non-White indigenous' and 'Catholics (non-Roman)' merged in the *WCE2* into the new and very significant category of 'Independents'.[57]

Independents are those Christians, churches, and networks that mainly rose in the twentieth century and that are unrelated to, and generally uninterested in, the churches and structures of historic, traditional, denominational Christianity. They include the house churches of China, the African Independent Churches, the house church movement of Britain, the Jesus-movement and Third-Wave charismatic churches of the United States (such as the Vineyard churches and the Calvary Chapel movement), and so on. Many African, Black American, Asian, Pacific, and Latin American indigenous church movements are here. Independents are predominantly, but not entirely, Pentecostal or charismatic. They include Apostolic churches, Full Gospel churches, Oneness Pentecostal churches, and Word of Faith/Prosperity churches; neocharismatic and signs-and-wonders church movements; grassroots, house-church, cell-based, radio/TV, and isolated church movements; ethnic churches; Messianic churches; Old Believer, Old Catholic, and Old Calendarist churches; mixed-tradition, conservative, united church, and community church movements; and Fundamentalist and dispensationalist church movements.[58]

Again, what holds these together in one category is their separation from, and rejection of, historic denominational Christianity. They all, to a significant degree, stand outside the four great denominational blocs (Roman Catholics, Protestants, Orthodox, and Anglicans). Another word for this Independent bloc, this huge global movement within Christianity, is postdenominationalism. Their patterns of organization, worship, leadership, training, affiliation, and mission differ from the various historic denominational patterns.

This is a huge and fast-growing bloc. At the start of the twentieth century it accounted for only about 1.3 percent of affiliated

Christians. By the close of the century it accounted for more than 20 percent of affiliated Christians and stood as the second largest ecclesiastical megabloc in the world, after only the Roman Catholics. So the Independent churches have surpassed the Protestants, the Orthodox, and the Anglicans in size globally. They also have the fastest growth rate by far. The postdenominational churches are the only Christian megabloc growing at a rate faster than the global population and the only megabloc growing faster than Islam. Some small religious movements in the world are growing at a faster rate than Independent Christianity, but none with more than 25 million adherents in 2000. Compare that to the 386 million adherents in 2000 of this Christian megabloc. So this is not just the fastest-growing bloc within Christianity, but the fastest-growing major religious movement of any kind in the world, when "major" is defined as anything over 25 million people in size.[59]

Nor is the growth of postdenominational Christianity largely driven by the more rapid rate of population growth in the Four-Fifths World (Africa, Asia, and Latin America; 82-plus percent of the world's population). At the close of the twentieth century the Four-Fifths World had 58 percent of the world's Christians but 72 percent of the world's Independent Christians. As noted above, the growth of global Christianity in the decade of the 1990s was driven 90 percent by natural increase and 10 percent by conversion. In that same decade the much more dynamic growth of the Independent churches was driven 53 percent by natural increase and 47 percent by conversion. That is an amazing number for a religious movement of any size, not to mention one with 396 million adherents.[60]

Another approach to the question, "What kinds of Christians are there?" requires us to recognize, with sorrow, that there are good Christians and bad Christians, faithful and hypocritical, holy and wicked, practicing and nonpracticing, those who attend church often and those who attend church rarely in their lives. There are Christians who live for Christ and Christians who live for the devil. For some, their faith means everything to them. For others, their faith means very little—but it is still, nonetheless, their faith. They are not Buddhists or Hindus because they are lax as Christians.

Global missions researchers are not unaware of the sins of the saints. Incidentally, one aspect of Christian disobedience that the WCE2 quantified and reported on is embezzlement, or ecclesiastical crime. Trusted Christian pastors, treasurers, and other workers steal more than US$16.7 billion of church and mission funds in an average year around the world. This is a larger figure than the total amount given by all Christians, globally, for foreign missions, which is close to US$15 billion.[61]

Jesus warned us not to try to tear out the weeds ourselves but to leave that to the angels at the end of the age (Matt. 13:24–30, 36–43). Maybe in normal conversation you will choose not to give the name 'Christian' to the untaught, the hypocritical, or the wicked. But here the sociological precision that we researchers are bound to forces us to use the term 'Christian' for all Christians, good and bad, righteous and evil. We cannot count the number of hypocrites. Please do not misunderstand our use of terms. The critics who complain to us, "How can you call those people Christian?" fail to see that when we say a country is 90 percent Christian, we are making a statement about religious adherence and not about religious obedience or devotion.

But we do also find ways to measure the more positive reality of Christian renewal. There are many important things in the hearts of Christians that we cannot see or count, but there are some important outward things that we can see and we can count. For some countries, statistics on church attendance are available; for many others they are not. So the WCE2 includes attendance numbers for certain countries in their individual country articles. Continental or global totals on attendance are, unfortunately, impossible; we can, however, quantify certain major international renewal movements.

First, Evangelicalism. The WCE2 distinguishes between capital-E Evangelicals and small-e evangelicals. Capital-E Evangelicals are members of that historic Christian movement, mainly within Protestantism, that began with the Wesleyan revival and that is connected with such international organizations as the World Evangelical Alliance. Small-e evangelicals are those Christians, in all traditions, who hold many of the same values as capital-E Evangelicals—especially a strong commitment to evangelism and missions—but who may or may not be part of the capital-E Evangelical movement. Thus nearly all capital-E Evangelicals are also small-e evangelicals, but many small-e evangelicals are not a part of the capital-E Evangelical movement.

Christians are counted as capital-E Evangelicals if they are members of denominations, organizations, or affiliations directly connected with this recognizable, observable movement.[62] We run into a problem here since many Evangelicals see Evangelicalism as equal to 'Christianity', whereas the WCE2 sees Evangelicalism as a renewal movement within Christianity. In the ordinary conversation of many Evangelicals, those who are not Evangelicals are not 'Christians'. At any rate, the research of the *WCE2* found a global total of 211 million Evangelicals at the close of the twentieth century, representing 3.5 percent of the world population and 10.5 percent of the world Christian population. Global Evangelicalism in the last decade of the century grew at a rate faster than Christianity overall, and faster than global population, but not as fast as Islam or the Independent churches. Only one-third (33 percent) of the world's Evangelicals are in the Western world; two-thirds (67 percent) are in Africa, Asia, and Latin America. The continent with the most Evangelicals was Africa, with 70 million; this compared to 41 million in the United States or 21 million in all of Europe.[63]

In the *WCE2*, small-e evangelicals are synonymous with the neologism 'Great Commission Christians', defined as "believers in Jesus Christ who are aware of the implications of Christ's Great Commission, who have accepted its personal challenge in their lives and ministries, are attempting to obey his command and mandates, and who are seeking to influence the body of Christ to implement it."[64] Assessment of the number of Great Commission Christians (GCCs) in any Christian population is drawn from their observable, measurable participation in evangelism and mission through a wide range of activities, including contribution of money and personnel. In 2000, 648 million of the world's Christians, or 32.4 percent, were GCCs.[65] On the one hand, one-third of the world's Christians are GCCs, which represents an enormous global force for evangelism and mission. On the other hand, two-thirds of the world's Christians are not GCCs, and they ought to be, which represents an enormous need for mission instruction, discipleship, and mobilization.

The third renewal movement reported on in the *WCE2*, one that cuts across the ecclesiastical megablocs of global Christianity, is the Pentecostal/charismatic movement. At the close of the twentieth century this movement included 524 million people, or 26 percent of all Christians. There are about two and one-half times as many Pentecostals/charismatics in the world as there are Evangelicals, with much overlap. This movement is growing at a faster rate than Christianity overall or than Evangelicalism, and with a higher percentage of its growth coming from conversion rather than natural increase. Though 10 percent of Christianity's growth in the 1990s came from conversion, 29 percent of Pentecostal/charismatic growth came from conversion.[66] Note that 'conversion' in the WCE2 includes converts from other Christian groups as well as converts from other religions or no religion.

Conclusion

The World Christian Encyclopedia tells us what happened in the twentieth century. We stand at the start of the twenty-first century. What will happen now? If Jesus has not returned by the year 2100, what will be reported as the demographics of world religions at the close of the twenty-first century? It is a question we would do well to think about. Month by month and year by year we could go about our missionary work, planting a few churches here and there, training some leaders here and there, serving the poor here and there—and feel content with that. But maybe, under God's direction and with the Holy Spirit's power, we could do more. Maybe we could do things that will seriously alter the charts of religious affiliation, globally, over the course of this century.

Consider: at the start of the twentieth century the world was 34.5 percent Christian; at its end, 33.0 percent. What would God be pleased for that number to be in the year 2100? Consider: at the start of the twentieth century the world was 4.4 percent Evangelical; at its end, 3.5 percent. What would God be pleased for that number to be in the year 2100? What could God do through our global Evangelical missions movement—through us—that would move those numbers in a serious way? Who is praying and thinking about these larger dreams and questions? Are we?

This essay looks at the world as it is divided into religions. In our Evangelical missionary efforts we made it our goal to proclaim the Gospel to every nation on earth. Then we made it our goal to proclaim the Gospel to every people on earth, and that is still very much a strategy in action. Let us now also consider how to bring the Gospel to every religion on earth. As missiologists we see that each religion needs its own sensitive, well-informed approach. Each needs its own apologetic. Each brings unique questions to the evangelistic encounter. Each challenges our faith on different points of theology, religious life, and practices. And many religions, even very large ones, are desperately neglected by Evangelical missionary effort.

We have some specialized mission agencies that focus their attention on single religions—some to Muslims and some to Jews. These not only bring the Gospel of Jesus Christ to members of these religions, but they also bring to the Christian world instruction, training, literature, awareness, and advocacy for the people they especially love. I would be pleased to see more specialized ministries to the Hindu world, missions that would study Hinduism, that would study the church-planting movements that have been most effective in attracting Hindus to Jesus, that would zealously advocate mission to the Hindu world, that would do fresh theological and apologetic work, that would offer training and literature, and that would recruit, send, and support more missionaries to the Hindu world. Other religions also deserve such attention. From such efforts comes this second blessing: serious encounter with other religions leads us to ask new questions and learn new things about our own.

Evangelicals disagree over which Christians are true Christians and which are false, over which are following the truth and which are deceived, over which are wheat and which are weeds. Our unity is much stronger on this point: that those who follow non-Christian religions or no religion are deceived, lost, and doomed. It is a spiritually dangerous business to approach them. Here there are demons. Despite this, with the help of God, let us come. Let us learn about them, love them, serve them, and tell them of the Way, the Truth, and the Life.

Notes

1. Parts of this essay appeared in my article, "The Statistical State of the Missionary Enterprise," *Missiology* 30, no. 1 (January 2002).

2. David B. Barrett, George T. Kurian, and Todd M. Johnson, *World Christian Encyclopedia: A Comparative Survey of Churches and Religions in the Modern World*, 2d ed., 2 vols. (New York: Oxford Univ. Press, 2001), 1:4; David B. Barrett and Todd M. Johnson, *World Christian Trends AD 30—AD 2200: Interpreting the Annual Christian Megacensus* (Pasadena, Calif.: William Carey Library, 2001), with accompanying CD-ROM.

3. Barrett, Kurian, and Johnson, *World Christian Encyclopedia*, 2d ed., 1:4; Barrett and Johnson, *World Christian Trends* CD-ROM.

4. Barrett, Kurian, and Johnson, *World Christian Encyclopedia*, 2d ed., 1:4, 412–13.

5. Barrett, Kurian, and Johnson, *World Christian Encyclopedia*, 2d ed., 1:4; Barrett and Johnson, *World Christian Trends* CD-ROM.

6. Barrett, Kurian, and Johnson, *World Christian Encyclopedia*, 2d ed., 1:4; Barrett and Johnson, *World Christian Trends* CD-ROM.

7. Barrett, Kurian, and Johnson, *World Christian Encyclopedia*, 2d ed., 1:4; Barrett and Johnson, *World Christian Trends*, p. 602 and CD-ROM.

8. Barrett, Kurian, and Johnson, *World Christian Encyclopedia*, 2d ed., 1:4.

9. Barrett and Johnson, *World Christian Trends* CD-ROM.

10. Barrett, Kurian, and Johnson, *World Christian Encyclopedia*, 2d ed., 1:674.

11. Barrett and Johnson, *World Christian Trends*, p. 611.

12. Barrett, Kurian, and Johnson, *World Christian Encyclopedia*, 2d ed., 1:4; Barrett and Johnson, *World Christian Trends* CD-ROM.

13. Barrett, Kurian, and Johnson, *World Christian Encyclopedia*, 2d ed., 1:4.

14. Toby Lester, "Oh, Gods!" *Atlantic Monthly* 289, no. 2 (February 2002): 38.

15. Barrett, Kurian, and Johnson, *World Christian Encyclopedia*, 2d ed., 1:4, 2:102–3; Barrett and Johnson, *World Christian Trends*, pp. 601–2 and CD-ROM.

16. Barrett, Kurian, and Johnson, *World Christian Encyclopedia*, 2d ed., 1:29, 2:667.

17. Barrett and Johnson, *World Christian Trends*, pp. 604–6.

18. Barrett, Kurian, and Johnson, *World Christian Encyclopedia*, 2d ed., 1:4; Barrett and Johnson, *World Christian Trends* CD-ROM.

19. Barrett, Kurian, and Johnson, *World Christian Encyclopedia*, 2d ed., 1:558.

20. Ibid., 1:4, 191.

21. Ibid., 1:6.

22. Ibid., 1:4, 13.

23. Ibid., 1:4, 13; Barrett and Johnson, *World Christian Trends* CD-ROM.

24. David B. Barrett, *World Christian Encyclopedia: A Comparative Survey of Churches and Religions in the Modern World, AD 1900–2000* (Nairobi: Oxford Univ. Press, 1982), p. 6.

25. Note that Oceania is counted as part of the Western world. Though this continental region includes the non-Western island nations of the Pacific, the overall population is dominated by the culturally-Western nations of Australia and New Zealand.

26. Barrett, Kurian, and Johnson, *World Christian Encyclopedia*, 2d ed., 1:4, 13–5, 191, 624, 772.

27. Todd M. Johnson, "Quantitative Futures for Christianity and World Religions, AD 1900–2200" (Ph.D. diss., William Carey International Univ., 1993), pp. 11–22.

28. Samuel P. Huntington, *The Clash of Civilizations and the Remaking of World Order* (New York: Simon & Schuster, 1996).

29. Barrett, Kurian, and Johnson, *World Christian Encyclopedia*, 2d ed., 1:4.

30. Ibid., 1:4, 360.

31. Barrett, Kurian, and Johnson, *World Christian Encyclopedia*, 2d ed., 1:4, 13–15; Barrett and Johnson, *World Christian Trends*, p. 400.

32. Barrett, Kurian, and Johnson, *World Christian Encyclopedia*, 2d ed., 1:4.

33. Thomas Wang, "By the Year 2000: Is God Trying to Tell Us Something?" in *Countdown to AD 2000: The Official Compendium of the Global Consultation on World Evangelization by AD 2000 and Beyond, Singapore, January 5–8, 1989*, ed. Thomas Wang (Pasadena, Calif.: AD2000 Movement), pp. xvi–xvii.

34. Barrett, Kurian, and Johnson, *World Christian Encyclopedia*, 2d ed., 1:4.

35. Ibid., 1:27.

36. Ibid., 2:655.

37. Ibid., 1:839.

38. "The reader should be assured that the total number of Christians in the world at AD 2000's midyear, which this survey puts at 1,999,563,000—or, when rounded, at 2,000 million—is a coincidental total arising as the end product of complex computerized subtotaling and totaling. No manipulation of any kind produced this startling figure, which indeed was only noticed by the authors shortly before publication"—from the Preface, Barrett, Kurian, and Johnson, *World Christian Encyclopedia*, 2d ed., 1:vii.

39. Barrett, Kurian, and Johnson, *World Christian Encyclopedia*, 2d ed., 1:4, 13–15.

40. Ibid., 1:4.

41. Ibid.

42. Ibid., 1:8.

43. Ibid., 1:13–15.

44. Ibid., 1:13.

45. Ibid.

46. Ibid., 1:13–15.

47. Ibid.

48. Ibid., 2:541.

49. Ibid., 1:4, 16, 839.

50. Ibid., 1:27.

51. Ibid., 1:4, 191.

52. Ibid., 1:29.

53. Ralph Winter, "Strengths of WCEII," *Evangelical Missions Quarterly* 38, no. 2 (April 2002): 161.

54. Barrett, Kurian, and Johnson, *World Christian Encyclopedia*, 2d ed., 1:360, 372.

55. Ibid., 1:4.

56. Ibid., 1:29.

57. Barrett, *World Christian Encyclopedia*, p. 6; Barrett, Kurian, and Johnson, *World Christian Encyclopedia*, 2d ed., 1:4.

58. Barrett, Kurian, and Johnson, *World Christian Encyclopedia*, 2d ed., 1:16–18.

59. Ibid., 1:4.

60. Ibid., 1:4, 13–15.

61. Ibid., 1:5, 839.

62. Ibid., 1:28.

63. Ibid., 1:4, 13–15, 772.

64. Ibid., 1:28.

65. Ibid., 1:4.

66. Ibid.